THE MOTOR CRUISING MANUAL

Also by John Mellor
Sailing Can Be Simple
Cruising – Safe and Simple

and contributions to
The Best of *Sail* Cruising
The Best of *Sail* Navigation

THE MOTOR CRUISING MANUAL

John Mellor

DAVID & CHARLES
Newton Abbot   London

For Linda

The following illustrations are reproduced by kind permission:
Hydrographers of the Navy: figures 41, 62, 63, 64 and 68.
MacMillan & Co: figures 65 and 72.
Stanford Maritime: figures 58, 60 and 61.

British Library Cataloguing in Publication Data

Mellor, John
  The motor cruising manual.
  1. Boats and boating—Great Britain
  2. Motorboats
  I. Title
  797.1′25   GV835.3.G7

ISBN 0-7153-8851-7

Phototypeset by Typesetters (Birmingham) Ltd,
Smethwick, West Midlands
Printed in Great Britain
by Redwood Burn Limited, Trowbridge, Wilts
for David & Charles Publishers plc
Brunel House Newton Abbot Devon

CONTENTS

1
LIFE ON THE WATER

For many of us, for many reasons, getting out on the water provides perhaps the truest of all escapes from the pressures of modern life. There is something about water – particularly sea water – that is curiously attractive to humans. Whether it be the buoyant motion, reminiscent perhaps of life in the womb, or simply the fact that we ourselves are composed mostly of water, or whether it be one or more of a million other reasons, I leave to the physicists, the physicians and the philosophers to resolve.

For myself, I think the attraction is a mixture of contentment and challenge. The contentment comes with being in an essentially simple environment in which the simple qualities and pleasures of life become paramount. There is no need to fly out to the Taj Mahal to see a beautiful sunset; they happen all the time at sea. The most dramatic and expensive Marineland can never show you dolphins as you will see them from the deck of a small boat, alone in a seemingly endless expanse of water. The finest and most sophisticated of dinner parties ashore will never give you the pleasure to be had from sharing a simple meal on board with convivial fellow sailors.

Even from a more practical and mundane viewpoint there are considerable benefits to be had from holidaying on your own boat, particularly if you have children. There are no expensive hotel bills to pay; no airport transfers and delays; no constant packing and unpacking, travelling, waiting or queuing. You do not have fixed meal times or prearranged tours to rigidly control your spare time. You can get up in the morning (or the afternoon!) and eat what you like, when you like, then browse through the chart, check the weather forecast and decide on the spur of the moment where you want to go for the day, and when. And if you do not feel like going anywhere you can simply sit on deck in the sun, or put a fishing line over the side, go swimming or pack a picnic lunch and row to a quiet nearby beach with the children. Your time is your own, and what you do with it is for you alone to decide. Which makes life afloat a real challenge.

The essential challenge of going to sea in a small boat, be it a sailing yacht or a motor cruiser, is that you, the skipper, are on your own. You, and you alone, are totally responsible for the safety and well-being of the vessel and her crew. Out at sea there are no garages, no boatyards, no doctors, no dentists, no corner shop for that jar of coffee you forgot, no plumbers, no engineers, no one you can pass the buck to when things go wrong. If one of your crew breaks his leg, *you* have to splint it; if the engine breaks down, *you* have to fix it; if the navigation lights fail on a wild, black night, *you* have to mend them; if an emergency arises, *you* have to deal with it. You cannot pick up a telephone and get an expert round within the hour to sort out your problems. The deep satisfaction obtained from taking a small boat to sea or even on the inland waterways comes directly from the independence and self-reliance fostered by this challenge. And self-reliance is a precious, all-too-rare quality in this regulated age of ours.

Challenge, self-reliance and independence; if these qualities attract you, it is very likely that taking your own small motor cruiser to sea will do likewise. In which case you will very quickly discover that life on the water is not always so intense. It is not to be confused with sailing backwards around the world single-handed while living on raw fish and rainwater. Self-reliance is essential, the challenge will always be there; but so will fun and laughter, relaxation, memorable evenings ashore in strange and exotic foreign parts, lazy days sunbathing on deck or deserted beach, leisurely walks ashore to explore new sights, new friends to meet who share your interest in boats.

You can have a wonderful time on the water, be it canal, river or sea, *so long as you know what you are doing*. It is not a fool's paradise out there, and messing about in boats can be fatally dangerous for the inexperienced or the incompetent. Much of your knowledge and ability to cope with the problems you will encounter on the water will come from experience, but it is nevertheless essential to have a solid grounding in the basic techniques before you start. The purpose of this book is to give you that. It does not claim to be an encyclopedia of motor cruising, and huge amounts of detailed and technical information will not be found in it. Excessive knowledge of a subject serves only to intimidate and confuse the beginner, who just does not need it. What is required is sufficient basic understanding (not just knowledge, but *understanding*) of everything necessary for pottering about safely in a canal,

river, harbour or estuary and, after some experience of this, to make a simple, short coastal passage in fine weather. This book, I hope, will give you just such understanding.

So what exactly is a motor cruiser? And why is it necessary to write a whole book on just the basic principles of how to drive one about? Perhaps the first thing that must be appreciated is that a motor cruiser (or any other boat for that matter) operates in a fluid environment in which it can be moved very easily by the wind. The environment itself – the water in which the boat floats – can also move of its own volition due to wind, current and tidal streams. Thus, controlling a boat, and making it go where you want it to is a far more complex matter than is driving a car. Not only have you to learn how to drive the boat itself, but also you must learn to predict and compensate for the effect that wind, current and tidal stream will have on the direction and speed of the boat. Add to this the fact that even the boat itself will not always go in the straight line that you expect it to, and you should begin to see that a certain amount has to be learned before you can safely move a motorboat from one place on to the next.

When you do get the boat to the place you want to reach you will discover that, due to all these factors, you cannot simply park it somewhere handy and put on the handbrake! It has to be berthed alongside or anchored using knowledge and techniques that likewise must be learned. Boats have to be tied up to a quay in a certain way or damage will be caused by them drifting or blowing about. They may have to be berthed or anchored in particular places if certain weather conditions are expected, so some simple weather forecasting knowledge is necessary.

Boats do not proceed along clearly defined routes like motor cars, so are in

constant danger of crashing into one another. The simple rules for avoiding this must be learned. Also, the water is not clearly signposted like the roads, so it is necessary to learn how to get from one place to another without becoming lost. Out at sea there are often waves, sometimes small and sometimes large. It is important that you know how to drive your boat safely over them without it being damaged or capsized. Particular problems attend entering strange harbours, motoring at night or in canals, and so on. All these things must be learned, as must a certain amount of basic routine maintenance and simple repair work.

In short, just as with beekeeping, flying or photography, the techniques must be studied if you are to make a success of it. Remember, a failure in a boat can cause people to be drowned. A photographer will begin a study of his craft by learning how a camera works; let us begin our study by learning how a motor cruiser works.

2
HOW A MOTOR CRUISER WORKS

We can say in simple terms that a motor cruiser is a floating box that can be moved by an **engine** driving a **propeller** (see figure 1). As the engine goes round so it turns the propeller round, and the propeller is so shaped that as it goes round it pulls itself along through the water, in much the same fashion that a screw, when turned in the right direction, will pull itself along into a piece of wood. As the propeller moves through the water so it pushes the boat ahead of it. If it is turned the opposite way it will move in the opposite direction and pull the boat behind it, as does a screw when it is being unscrewed. This, in principle, is how a motor boat is moved through the water. Turn the propeller one way and it goes forward; turn the propeller the other way and it goes backwards. How, in detail and in practice this is actually done we will look at in the next chapter. For the moment, let us keep things

simple until we understand the basic principles of how it all works.

In some boats the actual direction of rotation of the engine is reversed in order to turn the propeller the opposite way and drive the boat **astern** (backwards). In most boats, however, the engine rotates continuously in the same direction and a **gearbox** is used to reverse the rotation of the propeller. This is a much simpler gearbox than that used in a car as, there being no hills on the water, only one forward and one reverse gear are needed. No separate **clutch** is required either, as individual clutches are contained in the gearbox for engaging ahead and astern. When the **gear lever** is in **neutral**, the engine is disengaged from the **propshaft** and, although the engine continues to rotate, the propshaft and propeller do not. Push the gear lever into ahead and the clutch engages forward gear, thus turning the propeller in such a direction that it will push the boat ahead. To go astern the

Figure 1

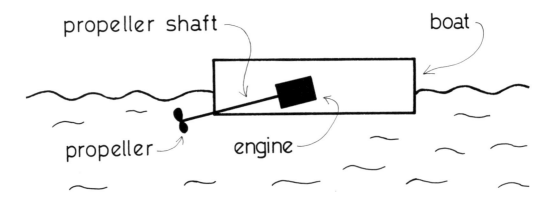

gear lever is pulled back into neutral to disengage forward gear, then pushed into astern. Another clutch then engages reverse gear and the propeller is rotated in the opposite direction, thus pulling the boat astern.

In simple terms, that is how it works. Often, however, it will be found that the engine rotates too quickly for the type of propeller and boat. If a propeller is turned too quickly it will not grip the water properly and thus will not drive the boat efficiently. To get round this problem a **reduction box** is often fitted between the gearbox and the propshaft. This is simply another gearbox that slows down the speed of rotation of the propshaft. The propshaft then goes out of the stern of the boat through a **stern gland**, which seals the rotating shaft against water leaking into the boat. On the end of it is fixed the propeller (see figure 2).

Clearly this neat collection of engine, gearbox etc does not just lie about in the

Photo 1 A fairly typical small traditional motor cruiser.

bottom of the boat. Not only must it be aligned properly and fixed in position so that it does not rattle around bending the propshaft and so on, but it must also be secured to the boat in such a way that the driving force from the propeller is transmitted firmly to the boat. In a small installation this is generally done through the **engine beds**. These are strong bearers securely fastened to the boat and carefully aligned to the propshaft, to which the engine is bolted. The force from the propeller is then transmitted along the propshaft to the engine and thence through the beds to the **hull** of the boat. In a larger installation, however, you may find this force transferred through a **plummer block**, as the strain may be too much for the engine mountings alone. A plummer block is a special bearing situated between the gearbox and the stern

11

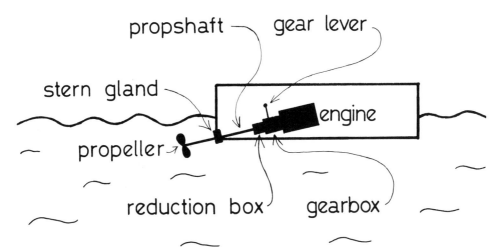

propshaft — gear lever

stern gland

engine

propeller

reduction box gearbox

Figure 2

gland which both supports the propshaft and transmits the force from the propeller directly to the hull. An extra advantage of this arrangement is that the engine, relieved of having to transmit the propeller force through its mountings, can be secured to its beds with **flexible mountings** which considerably reduce noise and vibration. A **flexible coupling** must then be inserted between the gearbox and the propshaft in order to allow for the movement of the engine. And there let us stop before we get too deep; the foregoing should be sufficient to enable you to understand the basic manner in which the propulsion system of a motorboat is arranged.

How the Machinery Works

Having put all this machinery, at vast expense, into our boat, how do we make it all go round? Well, unless you have in your boat a triple expansion steam engine or a gas turbine (in which case you are unlikely to be a beginner!) you will almost certainly have that fiendishly primitive and inefficient device known as an **internal combustion engine**, so called because it operates by exploding combustible things inside itself. The basic component of this type of engine is a **cylinder**, closed at the top and open at the bottom, in which a **piston** sits very snugly. The underside of the piston is connected fairly loosely by a **connecting rod** (*conrod* for short) to a cranked section of the **crankshaft** (see figure 3).

The crankshaft is the part of the engine that actually goes round. It pokes out of the back of the engine and is connected to the gearbox, from where the rotation is transmitted, as required, to the propeller. To make the crankshaft go round some sort of combustible fuel is mixed in a certain proportion with air and the resulting vapour is exploded, by one means or another, inside the cylinder above the piston. The force of this explosion drives the piston downwards, thus pushing the con-rod against the cranked section of the crankshaft. This, as can be deduced from figure 4, will make the crankshaft rotate.

Unfortunately, it will only make it rotate half a turn. The system is so constructed that when the piston is at the top of the cylinder the crank in the shaft is pointing vertically upwards. When the piston is driven downwards it pushes the crank until the latter is pointing vertically downwards. To continue the rotation of the shaft the crank must then move upwards on the op-

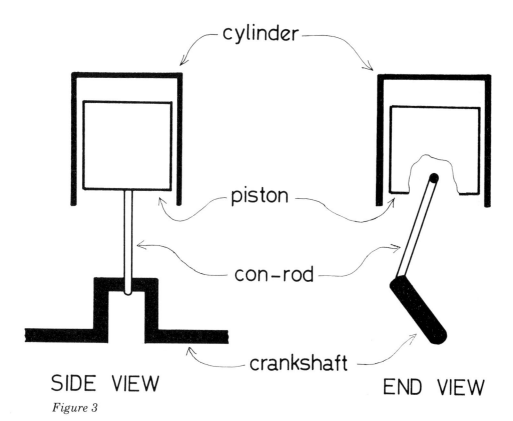

SIDE VIEW

Figure 3

END VIEW

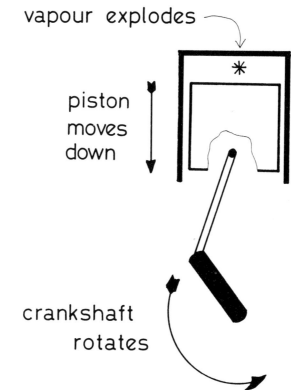

Figure 4

posite side. This is achieved by having a very heavy metal disc known as a **flywheel** fixed to the shaft. As the piston drives the crank round so it builds up sufficient momentum in the flywheel for the latter to continue the swing of the crank far enough to push the piston right back to the top of its cylinder in time for the next explosion to drive it down again. A continuing series of explosions will thus cause the crankshaft to spin steadily and constantly, and there we have an engine.

Types of Engine

Although some marine engines do have only one cylinder, most use a number of them set in line along the crankshaft, each driving a separate crank. There are certain advantages to this arrangement, although it is more complex than a single cylinder. The very heavy flywheel can be dispensed with, as the cranks are set at varying angles to the shaft thus ensuring that some pistons are being pushed upwards by others as they explode downwards (a lighter flywheel is retained in order to smooth out the roughness from all the explosions). The explosion itself becomes less severe as it is split into a number of small components and this, in conjunction with the flywheel, makes for a smoother running engine. It is also a more conveniently shaped one, being longer, narrower and lower, and it is not totally reliant on one cylinder working; a multi-cylinder engine will normally run even if some of the cylinders are not working for one reason or another.

Multi-cylinder engines come in various formats but you will almost certainly have an **in-line** configuration (cylinders in line along the crankshaft) on your small motor cruiser; we will leave the others where they belong – in the specialist manuals (see Appendix 3). You will find, however, that your small in-line engine is described as a

petrol engine or a **diesel** engine, and as a **two-stroke** or a **four-stroke**. The first two are different fuels; the last two describe different ways in which the fuel/air mixture is sucked into the cylinders, compressed, exploded and then removed as waste gases.

Petrol and diesel engines both work on the same basic principle described earlier, but there are important differences. The fundamental one is that while the mixture in a petrol engine is exploded by an electrical spark, that in a diesel engine is exploded by compression, the piston being designed to compress the gases in the cylinder so much that they spontaneously ignite and explode. In the petrol engine the designed compression is considerably less, and the gases are ignited by a very carefully timed spark. This spark is created by passing a very big electric current into a device called a **sparkplug**, that is screwed into the side or top of the cylinder. The electricity jumps across a gap at the end of the plug and ignites the mixture. Figure 5 shows how this current is produced, and delivered to each spark plug at precisely the moment that ignition in that cylinder is required.

The difference between two-stroke and four-stroke engines is rather more complex. As a piston goes up and down in its cylinder a certain cycle of operations takes place. First, the fuel/air mixture has to be drawn into the cylinder. Second, this mixture has to be compressed so that on exploding it can expand and push the piston down. Then it must be ignited, and finally the waste gases must be removed. This cycle is then repeated over and over at great speed in order to produce a steady rotation of the crankshaft.

A four-stroke engine is so called because this cycle takes place during four strokes of the piston. On the first stroke the piston goes down, and draws

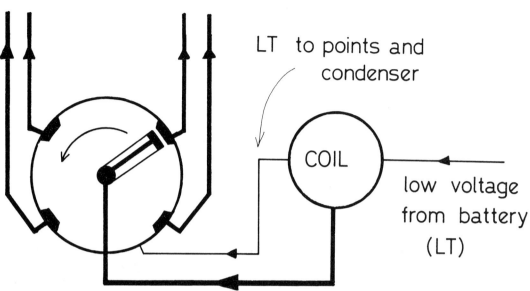

high voltage
to sparkplugs
(HT)

LT to points and
condenser

COIL

low voltage
from battery
(LT)

DISTRIBUTOR

in the fuel/air mixture through a valve in the top of the cylinder. This valve is opened automatically at the right moment through a series of cogs or chains from the crankshaft (to put it very simply). At the bottom of the stroke the valve closes. The second stroke is upward, during which the mixture is compressed. The mixture is then ignited and drives the piston down again for its third stroke. At the bottom of this stroke another valve is opened in the top of the cylinder and the fourth, upward stroke expels all the waste gases. Diesel engines actually draw in air only on the first stroke, the fuel being injected separately after the air has been compressed. More on this when we discuss the fuel system.

In a two-stroke engine all this takes place during two strokes of the piston, thus enabling the engine to fire (ignite the mixture) every time the piston

Figure 5 The coil is a simple device that converts the 12 volts fed into it from the battery (more on batteries later) into about 30,000 volts for the purpose of sparking across the gaps in the plugs. This very high voltage (known as HT – high tension; the 12 volts being the LT – low tension) is passed along a very thick wire to a revolving contact in the centre of the distributor. This contact is driven round by the engine, and is very carefully and accurately timed so that it passes the HT through each outer contact at precisely the moment that a firing spark is required at the plug to which the contact leads. The order in which the plugs fire is crucial, they do not simply fire in sequence along the engine, and details will be in the engine manual. The HT from the coil is activated at the required moment by the opening and closing of a small LT contact in the distributor (called 'the points'), which is operated by a cam revolving with the central contact (the rotor arm). Also in the circuit is a small condenser (which stores electricity), and this assists in the production of a large and sudden burst of HT to the plug lead.

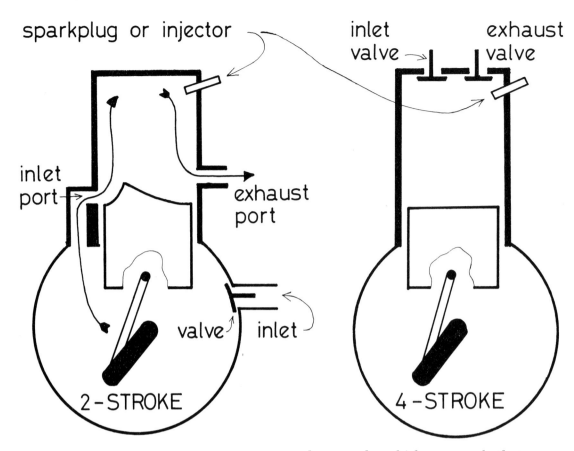

sparkplug or injector

inlet valve

exhaust valve

inlet port

exhaust port

valve

inlet

2-STROKE

4-STROKE

Figure 6

reaches the top of its cylinder instead of every other time as in a four-stroke. The design of the engine is quite cunning in order to achieve this (see figure 6). Instead of valves in the top of the cylinder that open and close to admit fresh mixture and discharge the waste, there are two holes (or ports), one for the inlet and one for the exhaust, situated on opposite sides of the cylinder. The inlet port leads from the **crankcase** (the chamber containing the crankshaft) and the fuel/air mixture is drawn into the crankcase before going to the cylinder.

For convenience let us begin with the firing stroke. With the piston at the top of the cylinder, having compressed the mixture, ignition takes place. The resulting explosion drives the piston

downwards, which process both turns the crankshaft and compresses the mixture that is in the crankcase. As the piston nears the bottom of its travel it uncovers the exhaust port and the residual pressure from the explosion begins to drive the spent gases out through it. Almost immediately afterwards, with the spent gases beginning to flow out, the piston uncovers the inlet port, which is slightly lower down the cylinder wall. The mixture that is now compressed in the crankcase will immediately begin to flow up and through the inlet port into the cylinder. As it does so it is deflected by the strange shape at the top of the piston so that, instead of flowing straight across and out of the exhaust port, it flows up behind the waste gases and pushes the remains of them out of the exhaust port. By the time all the waste gases have been displaced by the required amount of fresh mixture, the piston will be on its way up for the second stroke. The rising piston will shut off both ports at the beginning of its stroke, then continue upwards, compressing the fresh mixture as it goes. At the same time the rising underside of the piston will suck more fuel and air into the crankcase through a simple non-return valve. When the piston once more reaches the top of its stroke it fires again and the cycle continues. There are slight variations on this theme, but the principle remains the same.

And there we have the basic principles by which the various types of internal combustion engine likely to be met will work. The descriptions have been kept as simple as possible to avoid becoming bogged down in detailed engineering. It could be argued that a beginner has no real need to know how an engine works at all, but it is important to understand, at least roughly, what is going on inside your machinery. As you gain in experience and read more detailed books on the subject, so this basic knowledge of how it all works will help you appreciate the intricacies of, and need for, regular maintenance and troubleshooting – both absolutely vital if you are to be a safe and competent skipper of a motor cruiser.

Ancillaries
So far, then, we have one or more pistons firing up and down and driving a crankshaft round, which drives the gearbox ahead or astern, depending on which gear is selected, which drives the reduction box, which then drives the propshaft round at a slower speed than the engine (if such is needed), which in turn drives the propeller round, which finally drives the boat along. As you can imagine, with all this metal rattling around, and bits rubbing against each other, everything gets pretty hot. All

these bits of metal would also jam solid, or wear one another away, if they were not lubricated in some way. So we need some sort of cooling system and some sort of lubrication system.

Cooling of marine engines is normally done in one of three ways. **Air-cooled** engines drive a large fan that simply blows cold air over the hot engine. Heat is absorbed from the engine by the much colder air and carried away into the atmosphere. **Raw-water cooled** engines are cooled by pumping water in from outside the boat and round passageways in the engine. The water absorbs the heat from the engine and is then pumped back out of the boat. **Indirect water-cooled** engines are cooled by pumping fresh water round passages in the engine. The fresh water goes round the engine absorbing the heat and is then passed through a device called a **heat exchanger** before going back round the engine again and again constantly. The heat is removed from the fresh water by passing raw water (water from outside the boat: ie the water it is floating in) through the heat exchanger and then pumping the now hot raw water back out of the boat. The heat exchanger is a simple container through which the fresh water is pumped. The raw water is passed through a coiled pipe inside it to remove the heat, then round the exhaust as it comes out of the engine (to cool that), then usually pumped out through the exhaust pipe. If oil coolers are fitted to engine and gearbox, the raw water will cool these through individual heat exchangers (see figure 7).

Oil is used to lubricate the moving parts in engine and gearboxes, and it is important that it does not get too hot or its lubricating properties will suffer. The oil sits in the bottom of the gearboxes and is normally just picked up by the moving cogs and passed around to lubricate everything that needs it.

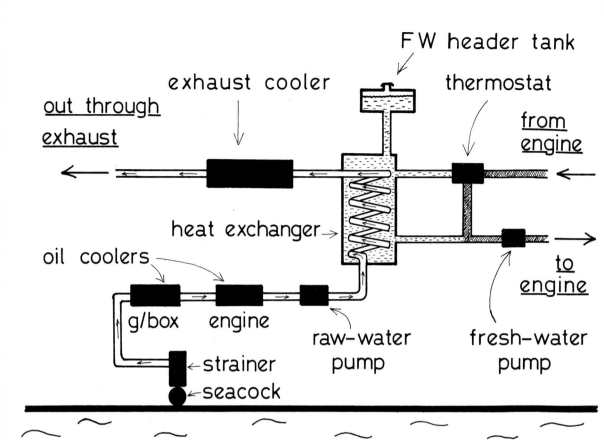

out through
exhaust

exhaust cooler

FW header tank

thermostat

from
engine

heat exchanger→

oil coolers

to
engine

g/box   engine

raw-water
pump

fresh-water
pump

←strainer

←seacock

Figure 7 The raw water is drawn in through a valve in the bottom of the boat, known as a seacock, then through a strainer to filter out weed and mud etc. After cooling the fresh water in the heat exchanger it is passed through a jacket around the exhaust manifold (a box connecting the exhausts from the various cylinders to the single exhaust pipe), and is then (to reduce noise and provide further cooling of the exhaust) injected into the exhaust pipe, which comes out of the side of the boat, usually just above the waterline. In a direct raw-water system, the water would pass through the engine instead of the heat exchanger. The indirect system reduces the corrosion that this hot sea water could cause in the engine. The fresh water is in a closed system, kept automatically topped up by spare water in the header tank. The thermostat is a heat-operated valve that remains closed when the engine is cold, thus diverting the fresh water straight back into the engine without going through (and being cooled by) the heat exchanger. This enables the engine to warm up quickly after starting. When the normal operating temperature is reached, the thermostat opens and passes the water round the heat exchanger for cooling. By opening and closing as the water temperature varies slightly, the thermostat ensures that the engine is always at its optimum working temperature. A variation on the indirect system, sometimes encountered when weed is a serious problem, is known as 'keel cooling'. Instead of passing the heat to the outside water via a heat exchanger, the fresh water is pumped through pipes fixed to the outside of the bottom of the boat, and transfers its heat directly to the outside water, thus avoiding the complexity of seacocks and raw-water pumping systems.

Engines are rather more difficult to lubricate due to their more complex construction. A pump driven off the crankshaft normally pumps the oil round passageways to lubricate the moving parts. It then drips back into the **sump** (the bottom of the crankcase) to be picked up once again by the pump and circulated. Two-stroke engines, however, cannot be lubricated in this manner as the fuel/air mixture is drawn through the crankcase. With two-stroke engines the lubricating oil is actually mixed with the fuel and does its job while the fuel is floating about in the crankcase. It then, unfortunately, gets sucked into the cylinder with the fuel and is burnt, but at least it ensures, en route, that the moving parts of the engine are lubricated. The actual amount of oil burnt each time the engine fires is fairly small, so this system is not quite as silly as it might at first seem.

So now we have most of the mechanics working. All we have left to do really is get the fuel and air into the cylinders in the correct proportions and quantities and then get it all out again after it has burnt. After that we had perhaps better see how the whole complex process is begun – how, in fact, we actually start the engine.

Fuel is normally stored in a tank and is either pumped or drained (if the tank is high enough) to the engine. Before it goes into the cylinders it passes through a metering device of some sort that ensures the right quantity being passed for each firing. In a petrol engine the fuel is fed into a device called a **carburettor** which mixes it with air in the correct proportions. The mixture is then sucked into the engine at the right moment by the piston. Diesel engines work slightly differently. In these, an **injector fuel pump** measures out the correct quantity of fuel and then pumps it, at the right moment, into each cylinder through little things called **injectors**, which screw in near the top of the cylinder rather like sparkplugs do in a petrol engine. The injector – which is a precision instrument – sprays the fuel into the cylinder after the air has been drawn in through the inlet valve and compressed. This spray, which is at very high pressure, is so fine that the fuel and air mix in the cylinder instantly and explode. Figure 8 shows a complete fuel system.

After a cylinder has fired, the spent gases are pushed out through exhaust valve (four-stroke) or exhaust port (two-stroke) and down a pipe (exhaust pipe) which carries them away to be vented in the open air. Somewhere along the exhaust pipe the gases will normally pass through a much fatter piece of pipe known as a **silencer**, which does exactly what its name implies. How it does it is quite simple. The reason engine exhausts are so noisy (as I am sure most of us have experienced with old motor cars!) is that the gases that were compressed in the cylinder suddenly, on being released through the exhaust, expand very rapidly. It is this sudden expansion of the gases that causes the noise. A silencer, basically by means of baffle plates, slows down this expansion so that the noise reaches an acceptable level. A silencer on a gun works in much the same way. If the exhaust is water cooled, however, the injected raw water does the silencing.

Starting and Stopping the Engine

We know now how engines go round, but how do we start them off? In theory, all we need do is turn the crankshaft physically through one cycle so that the engine will fire on one cylinder and then the beast should continue on its own. If you have any experience whatever of engines, marine or otherwise, you will know only too well that it is rarely so simple. Engines invariably

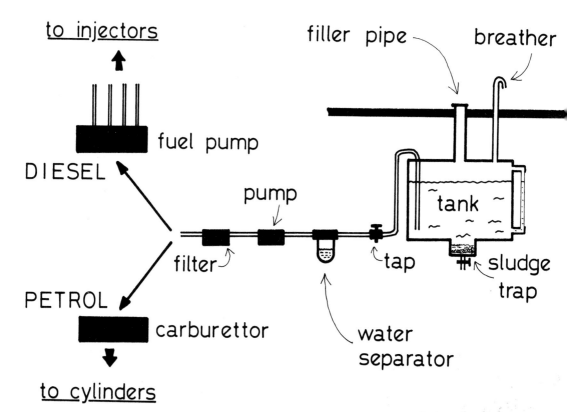

to injectors

filler pipe

breather

fuel pump

DIESEL

pump

tank

filter

PETROL

tap

sludge trap

carburettor

water separator

to cylinders

Figure 8 This shows the basic principles of a fuel system. A simple lift pump, driven by the engine, delivers clean fuel from the tank to the injector pump of a diesel or the carburettor of a petrol engine. The sludge trap collects the worst of any water and dirt in the tank, well clear of the pipe leading to the pump, and can be drained periodically to prevent the sludge building up. Any remaining water is removed by the water separator, and other impurities by the filter. This produces very clean fuel, as required by a diesel where the slightest impurity will clog the injectors. Petrol engines, which do not require the same degree of cleanliness of fuel, may have much simpler filtering arrangements – perhaps nothing more than simple gauze filters in the pump. A diesel system would have an extra pipe, re-

turning surplus fuel from the injectors back to the tank. Measuring the level of fuel in the tank can be done from a sight glass on the tank side (as shown here), or by poking a marked dipstick down the filler pipe. There will generally be baffles in the tank to stop the fuel sloshing about too much in a seaway. The breather allows air into the tank as the fuel is pumped out, so preventing the build up of a vacuum that would stop the pump drawing the fuel. The top of it is bent over to prevent the ingress of water and dirt. There should be some measure of flexibility in the piping between tank and engine, such as a series of large coils. If the engine is on flexible mountings, this will be insufficient and a length of suitable, approved flexible pipe should be inserted.

seem to need fiddling with in order to get them started from cold.

The basic reason for this is that engines are designed to run at a certain, quite hot temperature, and when they are cold the fuel has difficulty in vaporising, thus being quite hard to ignite.

Simple diesel engines do not suffer much from this problem as the very high compression ratio ensures that the gases are sufficiently pressurised to ignite even when cold. This is because increasing the pressure on a gas in a very small space raises its temperature.

Petrol engines (because of their lower compression ratio) and complex diesels (because of certain design peculiarities in the cylinder) do, however, need some sort of assistance to start from cold. On a petrol engine this is done by means of a device called a **choke**, which is generally in the form of a knob on the control panel. When this is pulled out it increases considerably the ratio of petrol to air in the mixture, making a richer mixture which will fire up much more readily when cold than the normal running mixture. It is exactly the same as the choke on a car, and should be progressively pushed in again as the engine warms up.

Diesels have a wider selection of starting aids, although you are most likely to encounter either an **excess fuel lever** or a **glowplug**. The former is very similar to the choke on a petrol engine in that it causes the fuel pump to inject extra fuel into the cylinders. The glowplug is a small electric heating element fitted inside each cylinder. To start the engine the glowplugs are switched on for maybe half a minute before turning the engine over. They heat up the insides of the cylinders thus causing the fuel to vaporise, and so ignite, more readily. Spray cans of easily vaporised fuel can be squirted into air intakes to assist starting, but if they are used frequently, engines get addicted to the stuff and will not start without it. If your engine is difficult to start, find out why before resorting to this.

Actually turning the engine over can be accomplished either manually, by turning a handle connected to the crankshaft, or by means of a **starter motor**. A starter motor is simply an electric motor with a cog on the end of the shaft, which engages with cogs around the flywheel. As the starter motor whizzes round, so it turns the engine over. When the engine fires, the starter motor cog is automatically pulled clear of the flywheel gears by a spring.

Small engines are generally hand-started for simplicity and reliability; larger ones have electric start, usually with an emergency hand-starting facility. A petrol engine can be turned over quite readily by hand due to its relatively low compression ratio, but a diesel cannot. Thus on diesel engines you will find on each cylinder a small **decompression lever**, which opens one of the valves, so preventing the piston from building up pressure in the cylinder. With these levers pushed over to open the valves the engine can be turned over very easily by hand. When some speed has been built up on the starting handle the decompression levers can be flipped back to compress the cylinders and the engine will then fire immediately and continue to run – we hope! The faster you turn over a diesel the more readily it will fire, as the heat generated by the compression will have less time to dissipate through the walls of the cylinder.

Finally, how do we stop the engine when we have finished with it? A petrol engine is stopped simply by switching off the electricity to the sparkplugs; with no sparks, the engine will not run. This is generally done by turning a key in the control panel, just as in a car. A diesel is stopped by switching off the fuel supply. This is generally done by pulling out a knob in the control panel which is connected to a valve in the injector fuel pump. With no fuel, the engine will not run. Remember to push the knob back in before starting again!

Electrical Systems

If you have a small hand-start diesel and no electric lighting or other equipment, you will not need an electrical system at all. Otherwise, you will have hefty batteries to store electricity in

21

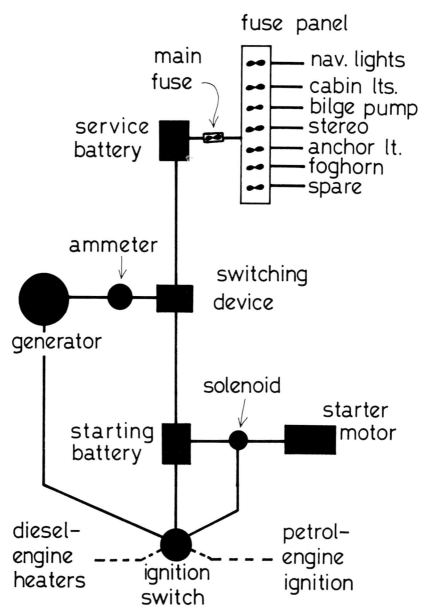

Figure 9 This is not a wiring diagram, but simply shows the basic way in which a fairly typical electrical circuit will be arranged. The ignition switch, as can be seen, does quite a lot of work. It activates the generator (through various voltage and current regulating devices); it activates the solenoid, which is a very heavy duty switch supplying the large current required by the starter motor; it supplies the LT to the coil of a petrol engine's ignition system (see figure 5), and it activates the glowplugs in a diesel starting system. Precisely how it does all these jobs will depend on the installation. The ammeter is a gauge showing the amount of electricity produced by the generator, in units known as amps. It may also be connected so as to show the amount of electricity being consumed by the services connected to the fuse panel. If these are taking more electricity than the generator is producing, the ammeter will give a negative reading – discharge instead of charge – and the battery will gradually run down. It will not be connected into the starter motor circuit, as the discharge of this is very high and of short duration. The battery isolating switches have been left out of the diagram for clarity.

and supply it when required, and an electricity generator driven by the engine to keep the batteries charged up with electricity while the engine is running. There are two types of generator – the **dynamo** and the **alternator**. The former is not often used these days as the alternator is much more efficient and produces a lot more electricity. It needs treating with care, however, for it can be ruined if you run the engine with the battery disconnected. The alternator must have something to pump its electricity into, whereas the dynamo is not so choosy. The **'ignition' switch** on a diesel-engine installation may start the engine, but it also connects the alternator to the battery. Thus it must always be on when the engine is running; never turn the switch off until after you have stopped the engine. This problem does not arise with a petrol engine as turning the switch off stops the engine anyway.

With an electric-start engine, you should have two quite separate banks of batteries – one for starting and one for lighting etc. This is to ensure that the **starting battery** does not get run down. There will be a box of tricks to ensure that the charge from the alternator goes first to the starter battery and only feeds the **service battery** when the former is fully charged, although some systems employ a complex switchboard enabling you to switch the charge to either battery, and either battery to the charging circuit or the service circuit. The service battery will feed a **fuse panel**, from which individually fused circuits will feed your various electrical bits and pieces. All the circuits (service, charging, starting etc) will have double wires, one to take the electricity to the device, and one to return it to the battery after it has been used. Electrical equipment works by a flow of electricity through it, coming out

of one end of the battery and back into the other end. There will be no 'common return', as there is on a car, with all circuits returning via the chassis, as this can set up terrible corrosion problems (see Chapter 13). For the same reason you must have **double-pole isolating switches** (disconnecting both feed and return wires) on both banks of batteries, so that there is no risk of electric current leaking out of them gradually while the boat is not being used. This will have the added benefit of preventing the starter battery from losing its charge if there are any leaks of electricity in the system. Figure 9 shows a typical electrical circuit. This will normally operate at 12 volts, like a car, but large installations may use 24 volts as it is more efficient.

Instrumentation

There are four basic items of information that must be known all the time the engine is running – the temperature of the engine, the pressure at which the engine oil is being pumped round, the amount of electricity being put into the batteries by the generator and the speed at which the engine is turning. On the control panel you should have gauges displaying all these values – **temperature gauge, oil-pressure gauge, ammeter** and **rev counter** (displaying the number of revolutions per minute the engine is turning at). Your engine manual will tell you what the oil pressure and temperature should be, and Chapter 13 discusses what to do if they are not. The electrical charging rate will vary depending on the state of charge of the batteries. A fully charged battery is like a fully filled tank of water – you cannot put any more in. Thus the charging rate will gradually fall as the batteries fill up with electricity. Some sophisticated installations may have **oil-temperature gauges, fuel-con-**

Photo 2 This is a very sophisticated instrument panel on a twin-engined motor cruiser. Most panels will be considerably simpler, but this one serves to illustrate just about everything you are likely to find on an instrument panel. The two large dials in the centre are clock and log/speedometer (see Chapter 11), and on either side of these two are grouped the instruments for each engine. The large dial is the rev counter and the small ones comprise (from top left) oil-pressure gauge, fuel-level gauge, engine hours recorder, water-temperature gauge, voltmeter and ammeter. The ignition switch is to the outside of the lower gauges and has three positions – run, heat (diesel engine) and start. The lower part of the console contains all the fuses and switches for the electrical circuits. The two gauges at the bottom show the angle of the trim-tabs (see Chapter 3) and the large switch between them controls the tabs. At the bottom right of the picture, below the consol, are two single-lever engine controls – one for each engine. Each lever controls both gears and throttle. To the left of these is the panel of an electronic Decca Navigator (see Appendix 2) and an echo-sounder (see Chapter 6). On top of the console are two compasses (see Chapter 11).

sumption gauges and the like, but the four mentioned are the basics.

Installations

There are a number of ways of installing these various types of engine in a boat, but the three basic installations are the **inboard**, the **outboard** and the **outdrive.** The inboard is the type of installation described at the beginning of the chapter, with engine, gearboxes and propshaft all fitted inside the boat and connected through the hull to the propeller. Normally all these are in line, but sometimes, if space is restricted or the installation awkward, you may find the drive transferred sideways by chain or offset gearbox, transferred anywhere by a **hydraulic drive** (the engine might be right forward perhaps), or even transferred through 180 degrees with engine and gearbox installed back to front. If you understand the principles of the com-

24

plete power train, as described in this chapter, you should be able to work out how yours is fitted if it is not standard.

The outboard installation is a very compact package of engine, gearboxes, propshaft and prop all contained in a single unit that fastens to the outside of the stern of the boat. Due to the need for light weight and small size, these are invariably two-stroke petrol engines driving small, fast-revving propellers, although some larger units may be four-stroke. They are normally raw-water cooled, with an intake down by the propeller and an outlet near the top of the unit where the water flow can be easily seen and checked on. Small ones are started manually with a cord that spins the engine round; large ones are usually electrically started in the manner described earlier. Fuel tanks are generally built into the unit in small outboards, while a separate portable tank is provided with larger ones. Large, electric-start outboards may have their own batteries and

Photo 3 This inboard engine is housed partly above deck in the large open cockpit of an angling boat. The removable cover makes access for maintenance extremely simple. A large, sheltered air vent can be seen at the rear end of the cover. The propshaft runs below the deck and a hatch flush with the deck can be lifted for access to it.

Photo 4 An outboard engine securely clamped to the stern of a small cruiser. The steering wheel and single-lever throttle/gear control are linked to the engine by cables and can be seen at the top left of the picture. The lever sticking up at the front of the engine can be swung down to provide emergency hand tiller steering (see Chapter 3). The cooling-water intake can be seen at the lower left side of the outboard leg, while the exhaust is directly above the propeller. The thick black pipe just below the steering handle is a fuel pipe from a separate tank situated in the boat. The angle that the outboard makes with the stern of the boat can be adjusted by fitting a retaining pin into different holes at the bottom of the bracket on the stern. The pin and three spare holes can just be seen at the bottom of the bracket directly below where the fuel pipe enters the engine. The use of this is discussed in Chapter 3.

Photo 5 An outdrive unit fitted into the stern of a planing boat (see Chapter 3 for details of this, and the trim-tabs that can be seen on either side of the unit). The propeller has been removed while the boat is ashore. The flat plate above the propshaft is an **anti-cavitation plate**. As the prop is very close to the surface in this type of installation it can have a tendency to suck air around itself instead of water, and this plate helps to prevent that. Note a similar plate on the outboard engine (see photo 4). The actual engine would be directly inside the stern. Note the difference with the position of the inboard engine in the angling boat (see photo 3).

chargers fitted, but small hand-start ones provide electricity to the plugs from a small device known as a **magneto**. As soon as the engine turns over, the magneto turns with it and produces electricity for firing. Propeller thrust is taken directly on the stern of the boat, where the unit is bolted.

The outdrive is a combination of inboard and outboard, the engine being installed inside the boat right at the stern, and connecting directly through the stern with an outboard type 'leg' containing gearbox, propshaft and propeller. This has the advantage of tucking the engine right out of the way in the stern leaving more space in the main part of the boat. The propeller, as with the outboard, has the advantage of being accessible and the disadvantage of being vulnerable. The installation of ancillaries will be basically the same as with an inboard, and most types of fast-revving engine can be used. Propeller thrust is taken on the stern, as with the outboard.

Propellers

The design of a propeller varies with the type of boat and engine, and it is most important for efficiency that they are properly matched. The amount of twist in a propeller blade is known as its pitch: the coarser the pitch, the further the prop will drive a boat in one revolution and the more power will be needed to turn it; the finer the pitch, the less power will be needed and the less distance it will push the boat with each turn. The heavier the boat, the larger prop it needs. Matching prop, engine and boat requires specialist engineering advice. However, see Appendix 5. See props in photos 4, 6 and 30.

3
HANDLING A MOTOR CRUISER

Before we go into the intricacies of manoeuvring and so on, it will be as well to learn a few basic nautical terms so that we can describe things as they should be described. Figure 10 shows that the front of a boat is known as the **bow** and the back as the **stern**. The left-hand side is called the **port** side and the right-hand side the **starboard** side. Anything at the front of the boat is referred to as being **forward** (or **for'ard**) and anything at the back is **aft**, if they are **inboard** (inside the boat). If they are **outboard** (outside the boat) they are more commonly referred to as being **ahead** or **astern**. Anything

in the middle of the boat is described as being **amidships**. Added to these, we call the side from which the wind is blowing the **windward** or **weather** side, and the other side the **lee** or **leeward** side. Other vessels etc may be noted as being to windward or to leeward.

And now to business. Figure 11 shows the basic tools available to assist us in manoeuvring a motor cruiser. The hull is pushed through the water by the propeller which is driven by the engine through a gearbox giving us ahead, astern and neutral. Behind the propeller is in essence a flat plate hinged on the stern and controlled by a stick. The plate is known as a **rudder** and it

Figure 10

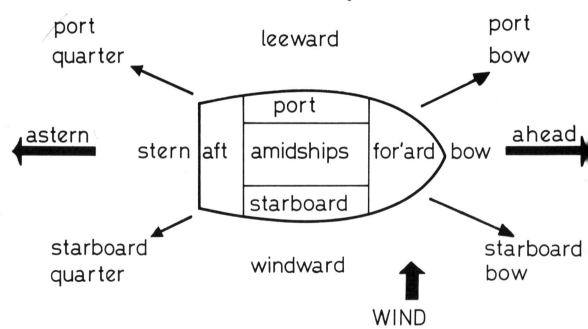

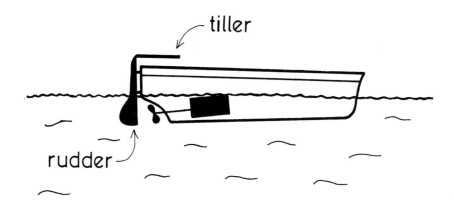

Figure 11

swings across the stern in order to divert the water stream, flowing from the propeller, to one side of the boat. This action pushes the stern the other way and thus enables us to steer the boat. It is most important to appreciate that a boat is steered from the stern and not from the bow, as a car is. A boat is steered round a corner by drifting the stern out until the whole boat is pointing in the new direction, then straightening up and proceeding. The process is similar to that adopted by a racing car in slippery conditions as it slides

Figure 12 With the tiller over to port, the bow and stern will swing as shown by the arrows, the boat pivoting around a point roughly one-third of its length aft of the bow. When going astern, this pivot point moves to a position one-third of the length for'ard of the stern (see figure 15).

sideways round the corner and then straightens up. The significance of all this if you are manoeuvring in close proximity to other boats, moorings, harbour walls and so on is that the boat will slide a long way sideways out of the turn, so room must be allowed for this.

The rudder is controlled by a stick called a **tiller**. This gets many beginners into all sorts of trouble because they are frequently told to 'push the tiller in the opposite direction from that in which you want to turn'. I am not at all surprised that they get confused in the heat of the moment. You should always remember that a boat is steered by swinging the stern away from the corner, and that the stern will swing in the direction the tiller is pushed (see figure 12).

Many, even small motor cruisers, have a **wheel** for steering, which is connected by some sort of linkage to the rudder, and this is used in the same way

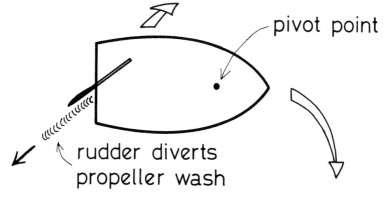

29

as the steering wheel on a car. You must still remember, however, that even though the wheel is simply turned in the direction you want to go, it still makes the stern swing out.

The other important point to appreciate about the rudder is that it will only push the stern across if there is a stream of water flowing past it. The faster the stream of water, the more rapidly will the rudder push the stern round. Thus a boat will turn more quickly if the propeller is pushing water past the rudder than it will if the boat is drifting along in neutral. The faster the propeller is turning the more effective the rudder will be. This, as we shall see, can be very useful when manoeuvring in tight spaces.

In conjunction with the rudder we have the propeller. One could probably write a complete book on its complex workings, but for our purposes we can say that, besides pushing us forward and backwards as we saw in the last chapter, the propeller can also push the stern of the boat sideways. What happens is that, because of its twisted shape, it tends to climb sideways through the water as well as forward or back. If you have ever had an electric

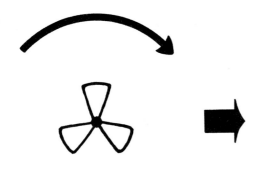

Right-handed prop ahead

Left-handed prop astern

Figure 13

drill slip you will know exactly what I mean!

This effect is known as the **paddlewheel effect**, as the propeller seems to act like a sideways paddlewheel. Like most things that affect the manoeuvrability of a boat it can be a nuisance or, as we shall see, it can be used to advantage. In the meantime, note that propellers can spin either clockwise or anti-clockwise to push us ahead. Those that turn clockwise (viewed from astern of the boat) are known as **right-handed props** and the anti-clockwise ones are called **left-handed**. As shown in figure 13, if we go ahead with a right-handed prop it will tend to paddle the stern over to starboard. The same thing will happen if we go astern with a left-handed prop, as it will turn in the opposite direction to normal. If we go astern with a right-handed prop the paddlewheel effect will push the stern of the boat to port, and likewise if we go ahead with a left-handed prop. Do not try to remember all this; just think which way the prop is turning and know that it will 'paddle' the stern in the same direction.

Finally, it is as well to know that the paddlewheel effect is at its strongest when the propeller first starts turning. This can be very useful as it enables us to swing the stern sharply while moving forward very little, simply by giving a short burst of power. This will create a strong paddlewheel effect while not being of long enough duration to get the boat moving forward very much. By putting the rudder hard over to swing the stern in the same direction, we can make the stern swing across even more, due to the sudden flow of water from the propeller impinging on the rudder.

You should now be beginning to see the basic forces that we can utilise in order to manoeuvre a motor cruiser. We can go ahead on the gear lever and move forwards. We can go astern on the gear lever and move backwards. We can also, by judicious use of rudder and paddlewheel effect, twist and turn the boat in all sorts of directions, remembering that all these rorces move the stern of the boat, not the bow.

These are all general principles, and the precise effect they have on the handling of your motor cruiser can only be determined by experience. The extent of the paddlewheel effect, for example, will depend greatly on the size and shape of the prop, its speed of rotation, and its precise positioning in relation to the underwater shape of the boat aft, as well as the underwater shape of the boat generally and the power of the engine. It can also be affected by external factors such as wind and the depth of the water, and we will look at these factors in later chapters.

The only sure way to find out precisely how a boat handles is to get out into open water where there is plenty of room to play about, and experiment. Go ahead and go astern; see how quickly she moves off and how quickly she stops. (Boats are always referred to as 'she' rather than 'it'; presumably because in the old days seamen were dependent on their boats both for their livelihoods and for their lives, and so would become very fond of a good boat, as they would of a good wife.) Play around with the **throttle** (the lever that controls the speed of the engine) and see how she accelerates; see how she behaves when you give her full throttle astern; how the paddlewheel effect varies when going ahead or astern, and how long it lasts; how the speed of the engine affects it; how quickly she turns under full rudder and at varying engine speeds; how she drifts on a turn, and how her turning will be different to port than it is to starboard, and so on and so forth. Think about what is causing all these effects. A few hours spent like this

on a quiet day – it is best to do this when there is no wind so that you can learn first how the boat herself handles before exploring the effect the wind will have on her – will teach you a great deal about your boat.

Twin Propellers
Many larger motor cruisers actually have two engines, generally installed side by side, each driving its own propeller situated on either side of the boat's centreline. There are various reasons for fitting twin **screws** (as propellers are often called), but the two main ones are ease of handling and safety. A twin-screw motor cruiser, as we shall see shortly, is considerably more easily manoeuvred than a single-screw one, and having two engines provides a back-up propulsion system should one break down.

As shown in figure 14, these screws are normally so installed that they turn in opposite directions, either **inward turning** or **outward turning.** The idea of this is that the paddlewheel effects of the two screws cancel each other out when motoring steadily, both engines turning at the same speed, which is how twin-screw boats normally go about their business. The turning moment of each prop (its tendency, because offset from the centreline, to swing the boat as it pushes her ahead) is also cancelled by that of the other. Thus a twin-screw motor boat will normally proceed steadily in a straight line with the rudder set amidships (lined up with the centreline), which single-screw boats will not, as they always need a certain amount of rudder on one side to counteract the paddlewheel effect, however slight. Twin-screw boats, incidentally, normally should have twin rudders, one behind each screw so as to gain maximum benefit from the flow of water out of the propeller.

So what is the difference between

31

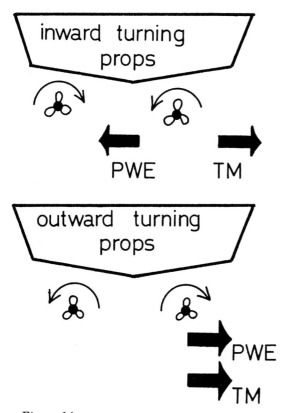

inward turning props

PWE   TM

outward turning props

PWE

TM

Figure 14

inward and outward turning screws? If you look at figure 14 again you will see that with inward turning screws the turning moment of each screw is opposed by its paddlewheel effect. With outward turning props these two forces push in the same direction. It would seem, on paper, that when manoeuvring on one screw, inward turning props would be more controllable. With paddlewheel effect and turning moment opposing each other it would seem that the boat would go in a straight line on one propeller, whereas the outward turning screw combines these two forces to create a strong sideways push at the stern. In practice it is not quite that simple. Because these forces are variable, and extremely difficult to predict, the effect of a single inward turning prop is almost impossible to foresee. Sometimes it will go straight,

sometimes it will swing to port – how far one never knows – and sometimes to starboard. Mostly it will vary its behaviour constantly throughout a manoeuvre. Clearly, this unpredictability could be an absolute menace in real life, so in practice twin screws are almost invariably outward turning. Although the sideways thrust of a single outward turning screw can be considerable, at least it is always in the same direction, so we can allow for it. In fact, not only can we allow for it, but we can actually use it to great effect when manoeuvring in a tight space.

The secret of handling twin screws successfully lies in understanding and using properly the sideways thrust of each propeller. These forces are so strong that much of the manoeuvring of twin-screw boats can, and should, be done using the engines alone, without recourse to the rudders. You should think of the boat simply as being powered separately on each corner of the stern. If you push the boat ahead with equal power on both quarters, she will move straight ahead. If you pull her astern with equal power on each quarter, she will move straight astern. Apply differing amounts of power to the quarters – by varying the throttle setting on each engine – and she will swing through differing degrees. If, for example, you go astern for any distance in a single-screw boat, you will find it virtually impossible to move in a straight line (however far you put the rudder over) because of the paddlewheel effect. In a twin-screw boat you should, in theory, go straight; in practice the shape of the hull will cause you to veer off somewhat to one side or the other. By manipulating the throttles, to put more or less power on the requisite corner, you will find you can continually swing her back into line. With experience, you will be able to anticipate any swing so early that a slight alteration of throttle setting will keep her straight before she has time to swing.

Clearly this swinging will be much accentuated if you put one engine in neutral. If you go ahead on one engine and astern on the other, you should be able to turn the boat round in less than her own length, ie without moving forward at all. The benefits of this in a crowded harbour or marina should be fairly obvious. Once again, the only real way of getting to know how your particular twin-screw installation works is to go out into open water and experiment. It is important to appreciate, however, that the overall turning movement of the boat is caused by the difference in the thrust of each propeller, not by the total amount of power applied to them. For example, you will not turn on the spot any more sharply by going full ahead on one and full astern on the other than by going slow ahead and slow astern. All you will do is create so much turbulence in the water that she very likely will not turn at all. If you are turning on one engine, however, then clearly an increase in power, coupled with putting the rudder over, will turn her more quickly. At the same time it will push her ahead more, so experience is needed before you can properly judge how best to use the combination of rudders, propellers and

engines in order to carry out precisely the manoeuvre you want.

Outboards and Outdrives
These handle rather differently to the conventional inboard installation, mainly because they do not steer with a rudder. Instead, they swivel the propeller (in fact the complete unit) so that the wash pushes the stern in the required direction. This makes them extremely manoeuvrable when under way, as all the wash is used for turning instead of just the portion of it diverted by the rudder. When the propeller is not turning, however, they cannot be steered at all, so a special technique has to be employed. Where a conventional boat could proceed slowly by coasting along in neutral and steering with its rudder, an outboard or outdrive boat must be motored very slowly in gear all the time, if steerage control is to be

Figure 15 With the engine going ahead, and the outboard positioned as shown, the boat will pivot around the white pivot according to the white arrows (compare with figure 12). With the outboard in this same position but going astern, the boat will pivot around the black pivot according to the black arrows. Any paddlewheel effect will be negligible compared to this swinging, the amount of which will depend on how far from the centreline the propeller is angled. With the propeller over the other way, all these swings will, of course, be reversed.

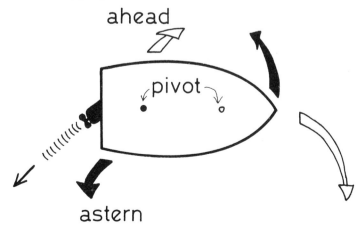

ahead

pivot

astern

maintained. They can normally be stopped very quickly, however, by going astern, as they are generally lighter in weight than an equivalent sized inboard boat. The weight of the latter, coupled with the fact that it is more deeply immersed in the water, causes it to gain considerable momentum, which makes it much harder to stop; hence the necessity for slowing down gradually with the engine in neutral.

The small, high-revving propeller found on outboards and outdrives produces very little paddlewheel effect compared with the large, slow turning and deeply immersed prop of an inboard-engined displacement boat. Where an inboard boat might use the paddlewheel effect to swing the stern in a particular direction (when going alongside a quay, for example; see Chapter 5), the outboard skipper must swivel his propeller in order to thrust the stern in the direction he wants it to go. He can do this with the engine going ahead or astern (see figure 15).

Displacement Boats and Planing Boats

Displacement boats are heavy and sit deeply in the water, which they push their way through. They are therefore slow, due to the resistance of the water. Planing boats are light in weight and sit lightly on the water; above a certain speed they actually rise out and skim over the top of it, thus reducing water resistance considerably and enabling much greater speeds to be attained than is possible with a displacement boat. Their relative merits are discussed in Chapter 14.

As far as handling is concerned, the former take a long time to speed up and slow down, while the latter accelerate very quickly and stop almost dead the moment the engine is put into neutral. Because a planing boat is so light and bobs on the surface, it is more prone to

being blown about by the wind than a displacement boat, and will skid sideways more readily in a tight turn as it has far less grip on the water. These points should be borne in mind when reading the next two chapters.

Trim

The way a boat sits in the water – known as her **trim** – can have a considerable effect on her handling. The trim of a displacement boat is governed by the shape of her hull underwater, and the distribution of weight along her length. The position of very heavy items such as engine, water and fuel tanks, and the like, will have a marked effect on whether she leans back with her stern deep in the water, or forward with her bow down. In the former case her bow will be more readily blown about by the wind (see Chapter 4), and in the latter, the deeply immersed bow will cause her to turn more sluggishly. In extreme cases the prop may lose some bite on the water by being too close to the surface.

The basic trim will be fixed by the designer, but it can be adjusted by

Photo 6 A typical sea-going displacement boat. Note the large amount of hull under the water and its soft, curving shape. The boat is clearly meant to sit in the water, not on top of it. Note the protected position of the propeller, tucked away safely right under the boat, and deep in the water. Note also the large sturdy rudder.

Photo 7 The typical hull of a planing boat – more or less flat bottomed, with little hull beneath the waterline. Note the square edge to the bottom of the boat (where the chocks are supporting it) and compare this with the shape of the displacement boat (see photo 6). This boat has twin screws and the near-side shaft and prop can just be seen behind the chock nearest the stern. Note its vulnerability compared with the single screw tucked away on the centreline of the displacement boat.

moving **ballast** around. This is simply heavy weight in the form of slabs of iron or lead (usually) put in the bottom of the boat, mainly to ensure that she floats deeply enough in the water to be stable and little affected by the wind.

Planing boats, because of their light weight, need to be trimmed differently. To a large extent this is done by the designer, but the trim of a planing boat will alter according to her speed and the sea conditions. Thus, planing boats are often fitted with **trim-tabs** – movable flaps jutting out from the stern under-water, which can be moved up and down from inside the boat. If she is skimming along the top of the water with her bow too high, angling the trim-tabs down-wards will make the flow of water force the stern up more, thus levelling the trim of the boat. If the bow is too low,

raising the trim-tabs will put things right. They will, however, have little effect at low speeds (see Photo 5).

A similar type of adjustment can be made with outboard and outdrive engines, the whole engine being able to tilt on its mounting bracket so that the thrust from the propeller can be made to push the stern slightly up or down. This will have more effect at low speeds than adjusting the trim-tabs.

So there we have the basic principles of handling a motor cruiser in still water and calm conditions. In practice, of course, we rarely get these ideals, and any wind or movement of water will affect the handling of a motor cruiser considerably. So before we make any attempt at getting alongside a jetty, we had better see how these outside influences will affect us.

4
THE EFFECTS OF WIND AND TIDE

Wind

The basic problem with wind, as far as a motor-cruiser skipper is concerned, is that it pushes against anything it blows towards. If that thing is movable, such as a boat floating in the water, the wind will move it. The stronger the wind, the more rapidly the boat will be moved. This is fine for a sailing-boat skipper, but for the motor-cruiser man it can be a right nuisance.

The problem of being simply blown away from where you want to be is generally compounded by two specific effects that the wind has on a motor cruiser, particularly when she is manoeuvring at slow speed – just the time, of course, when you are likely to be in a confined space surrounded by expensive or immovable objects which your bank manager would rather you did not hit! The first effect is caused by the fact that the hull of a motor cruiser is generally deeper in the water aft than it is for'ard. We need not go into the details of why this is so, other than to say that it is partly to get the propellers down into undisturbed waters well below the surface, where they will work more efficiently. The less deeply immersed bow can be more easily pushed through the water than the more deeply immersed stern, so a side wind (in practice one that blows from anywhere other than directly ahead or astern) will push the bow further than it does the stern. Thus, instead of being simply blown sideways, you will find your bow being blown,

embarrassingly quickly, round and away from the wind. At slow speeds, in all but the lightest of zephyrs, you will find this effect quite marked. In strong winds it can make many motor cruisers almost uncontrollable.

Even when motoring directly into the wind this effect can be so pronounced that just the slightest deviation from the course you are steering will allow the wind to 'grab the bow' and blow it right round. Bold action is required to counteract this, and you need the nerve – and the experience – to give her full throttle with the rudder hard over in order to get back on course. In a twin-screw vessel it may be necessary to stop the windward propeller in order to get the bow back round into the wind. As you can imagine, in a confined space this can be a real problem, not to say danger, and I would strongly advise that you avoid such places in strong winds until you have gained some solid experience in handling your boat. The best of skippers needs to plan a tricky manoeuvre very carefully in such conditions. The novice can lose complete control of his boat before even realising quite what is happening.

The other problem, paradoxically, can often provide an emergency solution to this first one. If you go astern in any strength of wind you will find the stern of the boat swinging quite sharply round towards the wind. This is often referred to as 'the stern seeking the wind', and is basically caused by the same thing happening as before – the

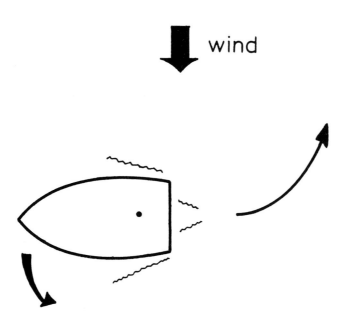

wind

Figure 16 As the boat goes astern, the wind blows the bow to leeward, the boat pivoting as shown by the black pivot in figure 15. This causes the stern to swing very sharply into the wind until the bow is pointing directly downwind. The wind, now blowing on both sides of the bow, holds the boat like that and she moves in a straight line directly upwind astern.

bow being blown off more rapidly than the stern (see figure 16). In strong winds no amount of paddlewheel effect or use of rudder will counteract it. However, when the stern is finally pointing directly into the wind, the boat will proceed in a straight line towards the wind regardless of paddlewheel effect or anything else.

There are times when this tendency can be put to very good use, for instance if you have had the bow blown off towards a wall or moored boats and there is no room for you to go full ahead with the rudder over to get out of the situation. If you then go full astern and say a little prayer, all being well the stern will pull round sharply into the wind and the boat will proceed astern in a straight line out of the impending disaster. When you get well clear of the

obstructions you will hopefully find space in which to go ahead and turn back towards where you were going in the first place.

Wind, then, can have a strong influence on the handling of your motor cruiser, and its effects need to be judged with some care and experience before you plunge into any tricky manoeuvres.

Tides, Currents and Tidal Streams
All these constitute movements of water and, as such, they have even more effect on our manoeuvring than the wind. Try to imagine driving your car at an angle across a moving conveyor belt and you will get some idea of the effect!

Although all three are movements of water, they differ one from another. Let us look at **currents** first as they are the simplest. A current is simply a more or less regular and permanent movement of water, such as you find in a river. Its effect on a boat, particularly if running strongly, is clearly considerable, but it is generally predictable and it moves the boat bodily in one direction without swinging her as the wind does. Making allowance for the effect of a current on the direction we are trying to motor in is not difficult (see page 43). Around the British Isles currents will only be found noticeable in rivers, although strong currents occur at sea in other parts of the world. For us, the major movements of water are caused by **tides**.

Tides differ from currents in that they are actually a vertical movement of water caused by the sea being pulled away from the earth by the gravitational force of the moon and the sun. The moon, being very much closer than the sun, has the greater influence; roughly what happens is shown in figure 17. At points on the earth's surface in line with the moon the water is pulled up, so raising the sea level. Elsewhere the level is lowered as the water is drawn away to where it is being raised. When the water reaches its maximum height it is said to be **High Tide** (or **High Water**); its lowest point is called **Low Water** (or **Low Tide**).

As the earth revolves completely once every twenty-four hours, it should be apparent that during this period both High and Low Waters will occur twice at any one place. Look at the X marked on the earth in figure 17 and imagine it moving right round the circumference once and back to where it is now. It will pass through a sequence of High Tide, Low Tide, High Tide and Low Tide during the twenty-four hours that it takes to do this. At the end of twenty-four hours it returns to High Water and the sequence repeats itself. In between times the water level gradually changes from High down to Low and back to High (see figure 18).

Now, if the earth rotated in exactly twenty-four hours and the moon stood still in the heavens that would be that and we could move on to the next chapter. However, the universe is not quite that simple. The earth does not rotate in exactly twenty-four hours; the moon actually rotates around the earth;

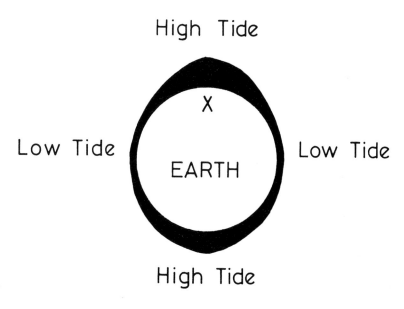

Figure 17

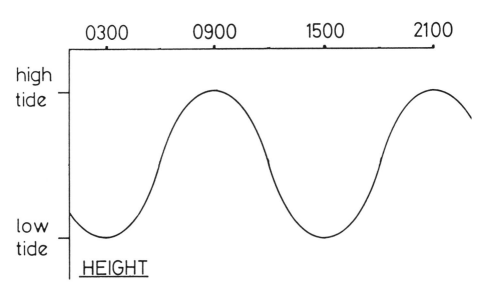

Figure 18

the whole shooting match rotates around the sun, and I do not think even the astronomers know what the sun rotates round, although it clearly does not simply hang in the sky. What all this means is that the tides unfortunately do not adhere to a fixed time-table like the trains.

What happens, as far as it concerns us, is that the moon takes approximately one month of twenty-eight days to rotate around the earth. As the apparent movement of the sun is fairly small during this period we find that, roughly speaking, the gravitational pull of the sun and the moon on the tides is in line twice and at right angles twice (see figure 19). When sun and moon are in line the pull on the tides will be greatest, making High Water very high and Low Water very low (the latter because more water will be pulled away to make the high High Water elsewhere). When sun and moon are at right angles (after 1 week and 3 weeks in figure 19) the total pull will be least, giving a relatively low High Water and

relatively high Low Water, there being less overall movement of water. The very high High Tides, that occur roughly once a fortnight, we call **spring tides**. The low ones, occurring one week after the spring tides, we call **neap tides**. So you can see that not only does the height of the water – as experienced at sea, on coasts, in harbours and estuaries – change during each period of twelve hours, but the amount by which it changes also alters steadily over a period of two weeks. The **range of the tide** (the difference in height between High and Low Waters) is considerable during spring tides and gradually decreases to a minimum at neap tides, before increasing again to the next spring tide.

As if this was not sufficiently complicated for us poor sailors, we also find that, due to the various irregularities mentioned, the time of High Water each day is not the same. It is actually nearly an hour later each day (24 hours) – 50 minutes, in fact – largely due to the movement of the moon around the earth. If you look again at figure 17 and visualise the X moving full circle in 24

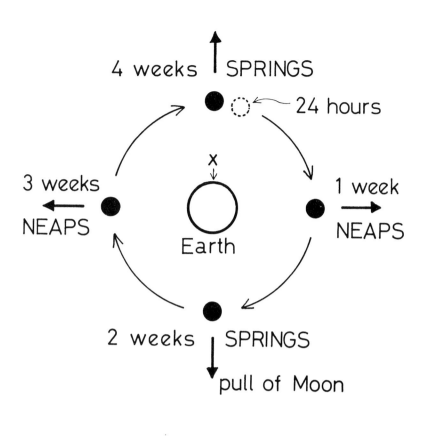

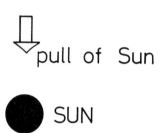

Figure 19

hours, then look at figure 19 and see how far the moon will have moved during this same period, you will see that the point marked X has to travel a bit further round to catch up with the moon before it can experience its next High Tide. Those who are mathematically inclined should be able to calculate that the earth will have to revolve for just less than an extra hour in order to catch up with the moon.

(During one day the moon will move $\frac{1}{28}$th of its 28-day rotation. Thus to catch up with it the earth will need to move a further $\frac{1}{28}$th of its 24-hour rotation, ie 51 minutes or so).

The reason I go into this theory – albeit roughly – is that if you understand basically why the tide varies so much in its height and its timing you will find its variations very, very much easier to remember. But bear in mind that even all this is only part of it. As the earth and the moon together re-

41

volve around the sun in one year, so the timing and heights of tides vary on an annual basis. In fact they vary on all sorts of bases, so that every spring tide, for example, is not the same height. When sun and moon are in opposition, spring tides are not quite as high as when they pull together. Mostly these variations are too small to concern us as seamen, but the **equinoctial tides** (or **equinoctial springs**) should be remembered. These are extremely high spring tides that occur in spring and autumn when the sun crosses the equator. These crossings are known as the **equinoxes** – the **vernal equinox** on 21 March and the **autumnal equinox** on 23 September. The nearest spring tides to these dates will be the equinoctial tides. Many old sailors claim, incidentally, that the equinoxes also bring bad weather – the so-called **equinoctial gales**. Many modern sailors, and meteorologists, deny it.

To sum up, we can say that we have a High Tide twice a day with a Low Tide coming roughly 6 hours after each High Tide. The first High Tide the next day will be roughly 50 minutes later than the time of the first High Tide the preceding day. (If it is at 0610 one day, it will next be approximately at 1830, and then 0700 the next day). Every month a couple of days after the **full moon** (when it shows as a complete white circle) we have spring tides, when High Tide is very high and Low Tide very low. The range of the tide (difference in height between High and Low Tide) will then gradually decrease over a period of a week to a minimum at neap tides, when High Tide is relatively low and Low Tide relatively high. It then increases again over the next week until a couple of days after the **new moon** (when only a very thin line round the edge of the moon can be seen) to a maximum again at the next spring tide. It then falls again over a week to

the next neap tide (at the neap tides the moon shows as a crescent), and so it goes on. You will find that spring tides always occur at much the same time, as do neap tides. If one spring tide is at midday at one place, all spring tides there will be at about midday.

Information on times and heights of High and Low Tide each day can be found in **tide tables**, published annually for various places. Not only do the times of High and Low Water vary from place to place, but the range of the tide can vary dramatically, due to geographical influences. The **spring range** (range at spring tides) at Gibraltar, for example, is little more than one foot, while that in the Channel Islands can be as much as forty feet. From the tide tables, using a simple formula, we can actually calculate the exact height of the tide at any time between High and Low Water, and we will look at this in Chapter 6, when to anchor we need to know the depth of water.

Our main concern at the moment, however, is the fact that as the water is pulled up and down by sun and moon, so it is also moved along horizontally (how else would it get from the low area to the high area). What this means is that as the tide rises in a harbour, for example, the water is drawn in from the sea. Or perhaps we should look at it the other way round. From Low Tide onwards the water flows into the harbour, gradually building up the level until High Tide is reached. It then pauses for a few minutes (sometimes much longer, in which case it is said to **stand**) before running back out, so lowering the level gradually until Low Tide is reached again. Thus, at sea, and in harbours, estuaries and anywhere else connected to the sea, we experience, in effect, a current that flows in from Low Tide until High Tide, then out again; the complete cycle occurring twice a day.

This current is known as a **tidal stream**.

Clearly the speed and direction of tidal streams change constantly and if we are to make allowances for them when manoeuvring (as obviously we must, just as we do for currents), we must be able to calculate both speed and direction at any time. This information can be found on charts, in **Pilot Books** (guide books for harbours and coast-lines etc) and also in special little books called **Tidal Stream Atlases**. The latter show simple maps of an area – one for each hour of the twelve during which the tide goes in and out – on which are little arrows giving the speed and direction of the tidal streams all over the area. This detailed information is essential for navigation (see Chapter 11). For manoeuvring in and around harbours, rivers etc, however, we must learn to judge speed and direction by eye – partly because there is no time when manoeuvring to calculate these things precisely, but also because in restricted spaces the tidal stream will be deflected by jetties, rocks, sandbanks and what-have-you, slowed down and accelerated and generally swirled about so that it will not behave quite as expected (see figure 20). However, knowing whether the tide is **flooding** (coming in towards High Water) or **ebbing** (running out towards Low Water) will get us off to a good start. The flooding tide is known as the **flood tide** and the ebbing tide as the **ebb tide,** often referred to simply as the flood and the ebb. Tide tables and Tidal Stream Atlases for the whole country will be found in a Nautical Almanac. This is an essential publication if you are to cruise beyond inland waterways as it contains a wealth of detailed information for which there is no room in this book. Geographical and other influences can sometimes have a con-siderable effect on the basic behaviour of the tides as discussed in this section, and details of these are in the Almanac (see Chapter 11 and Appendix 3).

Allowing for Current and Tidal Stream

In the simplest situation we can say that when motoring directly into a current or tidal stream it will slow us down by an amount equal to the speed at which it is flowing. If we are doing 8 **knots** (a knot being a nautical mile per hour) and the current is directly against us at 2 knots, then we will end up travelling at 6 knots past the land. (A knot is slightly faster than a land mile per hour because the nautical mile is rather longer than a land mile.) You should think of the water as moving *en masse* rather like a conveyor belt. If you run at 8 miles an hour along a conveyor belt which is doing 8 miles an hour in the opposite direction, you will remain stationary in relation to the ground. Thus your boat, in the example, will be doing 8 knots 'through the water', but only 6 knots 'over the ground'. If the tide or current is with you, however, you will do 10 knots over the ground but still only 8 knots through the water.

This may sound very simple, but it is important to understand the distinction between speed through the water and speed over the ground. Your speed over the ground dictates how soon you will get to where you are going, but your speed through the water is what will affect your manoeuvrability, as this is the speed at which the water is flowing past your rudder. If, for example, you are motoring at 6 knots against a 6 knot tidal stream, you will remain station-ary in relation to the land. At the same time, however, the water will be rush-ing past your rudder at 6 knots giving you considerable steering control. Thus, while remaining stationary in relation to the jetty that you wish to avoid hitting, you can twist and turn your

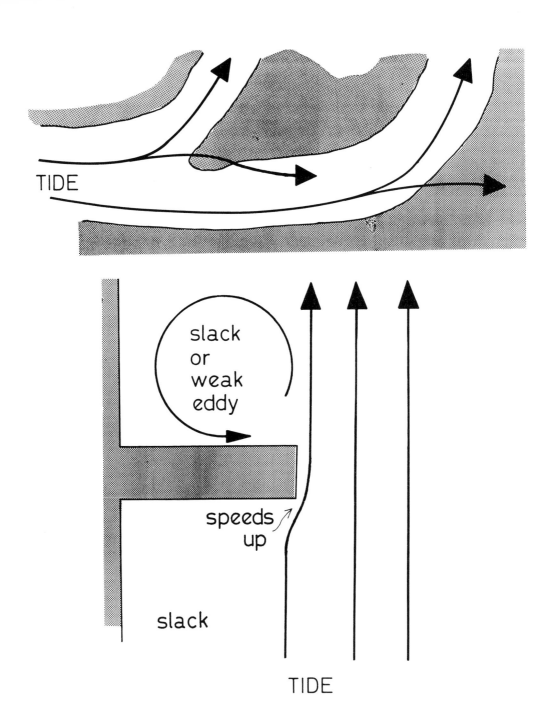

TIDE

slack
or
weak
eddy

speeds ↗
up

slack

TIDE

Figure 20 Tidal streams are generally strongest in the middle of a deep channel, where there is nothing to hinder them. Close to the banks they are slowed considerably by friction against the land, and will be almost slack, even occasionally forming back eddies. Whenever a stream is bent – round an obstruction or bend in a channel – it will be forced to speed up round the outside of the bend as it has further to travel. It will drift across into a bay or side channel, sometimes creating quite a noticeable sideways pull that must be guarded against when proceeding along the main channel.

boat in all sorts of directions and make her crab sideways towards where you want to go. Speed up a little and you will move forwards; slow down a little and the current will carry you astern. With a little practice and experience you will discover that with a fairly strong current against you, you can manoeuvre your boat virtually anywhere you wish under complete control.

If the current is with you, however, it is a very different story. To go backwards over the ground you must go astern faster than the current is running, and most boats have very little power in astern gear compared to the amount they have in ahead. Most boats also have little control over direction when going astern. Even twin-screw boats have far less control than when they are going ahead. It is extremely difficult, even for an expert, to manoeuvre a boat safely and in a controlled manner when motoring in the same direction that a current is running. Thus, all manoeuvres – getting alongside a jetty, anchoring, mooring, creeping through narrow gaps and so on, should be carried out motoring into the current or tidal stream, if at all possible.

If you are motoring across a current you will, of course, be set sideways in relation to the ground. The precise amount and direction of this set is, naturally, extremely important to calculate accurately when navigating along the coast or out at sea, or you will not arrive at the place you are aiming for. In Chapter 11 we will see how we can calculate this set using chart, Pilot Books and Tidal Stream Atlas, and then make allowance for it when working out the direction we should steer in.

When manoeuvring, however, we must estimate this set, constantly gauging it by eye as we move towards a berth or a mooring, or through a narrow entrance into a crowded marina. The

basic way to do this is to line up two objects at the place we are heading for, and keep them in line as we make our approach, even if it means steering towards somewhere else. Figure 21 shows that in order to reach point B we must steer towards some point upstream of it such that by the time we reach the shore, jetty or whatever it is, the stream will have pushed us sideways down to point B. If we gauge our speed and the angle of our course to the current correctly we should move steadily crabwise along the line between us and point B. It should be apparent from the diagram that as long as we are on this track – regardless of which way the boat is actually pointing – the two objects ashore will remain in line. The converse is that as long as we keep these objects in line, we will know that we are on that direct track to point B.

In practice you will find it necessary to juggle with your course and speed,

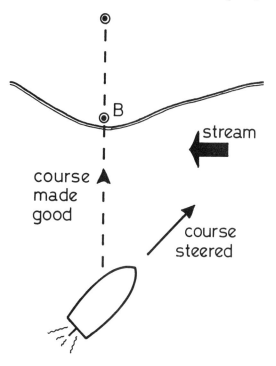

course made good

stream

course steered

Figure 21

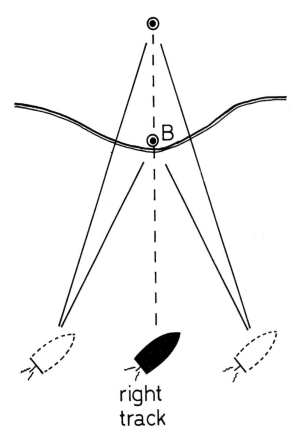

right
track

Figure 22

probably constantly, in order to keep the objects in line, and thus the boat on track. If you look at figure 22 you will see that if the boat drifts to port of her track the object at the back will open out to the left of the front one; if she drifts to starboard it will open out to the right. If this happens, you should make a bold alteration off course to get back on track as quickly as possible. There may be rocks or other dangers close to either side of the line, or for other reasons it may be very important that you keep closely aligned on the direct track. As soon as you are back on this you can resume the original course you were steering, with an allowance for the previous under- or over-correction that you had made for the stream. The best

way to remember this is to always steer towards the nearer object when you get off track.

Two shore objects aligned like this, to guide us along a particular line, are known as a **transit**. You will find them much in use for marking safe courses into harbours, past rocks and so on, and there will be more about them in Chapter 11. A similar result can be obtained by lining up one object ashore with a part of the boat between your eye and the shore. As long as your eye remains in the same place on the boat, keeping the two objects in line will ensure that the boat moves directly towards the shore object, just as it did by aligning two objects ashore. What you are doing, in effect, is setting up the transit on the boat instead of the shore. Look at figure 21 and imagine the shore (with the transit) moving towards the boat, instead of the other way round. The end result is the same. This is a very useful trick in tidal waters, and you should practise it. If the marks get out of line in this case, you should steer towards the shore mark. The same trick can be used to check if you are drifting sideways onto a buoy or a moored boat. In this case, when you line up the buoy (or whatever), you want it to drift off the line towards your bow or stern, thus indicating that it will pass safely ahead or astern of you. If it remains steadily in line with your eye, it will hit you!

You should now, I hope, have a fair understanding of the effects that wind and current will have on your boat while motoring around, and particularly while manoeuvring. So let us put it all into practice and look at how we go about putting our motor cruiser safely and neatly alongside a jetty. And then getting equally neatly and safely away again. We generally refer to good boathandling as being **seamanlike** or good **seamanship**.

5
BERTHING ALONGSIDE

By now you should have a clear idea of how to go about handling a motor cruiser, and the ways in which wind and tide can affect manoeuvring. Let us assume that we have spent the afternoon out in the open harbour practising our boathandling and now the time has come to return to our berth and go home for tea. Needless to say, there is rather more to getting a motor cruiser alongside the quay in a seamanlike manner than there is to simply parking the car. How do we do it?

The first thing to appreciate is that there are two clear stages in getting a

boat alongside – the initial approach to the berth, and the final manoeuvring. If you observe others berthing their motor cruisers you will notice that all too many totally ignore the second stage, being content merely to get close enough to the quay to throw a line ashore, with which they then drag themselves alongside. This is sloppy, unseamanlike and unsatisfying for a skipper, and there will be none of it in this book!

The object of the initial approach is simply to place the boat in a position from which she can be easily manoeuvred alongside and stopped. Thus, with very few exceptions (and these for

Figure 23

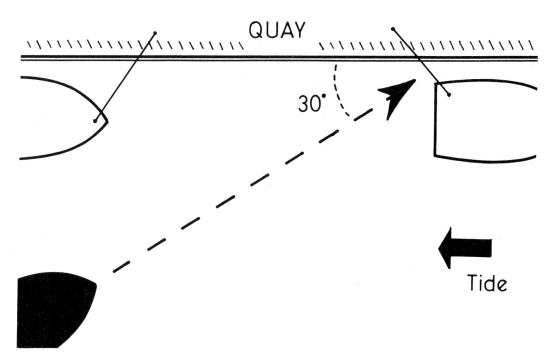

experts only), this initial approach is always made heading into the tide. The benefits of this are two-fold. Firstly, as we saw in the last chapter, it is much easier to manoeuvre at slow speeds when **stemming the tide** (heading into it) and this slow, controlled approach also gives us plenty of time to see how the boat is shaping out for the berth, and adjust our course accordingly. Secondly, it is much easier to stop when heading into the tide.

Figure 23 shows a fairly typical berthing situation where we have to slot into a space between two other boats already alongside. We should make the approach at about 30 degrees to the line of the quay and aim for the far end of the berth, stemming the tide as we go. This will put us in just the right place on arrival to slot neatly in alongside. Remember, however, that if

the tide is strong we will have to steer uptide of this course in order to move the boat along the line illustrated. On arrival off the berth we put the **helm** (wheel or tiller) over to swing her parallel to the quay and at the same time go astern.

If we have judged everything correctly, the boat will then swing neatly and stop precisely in the berth, close enough to simply step ashore with the mooring lines and secure her alongside. Practice, of course, is needed to judge the correct approach speed so that **steerage** (sufficient speed to steer the boat) is maintained all the way and the boat can also be stopped without having to give too much power astern. Too strong a burst astern will likely throw the boat all over the place, while too little will probably fail to get the stern in properly.

This basic example has assumed a single right-handed propeller which

Figure 24

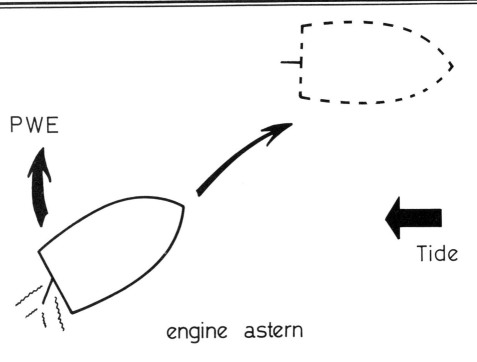

QUAY

PWE

Tide

engine astern

will throw the stern to port on going astern (see figure 24). The technique, however, gives a basic principle that can be varied and modified to suit the circumstances. There are so many variables involved in handling a power-boat – wind, tide, propellers, hull shape etc, that it is not possible to lay down hard and fast techniques to cater for every situation. It is important to understand the principles involved so that you can make your own judgement at the time as to how best to approach a berth.

If, for example, we have a left-handed propeller, going astern on approaching a berth port side to will cause the stern of the boat to swing *away* from the quay, thus the basic approach needs to be modified to allow for this. There are two ways of doing so, depending on the situation. One is simply to approach at a much shallower angle and put the helm hard over to get the stern swing-

ing in before going astern to stop. This initial swing, if judged correctly, should then be slowed by the paddlewheel effect until the boat stops in just the right place, forward movement and sideways swing coming to a halt at the same moment.

There will be occasions, however, when this method cannot be used due to the shallow approach line being restricted – by other berthed boats, for example. In this case we go to the other extreme and make the approach at a steeper than normal angle (see figure 25). This gives us room in which to get a powerful inward swing imparted to the stern while still some way off the berth. When the time comes to go astern and stop, this inward swing should then be sufficient to overcome the paddlewheel effect that is pulling the stern out. If everything is correctly judged, and only

Figure 25

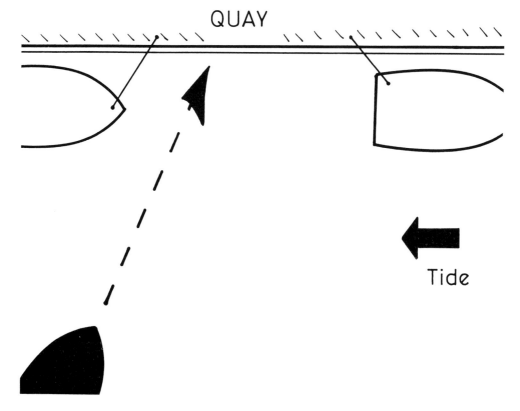

QUAY

Tide

49

practice can teach us this, the boat will once again come to a neat halt parallel to the quay and in just the right place. It may even be found necessary with some boats to give a slight kick ahead on putting the helm over, in order to increase the swing in before going astern. In this case the forward speed should be reduced as much as possible just beforehand, to ensure that this kick ahead does not get the boat going too fast in the final stages. The less stern power needed for stopping, the less will be the paddlewheel effect pushing the stern out. Note that in this instance the approach is made towards the near end of the berth rather than the far end. This is to give more room for the long, powerful swing that is necessary.

These, then, are the two basic techniques for getting a single-screw boat alongside a wall – with the paddlewheel effect pulling the stern in, and with it pulling the stern out. With twin screws we are, in effect, always dealing with the first situation, as going astern on the outboard propeller (assuming outward turning propellers) will pull the stern in whichever side we intend laying alongside the wall. The technique employed with a twin-screw vessel is to make the final approach going ahead on just the inboard engine. This will assist the initial swing as we put the helm over. This engine is then put into neutral to slow the boat, then the outside engine put astern to swing us in and stop us (see figure 26). Any manoeuvring required during the approach should be carried out with the engines as discussed in Chapter 3.

With an outboard engine, the final swing in will be carried out by swivelling the propeller on going astern, so that the prop pulls the stern in as we saw in Chapter 3 and figure 15. Twin outboards will swivel together, and should be treated as one for the purpose of this sort of manoeuvre, although the throttles can be adjusted during the approach in order to keep the boat aligned on track for the berth. Practise with your own boat and see how the various combinations of throttle and steering affect you.

Figure 26

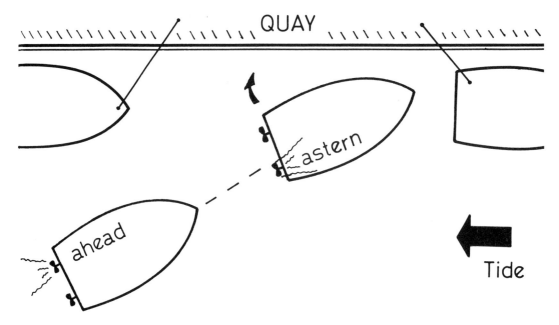

QUAY

astern

ahead

Tide

Wind and Tidal Stream

These techniques, of course, presuppose that there is no outside influence other than the straightforward tidal stream running against us. The chances are that in real life we will rarely encounter such simple and ideal situations. The tidal stream will not be running precisely along the quay and there will probably be a wind blowing from somewhere. We dealt with the effects of these, and ways in which to handle them, in Chapter 4, so let us briefly consider some berthing situations in which wind and cross tides will influence our techniques.

Cross tides are only likely to be a nuisance during the very early stages of an approach, as the tide will almost certainly be running more or less directly along the wall by the time we are close enough to be actually manoeuvring into the berth. Thus all we need do is set our course to make allowance for the tide, as discussed in the last chapter, so that the course we make good will take us towards the far corner of the berth. As we get closer to the wall so the cross-tide influence should decrease and we can then gradually correct the attitude of the boat so that she is pointing in the right direction when we get to the final manoeuvring stage.

The wind, however, is quite a different matter. Not only is it likely to influence us during all the stages of the approach, but it is quite possible that it will change strength and direction as we get nearer the berth, particularly if the quayside is surrounded by high buildings. Thus great care needs to be taken, and great attention paid, when approaching a berth in strong winds. Let us look at some typical situations.

If the wind is blowing in the same direction as the tide is running, the initial approach will be little affected; though we may have to keep the bow up into the wind a little to avoid it blowing off course. As we approach the final manoeuvring, however, and slow right down in readiness for swinging into the berth, the effect of the wind will become far more noticeable. The problem will be to prevent it from blowing the bow round and onto the wall when it is the stern that we want to push in that direction. This problem will be compounded by the fact that the moment we go astern, the stern will tend to seek the wind and thus pull itself away from the wall. The difficulty, in fact, is comparable to getting alongside with the paddlewheel effect in opposition, and the solution to it is much the same. A strong, quick burst ahead with the helm hard over just before arriving at the berth should overcome the effect of the wind, the sharp inward swing of the stern that this will induce being counteracted by both the wind blowing the bow in and the stern trying to swing away and into the wind. Fine judgement is required to get this sort of manoeuvre right, and practice is the key to success.

If the wind is blowing against the tide, we have to decide which of the two will have the greater effect on the boat. Although it is said that about eleven knots of wind are equivalent to one knot of tide, in practice it very rarely makes sense to approach into the wind rather than the tide, however strong the wind may be. The reason for this is the difficulty of maintaining a straight, steady course at slow speed into a strong wind just off the bow – all the problems described in the last paragraph, in fact, combined with the difficulty of maintaining attitude at slow speed when the tide is from astern. The moment you go astern to stop in this sort of situation, the combined effects of wind ahead and tide astern will throw you all over the place in a manner almost impossible to predict.

Approaching downwind and into the tide, however, will give you infinitely more control over the boat. The **foul tide** (tide against you) will give plenty of water flow over the propeller at the slowest speeds, while the following wind will always tend to attract the stern. Thus any slowing down that may be required due to the wind pushing you ahead can be accomplished quite simply

with a burst astern. This will slow you down considerably and at the same time the stern will seek the wind which is right behind you. The boat will maintain her attitude pointing towards the end of the berth, and keeping the right attitude to the berth during the approach is half the secret of success.

Crosswinds can be a problem if they are very strong, requiring a little forethought and planning. If a wind is blowing strongly off the quay, the basic 30 degree approach will find you about 20 yards off the quay and shooting sideways out into the harbour by the time you have stopped. The secret here is to avoid getting beam on to the wind until the last possible moment. Approach as steeply as possible (see figure 25), and only when your bow is almost touching the quay should you put the helm hard over and kick her ahead to swing. Go astern immediately and get your lines ashore as quickly as possible. What lines and where to put them are discussed later in this chapter. A little nerve is required here, to keep her going right up to the wall before swing-

Photo 8 A motor cruiser coming alongside a quay. The skipper is approaching at a fairly shallow angle and aiming beyond his berth (which is just ahead of the sailing boat) so as to allow the strong tidal stream to gently edge him sideways into it. The crew has led the head rope correctly beneath the guardrail, but she should really have coiled it more neatly to prevent the risk of a tangle. The skipper will step ashore from the cockpit with the stern rope when the boat is alongside. It would be advisable to have extra fenders well for'ard and aft in case the boat suddenly slews at an angle to the quay, and also springs prepared in order to hold her firmly in position in the strong stream. The strength and direction of the stream can be gauged from the way the moored boats are lying.

ing away. However, you will soon develop that nerve with experience of your boat and the ignominy of blowing away into the harbour a few times before ever reaching the wall!

If you misjudge things when a strong wind is blowing onto the quay, you will likely end up with a large boatyard bill rather than mere embarrassment. A shallow approach is generally best in this situation. Aim to land up a few feet clear of the wall so that the boat can drift down on the wind as you go astern and stop. Do not aim too far off the wall though as the boat will then drift onto it gathering momentum all the way. If you arrive five or six feet off in a very strong wind you could end up clobbering the wall pretty hard. Keep a very close eye on the track you are making good during the approach, and correct immediately if the wind is carrying you in too quickly. Have plenty of good fat **fenders** ready over the side.

Clearly it is not possible to lay down hard and fast rules for getting alongside in all conceivable circumstances. In many ways the contents of the previous two chapters are more important than the specific methods described here, as they outline the principles on which the handling of a motor cruiser is based. However, these techniques do provide guidelines around which to operate. The precise manner in which they are carried out must be judged at the time according to the layout of the berth, the

wind and the tide conditions, the handling characteristics of the boat and your own experience. Better to adopt a reasonable method that you know you can handle, than try a brilliantly clever one and bodge it up. Do not be afraid of hanging around the berth – going round in circles if need be – while you take your time assessing the situation before going in. Try a couple of dummy runs, to come alongside well clear of the berth, and see how wind and tide affect you. This will also give you a chance of a close look at the berth itself to see if there are any obstructions. Check the positions of other moored boats, and look for suitable places to secure your mooring lines to. The more prepared you are, the better job you are likely to make of getting alongside.

Staying in the Berth

Having got alongside safely and in a seamanlike manner, how do we keep ourselves there? Figure 27 shows the four basic ropes with which we moor up a boat. They do not simply tie her to the quay as you would tie up a horse; each has a very specific purpose. The head rope is there to hold the bow into the quay, but it is led for'ard as in the diagram so that there is some give to allow for the boat's movement in the wash of passing craft and so on. The same applies to the stern rope. Leading them both away at this sort of angle will also allow for a certain amount of rise and fall in the tide, especially if some slack is left in them as it should

Figure 27

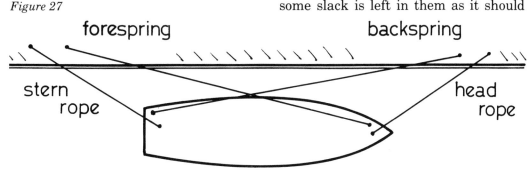

forespring   backspring

stern
rope

head
rope

be. It is important to realise that head and stern ropes are not there to pin the boat tightly into the quay; they are there to stop her floating away. Therefore give them a bit of slack so that the boat can move.

The forespring and backspring are the ropes that should be used to pin the boat in to the wall. These prevent her from surging back and forth along the quay, so should be hauled in as tightly as possible. In order to provide some give for movement and tidal range they should be as long as you can get them and be led to securing points close to the edge of the quay and as far from the boat as you can sensibly take them. They will then provide a pull as nearly as possible in line with the boat, and the length will give the necessary elasticity to cope with movement and the rise and fall of the tide (see Chapter 6), unless the range is very great, when you may have to leave some slack in these too. In extreme cases, you may even have to adjust them from time to time, to ensure that the boat is not left hanging in mid-air on her warps when the tide falls.

Figure 28 It is important to secure the forespring right for'ard or the bow will pivot in around it and jam against the wall, thus preventing the stern from swinging out properly.

You should now have a good picture of the basic principles that lie behind berthing alongside. Mundane details such as handling fenders and mooring **warps** (ropes), the correct knots to use when securing the warps, and so on, are dealt with later in the chapter. For now, let us consider, having got alongside, how we are going to get away again. This often involves much shouting and pushing and general chaos, for the simple reason that too few skippers understand the principle of 'springing'.

Leaving the Berth
Springing is an extremely useful technique that the expert uses to achieve all manner of amazing manoeuvres. It consists in essence of operating engines and rudder while keeping a line made fast to the shore, so that the boat can turn on the spot without moving ahead or astern of her position. For the time being, although its applications are almost limitless, we shall confine ourselves to its use for getting clear of a berth.

Have a look at figure 28. In order to get clear of the quay, especially when hemmed in by other boats, we can simply cast off all the mooring warps

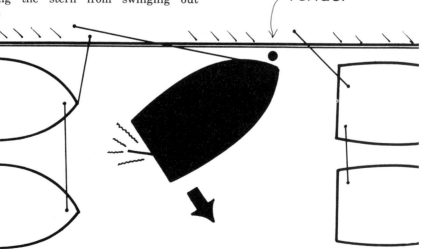

fender

except the forespring. With a good, fat fender right up for'ard we can then go ahead slowly with the rudder hard over to steer us in towards the wall. The forespring prevents the boat from going ahead and the result is that she turns on the spot, the stern swinging out and away from the wall. Having swung her out as far as we need, or as far as we can as the case may be, we can then let go the spring and motor astern clear of the berth. How far the stern will swing out depends on a number of factors – wind, tide and paddlewheel effect (whether it is helping the swing or hindering it). From what we have discussed in the last three chapters you should be able to work out roughly how each of these influences will affect the amount of swing and how the boat will behave on going astern. Practice and experience will show you.

With what we have learned so far you should now be able to make a competent and seamanlike job of getting in and out of most reasonably straightforward berths, and I would suggest that you try to avoid the more difficult ones until you have had some experience with the simpler variety. In time, however, with an understanding of the principles involved, and a thorough practical knowledge of how your own boat handles under a variety of conditions, you should be able to take her more or less anywhere with confidence.

Particular Berths
Let us now finish off with a brief look at a couple of particular berthing situations that you will probably be faced with in the early days of your motor cruising. The first is the ubiquitous marina berth, in which you will very likely be keeping your boat. In an attempt to make as much money as possible, most marina owners cram so many berths into a small space that it often requires quite expert boat-

handling, in all but the quietest of conditions, to get in and out at all. One cannot blame them, I suppose, but it does make life difficult for the beginner.

The basic problem is that there is hardly ever sufficient room to actually make a steady approach as we have described. Usually it is a question of nudging and nosing your way round a multitude of tight corners until you can get close enough to your berth to get a line ashore, after which much pushing and heaving and occasional touches on the engine will eventually get you into the berth. There is very little else you can do unless you are a real expert, but there are some useful guidelines that you can bear in mind. The first is to think of all the factors already discussed – how your boat behaves in wind and tide, the paddlewheel effect, your stopping distance and so on – and do not attempt to formulate a technique for berthing in a marina; there is no such thing. You may find a particular approach works for your own marina, but you can be sure it will not work anywhere else.

Take things as slowly as you can, consistent with maintaining control. Wind is generally the biggest problem in these situations, and you must bear in mind that, with much wind effect, going too slowly can be as bad as going too quickly. If you have to motor along a stretch with a strong wind on the beam, you will not have room to drift much. It will pay you to motor along there as quickly as you safely can. Keep as close to the windward side as possible. Remember the 'windseeking' effect when going astern; this is very often the best way of getting yourself out of trouble if you find yourself drifting onto a row of moored boats and space does not permit you to swing the bow up into the wind. And remember the drifting effect when you turn. The only technique that will help you in these tight situations is an absolutely thorough knowledge of your boat's behaviour under all circumstances.

The other particular berthing situation you may find is having to 'raft up' alongside other boats when berthing at a quayside. The only difference between this and berthing directly against the wall is that if you crunch him, an owner is unlikely to invite you aboard for a drink. Having safely got alongside him, however, there are one or two courtesies that should be observed. After mooring up to him with head and stern ropes and springs, you should then take further head and stern ropes to the shore so that the full weight of your boat is not taken by his warps and **cleats** (fastening points – see figure 32) if the weather

Photo 9 The second eye to be placed on the bollard is tucked up through the first one before being slipped over the top of the bollard. This way either can be removed without disturbing the other. This should be normal practice, whether mooring to the quayside or to another boat.

gets bad with wind and waves pushing and jostling you all about. When you go ashore, ask permission to cross his boat, and do so as far from his cockpit as possible, so as to create the least intrusion on his privacy. And don't go trampling all over his beautiful varnish work in your ordinary shoes. Put out plenty of fenders; it is not reasonable to use only his, if he has some out.

Tying the Boat Up

The *Ashley Book of Knots* lists some 3,854 different varieties, of which only 3 – you will be relieved to hear – are needed for securing your boat alongside. The clove hitch (see figure 29) is a simple knot that can be quickly tied round a bar or railing and easily adjusted. It is ideal for securing fenders to the guardrail so that their height above the water can be quickly altered if necessary. It is not, however, a very secure knot if there is any load on it, and it should never be used for tying up the boat.

Boats should be tied up using either a bowline or a round turn and two half hitches. The former (see figure 30) makes an eye in the end of a rope, of whatever size you need, that can be simply dropped over a **bollard** (a tall round object for tying ships to). If another boat is already secured to the bollard with an eye, you should 'dip' yours up through his from underneath before dropping it over the bollard. This will enable him to lift his off without having to try and remove yours if it is under strain.

The round turn and two half hitches (see figure 31) should be used for tying

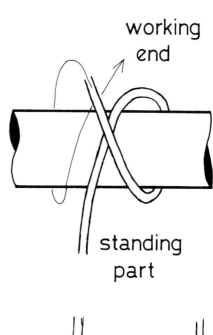

Figure 29 Wrap the rope around the bar, then lay the working end across the standing part (the end you are not working with) as shown. This can be done either to the left (as here) or to the right. Then take the working end round the back of the bar again, up the front, and underneath itself, as shown by the thin arrow. Pull taut on both ends. The fender will be hanging from the standing part, and its height can be raised by pushing the standing part into the knot and pulling out the slack with the working end. To lower the fender, push the working end into the knot and pull out the slack with the standing part. The knot must be kept tight.

Figure 30 Form a small eye in the standing part about twice as far from the working end as the diameter of bowline required. The standing part should emerge from the back of this small eye, so that the finished knot will hold it tight against the eye (see left-hand drawing). Then feed the working end up through this eye from the back, round the back of the standing part, and back down through the eye from the front, as shown by the thin arrow. Work the knot tight, as shown in the right-hand picture, by pulling down on the working end and the right-hand side of the main loop with one hand, and up on the standing part with the other. Leave a few inches of working end hanging from the knot to make sure it cannot shake apart. A much quicker way to make a bowline is to simply hold the working end in the right hand, lay it across the standing part where you want the small eye, then twist the two together down to the right. It is very difficult to explain this, but if you do it slowly and watch carefully what is happening, you will realise that you are attempting to twist the small eye into the standing part, with the working end already tucked up through it. You can then pass the working end round the back of the standing part and back down through the eye. With experience the whole thing can be done one-handed.

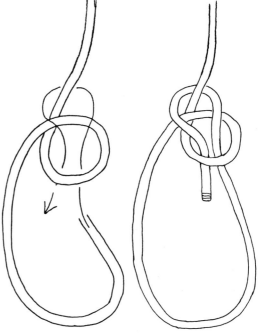

working
end

standing
part

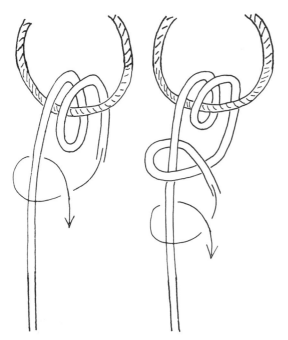

Figure 31 Pass the working end twice round the ring (or whatever) as shown in the left-hand picture, to make one complete 'round turn'. Then 'half hitch' the working end round the standing part as shown by the thin arrow, and draw the whole knot up tight. Finish with a second half hitch as shown by the thin arrow in the right-hand picture.

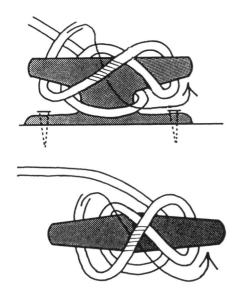

Figure 32

up to rings etc that a bowline cannot be dropped over. A bowline should never be tied into anything from which it cannot be lifted off, as it is not possible to undo it when it is under strain. After a lot of strain it can jam up quite solidly and be almost impossible to undo even when slackened off. It can also cause the rope to chafe quite badly if looped over anything small and rough, such as a wooden post, as it sits loosely round the object and can therefore move and rub on it. A round turn and two half hitches can be undone under tension and will not cause rope to chafe, as it is tied tightly round the object you are mooring to. It is an excellent general purpose knot.

If you have to secure to a cleat, turn the rope round it in a figure of eight a number of times, taking care not to jam any part of the rope under the bit that leads out and is under strain. If you do, you will not be able to uncleat the rope. It is a good idea to twist the last turn before putting it over the cleat, so that the end comes out as under the shaded section of rope (see figure 32). This will avoid any risk of the rope unravelling from the cleat. This should never, however, be done with old-fashioned natural fibre, as that swells when wet and will jam solid.

Where possible, warps should be led through **fairleads** before going to the shore. These vary in design, but are generally smooth, half-round objects fastened at the edge of the deck. They ensure that the warp leads from the right part of the boat (wherever the cleat may be) and that it does not rub against the boat, chafing both (see the photograph). As you approach a berth have all your mooring warps neatly coiled (clockwise) on deck in the places they are to be used. The end to go ashore should be on top, and the bottom end should be carefully pulled from under the coil, passed over the top of the

Photo 10 This fairlead is far too small for the size of rope and would chafe it if a length of plastic pipe had not been fitted over the warp.

guardrail then back inboard under the bottom rail, through the fairlead and secured to the cleat (see figure 33). The whole coil can then be thrown or taken ashore and secured, and the warp will automatically lead correctly under the guardrail, through the fairlead to the cleat. It can then be uncleated, hauled in and cleated again when the length is right. It is always wise to cleat the end before throwing, or the whole warp may disappear onto the shore or into the water.

Make sure fenders are positioned at the right height for the structure you are to lie alongside. Spread them out

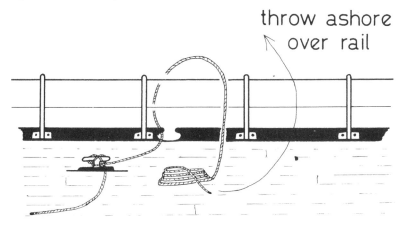

throw ashore over rail

Figure 33

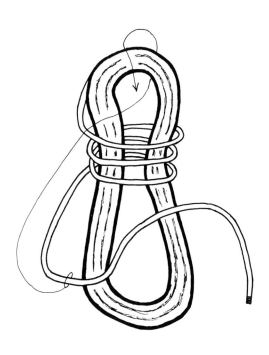
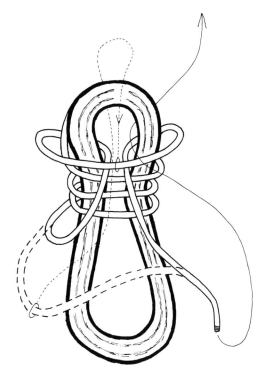

Figure 34 Hold the coil in your left hand. Take the end from the back of the coil in your right hand and wrap it round the whole coil a few times as shown in the left-hand picture (a fairly long length will be needed). Pull these lashings fairly tight, then pass the bight (middle bit) of the working end through the top of the coil, as shown by the thin arrow. Leave the actual working end dangling down the front. Pull the bight (like a loop) over the top and sides of the coil so that it sits round it as you can see in the right-hand picture. Pull it all tight, then pass the working end through the top of the coil, as shown by the thin arrow. The coil can then be carried, or hung up, by this working end, and will remain secure.

evenly along the boat – including right for'ard and aft in case the boat swings bow or stern against the wall – and try to position them at a strong part of the hull (where there is an internal partition which will help to take the weight off the hull itself). Always keep one or two spare on deck so that they can be quickly put over anywhere if things go wrong. Occasionally you may have to moor against an open jetty supported on piles instead of a solid wall. This can make fendering a problem as the slightest movement of the boat will roll the fender off the pile. If you can carry a plank of wood with a length of rope tied to each end, this can be hung down between the fenders and the piles to prevent that trouble. If it is big enough it can double as a gangplank. Failing that, try to hang long fenders horizontally across the piles.

When your warps are not in use they should be coiled neatly – always coil ropes clockwise as they lie more easily in a coil that way due to their con-

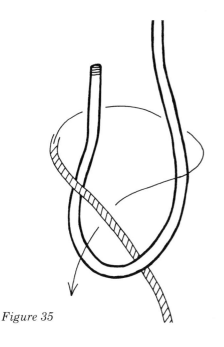

Figure 35 Put an open loop in the end of the thicker of the two ropes to be joined. Pass the other rope up through and round the back of this loop, from the short working end to the standing part, as shown. Then bring it back across the front of the rope, passing under itself, as shown by the thin arrow. Draw the knot up tight, careful to keep its shape. The two short ends should emerge on the same side, otherwise it is not a sheet bend but a weaver's knot – excellent, I've no doubt, for weaving, but not so good for tying ropes together. The knot is most secure if the loop is in the thicker of the two ropes. You can see the finished knot (bend, to give it its correct name) in the photograph in figure 36, where it has been tied into an eye in the end of a rope. Clearly, in this instance it can be made either way round. Figure 37 shows a double sheet bend (with the working end passed twice around the back of the loop) which is more secure, especially if there is much difference in thickness between the ropes.

Figure 35

Figure 36

Figure 37

struction, tied up securely (see figure 34) and stowed away in a cockpit locker or somewhere handy where they can dry off. If you have a permanent berth in a marina, you can save a lot of trouble by having short warps permanently secured to the pontoon in the right positions and just long enough to secure on deck. They can then be simply cast off whenever you go out and picked up again on your return. This will save you all the bother of heaving warps out of lockers, coiling them up and stowing them again every time you go out.

If you ever need to tie two ropes together to make a long one, it should be done with a sheet bend (see figure 35). The reef knot (see figure 38) is very

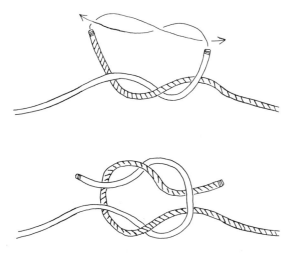

Figure 38 Take an end of the line in each hand. Lay the left one over the right one in a cross, then tuck it round the back of the right one and up the front, as in the top picture. Take this same end and cross it over the one now on the left, tuck it round the back and up the front as you did before, as shown by the thin arrows. The knot should now look like the bottom picture, and can be tightened by pulling on the two working ends.

handy for tying parcels and the general lashing of things, but is not safe for joining ropes that will come under strain. It can easily topple and come apart.

Finally, a few hints when coming alongside. Keep arms and legs well clear of the deck-edge in case the boat suddenly swings hard into the wall. Make sure no mooring warps can rub against sharp edges on the boat or the quay – they could chafe through and part. Do not throw ropes ashore unless the boat is drifting away; wait until she arrives, then calmly pass or take them ashore. If you need to hold the boat urgently, and haven't time to tie a knot, wrap at least a couple of turns of the rope around a bollard, or anything handy, and hold on tightly. If you need to throw a rope a long way, divide it into two small coils, one in each hand, and throw one, letting the rope run freely from your other hand. If the end of a rope becomes unravelled, cut off the rough bit and melt the clean end with a match or in a gas flame. This will keep it tidy and prevent it unravelling again. Wet your fingers and rub the molten rope to make sure the end is sealed completely. There is no need to set the rope on fire!

Restricted Waters: At all times when in restricted waters, such as harbours, rivers etc, your anchor should be cleared away and ready for instant use; in case of engine breakdown or the need to suddenly stop in an emergency. See Chapter 6.

6
ANCHORING AND MOORING

There will be many times, for various reasons, when you will be unable to tie up to a convenient wall or jetty. There may not be one in the harbour, the depth of water may be too shallow alongside it, it may be too busy, or you may simply want peace and quiet out on the water. In this case you will need to go out into the harbour somewhere and tie yourself to the seabed so as not to drift about. You can either do this with your own equipment or you can use something already fixed out there.

Anchoring

Your own equipment will consist of a heavy metal object known as an **anchor**, designed to hook itself into the sea bed, and a long length of either chain cable or springy nylon rope with which you can secure your boat to the anchor. This latter, whether it be chain or nylon, is generally referred to as the **anchor warp**. Anchoring a boat consists, in essence, of slinging the anchor over the side into the water (attached to the warp, of course) and then tying the warp to the boat when you have let out sufficient to reach the bottom.

Endless work and trouble are caused to harbourmasters and other boat-owners the world over by people (I will not call them seamen, for they are not) who literally do no more than this. Anchoring properly requires just as much care, thought and knowledge as does berthing alongside a quay if we are to be safe, comfortable and not a danger to other boats. Our anchoring equip-ment must be sound and suitable for the job – the right type and weight of anchor, and sufficiently strong anchor warp to hold the boat safely in all conditions (see photos 11, 12 and 13). The place we choose must be deep enough for us to float at Low Water; sheltered from waves that would make life most uncomfortable on board and also put a lot of sudden, jerking strains on the anchor and warp; it must also be far enough away from other boats, the shore, rocks etc so that as we swing around in the wind or in the changing tidal stream we will not clobber them. Let us see how we go about anchoring properly.

Figure 39 shows a boat anchored the way it should be. The anchor is firmly dug into the seabed and the chain cable is neatly laid out in a line along the bottom. There are three reasons for laying the anchor warp out tidily like this as opposed to simply throwing it over the side in a big heap on top of the anchor. First it ensures a horizontal pull on the anchor which will tend constantly to dig the anchor in more deeply. If the chain pulled more vertically on the anchor it would tend to loosen the latter's grip, perhaps pull it out of the bottom altogether. The second reason is that the weight of the chain itself creates a lot of friction against the seabead, and this reduces much of the load on the anchor. Thirdly it ensures, as the boat rises and falls with the tide, that the chain always hangs in a gentle curve from seabed to stem. This curve,

Photo 11, 12, 13 Three different types of anchor commonly used in small boats. The **Danforth** anchor at the top and the **CQR** anchor on the right are generally used as main anchors due to their very effective holding ability. The traditional **fisherman's** anchor (bottom right) is commonly used in small boats and as a **kedge**, or spare, anchor in larger boats, as it folds up to stow in a very small space. It also has the advantage over the others that it holds very much better in rocky or weed-strewn bottoms, so it is good policy to carry a fisherman's as the spare. As a general guide, the weight of an anchor in pounds should be rather more than the length of the boat in feet. A 30ft boat should carry about a 35lb anchor. The kedge anchor is generally somewhat lighter than this, so that .it can more easily be manhandled or taken away in the dinghy if you run aground (see Chapter 12). Suitable sizes of warp or chain will be recommended by the anchor's manufacturer, and advice should be taken from your local chandler or boatyard. Although much research is done into the holding powers of various types of anchor and warp, there is little doubt that the more weight you have on the bottom, the better it will hold you (assuming the gear has been laid properly). I would suggest that your main anchor and chain be as heavy as you can manage, your kedge likewise but used with nylon warp, which will make it very much easier to take away in the dinghy. This operation will be made very much easier still if you coil the warp in the dinghy, then pay it out as you row, rather than try to drag all the warp through the water from your cruiser. Light planing boats, being very easily upset in trim by surplus weight (especially for'ard), will probably have to settle for the minimum efficient weight of anchor, and nylon warp.

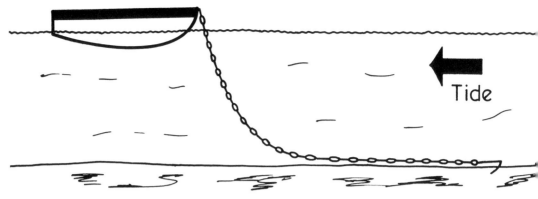

Tide

Figure 39 This boat is anchored with chain cable, which should be at least three times as long as the depth of water. With nylon warp, this 'scope', as it is called, should be at least five times the depth, as nylon, being much lighter than chain, will tend to go straight from the anchor to the boat, rather than lie on the bottom as the chain does here. The longer scope will help to create a more horizontal pull on the anchor. A nylon warp should have at least 5 metres of chain 'leader' between the end of it and the anchor – partly to improve the horizontal pull, partly to prevent the nylon from chafing on the seabed. Because of the much longer scope, and the lack of weight dragging on the bow, a boat anchored with nylon will swing and roam around over a much greater area of water than will one anchored on chain. The amount of warp let out can be gauged by having it marked at intervals of five metres. Use paint on chain and small line securely tied through the lay of nylon.

and any wind will, unless blowing from right ahead, push on her bow and make her lie crossways with her bow pointing away from the anchor. If there is a strong wind from astern she may even blow forward until she lies virtually above the anchor, and will probably sheer about from side to side as well. With sufficient cable out and the anchor laid properly as we have described, none of this should affect the security with which she is attached to the bottom. If the anchor and cable are not laid out properly then the boat sheering and moving in a strong wind could easily loosen the anchor. When the tide turns, changing from flood to ebb or vice versa, the boat simply swings round with it and points in the opposite direction until it turns again.

known as the **catenary** of the chain, can then straighten and slacken as required to absorb shocks caused by violent movements of the boat in waves and strong, gusty winds. This reduces considerably the risk of a sudden jerk loosening the grip of the anchor. Nylon absorbs these shocks by stretching.

The boat will lie like this, pointing into the current or wind (whichever has most effect – usually the current), as one or other of these will tend to sweep the boat away from the anchor. What is usually found in practice is that the boat will lie back from her anchor in the direction the current is sweeping her,

Depth of Water
As the tide changes from flood to ebb and back again it will also change in height, and this will alter the actual depth of water underneath the boat. Thus, when we pick a spot at which to anchor we must be sure that the boat will still float at Low Water and that she will have enough cable out at High Water. This means that the amount of cable that should be **veered** (let out) is at least three or five times as much as the depth will be at High Water, not the depth at the time of anchoring. This is the total depth of water, not just the height of the tide. The height of the

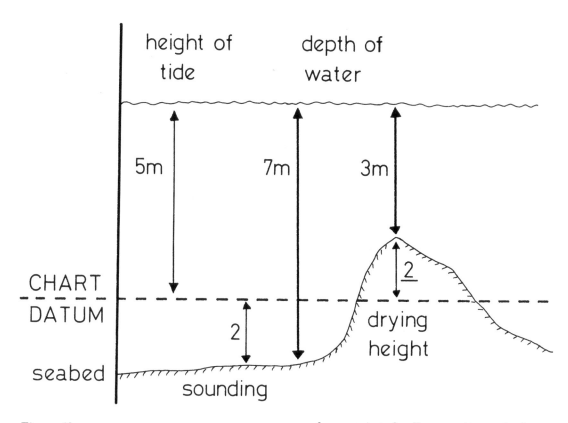

height of tide

depth of water

5m

7m

3m

CHART DATUM

2

drying height

2

seabed

sounding

Figure 40

tide, as given in the tide tables, is measured from some particular point, normally below the level of Low Water, while the depths of water marked on **charts** are measured below this level or, if the seabed comes up high enough, above it. This level is known as **Chart Datum** (see figure 40). Charts are simply maps of the sea and surrounding land, and we use them to find our way about on the water. They give us all sorts of useful information and we shall look at them in some detail in Chapter 11. For the time being, let us see how they can help us in anchoring.

Have a look at the chart of Runswick Bay, North Yorkshire, in figure 41. The area at the bottom and on the left is land – you can see Runswick Village on the left. Beyond the thick line surrounding the land is the sea, and the first thing to notice is the mass of

numbers printed all over it, and the lines that weave in and out of the numbers, roughly following the shape of the coast. The numbers signify depths in metres and tenths of metres below the level of Chart Datum, and the lines (known as **depth contours**) simply join up equal depths. You should be able to pick out the 1 metre line (dotted), the 5 metre line, the 10 metre line, the 15 metre and 20 metre lines. Inside the 1 metre line you can see a ragged, rocky looking line running round the bay. In places it is interspersed with short lengths of contour line, and on one such length at the top left of the bay you will see the figure 0. This is, in effect, the zero metre line, ie Chart Datum. Inshore of this line, at various places around the bay, **soundings** (depths) are underlined. These are parts of the seabed that rise above Chart Datum by the amounts marked (see figure 40). Some old charts may

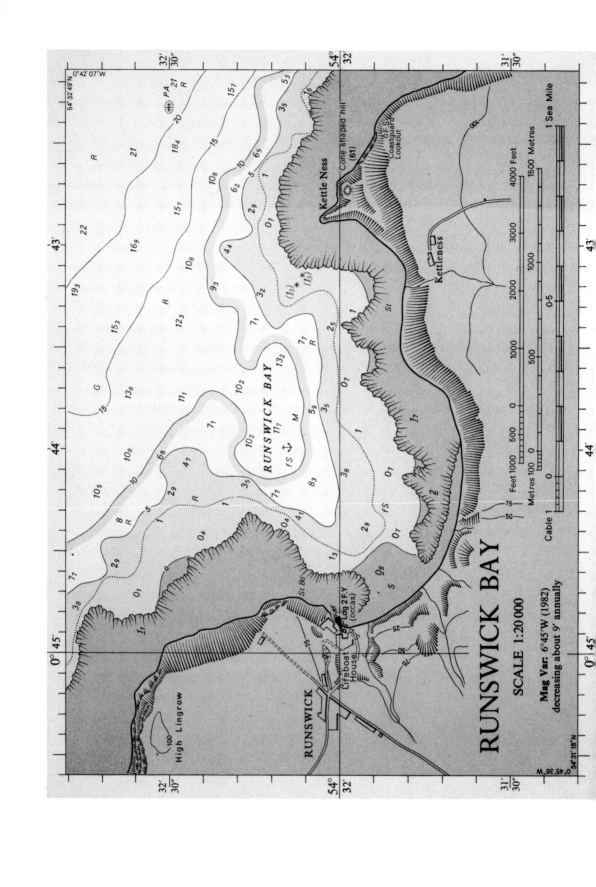

RUNSWICK BAY

SCALE 1:20 000

Mag Var: 6°45'W (1982)
decreasing about 9' annually

RUNSWICK BAY

RUNSWICK

High Lingrow

Lifeboat House

Kettle Ness

Cone shaped hill (61)

Kettleness

Coastguard Lookout

F.S.

show depths in feet and fathoms (6 feet). The units used for depths will be noted under the title of the chart.

Thus we can see that, where there is an ordinary sounding on the chart, the actual depth of water at any time will be the height of the tide plus the sounding. Where the soundings are underlined (known as **drying heights**) the actual depth of water will be the height of the tide minus the charted sounding.

Before we can safely anchor the boat, we must know not only the actual depth of water there at the time, but also how much higher it might rise and how much lower it might fall while we are there. Finding the actual depth of water can either be done 'on site' by motoring into the anchorage and measuring it (we shall see how in a moment), or by picking a suitable spot on the chart and calculating what the depth will be when we get there. Precisely how we get

Figure 41
Figure 42 This shows a 20-metre leadline, which should be long enough for your purposes. It can be made up quite simply from braided, pre-stretched terylene rope (it must not stretch or shrink in water) attached, as shown, to a lead. A good chandler will supply you with both. The simple knot used for attaching the eye to the shackle on the lead is called a 'cow hitch'. The line should be stretched out and the markings sewn on at the required distances, measured from the cow hitch to allow for a safety margin. There should be a hollow in the bottom of the lead and this can be filled with tallow, lard or even thick grease, to pick up a sample of the seabed – sand, shells, mud or whatever (see page 72). To take a sounding, the lead should be swung

out ahead of the boat so that by the time the boat catches up with it, it has reached the bottom and you can get an accurate sounding with the line vertical in the water instead of strung out astern. If you lift it up and down you will feel when the lead touches the bottom. The versatility of the leadline is that it can be used away from the boat – to sound out an uncharted creek from the dinghy, or check the depths alongside a quay before bringing your boat in. If used carefully, it can also warn of large boulders on the seabed or protuberances sticking out of the quay wall below the water, which could be dangerous to the boat when berthing. You can use what you like for the markings – different colours, shapes and materials. Traditional markings, however, will be found in the Almanac (see Appendix 3).

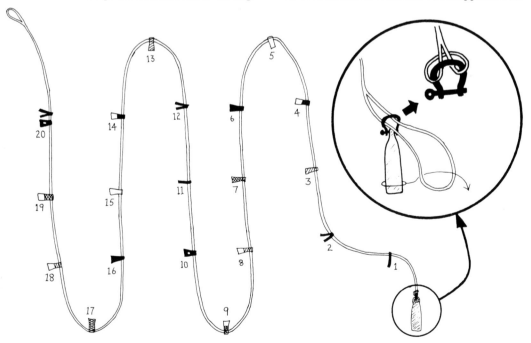

69

ourselves to a particular spot on the chart will be looked at in later chapters.

To find the actual depth of water in which we are floating we can use either a **leadline** or an **echo-sounder**. A leadline is simply a piece of rope, marked at certain intervals, with a lead weight on the end. We lower this over the side until it touches the bottom and read off the marked depth at the surface of the water (see figure 42). An echo-sounder is an electronic gadget that sends a pulse of sound downwards from the bottom of the boat. When this hits the seabed, it rebounds and is picked up

Photo 14 A common type of echo-sounder sensibly situated right in front of the helmsman. The depth is shown clock-face fashion by a red neon light, and its sensitivity can be controlled so as to prevent echoes from fish etc. This one has an audible alarm that can be set to warn you when the depth falls below a particular figure.

again by the **transducer** of the echo-sounder (the fitting in the bottom of the hull from which the sound signal is transmitted). The electronic gadgetry in the sounder then times how long the pulse has taken to go to the bottom of the water and back and calculates (knowing the speed of sound) how far the pulse has travelled. It then divides this by two (to allow for the return journey) and displays the answer on a dial as the depth of water. The sounder will display the depth continuously with no effort on the part of any human, so is a most useful device. It can be adjusted to show depth below bottom of boat or depth below surface of water. It is most important, clearly, that you know which yours shows, although which you select is a matter of personal preference. Some skippers like to see at a glance the depth below the boat, whereas the depth below the surface is

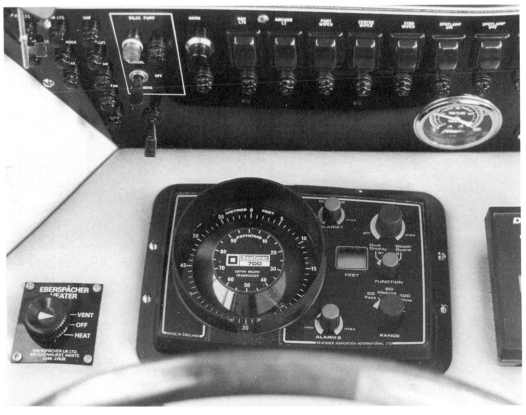

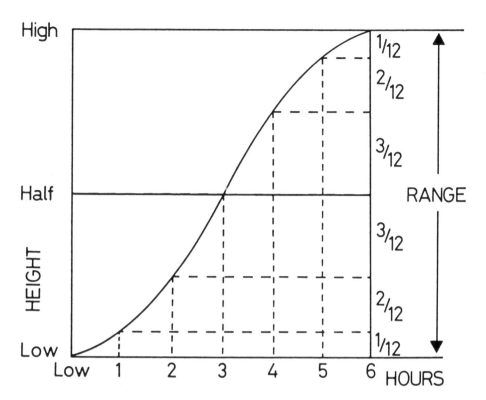

High

Half

HEIGHT

Low

1/12
2/12
3/12

RANGE

3/12
2/12
1/12

Low   1   2   3   4   5   6 HOURS

Figure 43

more convenient for tidal calculations. Whichever you use, remember that electronic things can break down or go haywire without warning. Always carry an accurately marked leadline as a standby, and also to periodically check the accuracy of the sounder. As you gain experience, you will discover certain things that a leadline can do that a sounder cannot.

To find out how much this depth will alter while we are at anchor, we must know how the tidal height will vary – as the sounding, with the boat remaining in one place, will not change. If we anchor at exactly High or Low Water, the tide tables will tell us the height of the tide. If we anchor at any other time, we will have to work it out. Fortunately the height of the tide changes in a predictable manner between High and Low Water, so this is quite easy to do.

You can see from figure 43 that the tide rises slowly to begin with, increases speed considerably over the period around half tide, then slows down again as it reaches High Water. The same happens when it falls. If we divide the range by twelve, you can see that in the first hour after Low Water the tide will rise by one-twelfth of the range; in the second hour by two-twelfths and in the third hour by three-twelfths, making six twelfths (a half) in all by half-tide. It then slows down, rising three-twelfths again in the fourth hour, then two-twelfths in the fifth, and one-twelfth in the last hour. This is known as the **twelfths rule**, and it is most important that you remember it. It is not scientifically accurate for a number of reasons, but it is perfectly adequate for our purposes, as a good safety margin of depth should always be allowed because of waves, atmospheric conditions affecting the predicted height of the tide, and so on. (See Chapter 11.)

71

The Anchorage

As mentioned briefly earlier, choosing a spot in which to anchor has to be done carefully, taking into account certain considerations. Let us imagine we want to anchor in Runswick Bay (see figure 41). The first thing we must ensure is that we will be sheltered from wind, waves and strong tidal streams. Any of these could make an anchorage uncomfortable or even dangerous.

The shore around the bay is quite high, as we can see from the hill contours, so it would give us very good shelter from a wind blowing off the land. If the wind was off the land (an **offshore wind**) there would be no waves in the bay, so it would be very calm and peaceful on the water. Any strong tidal streams running along the coast outside would shoot straight past the mouth of the bay, so there would be negligible tidal stream inside. With the wind blowing off the land and no **swell** (waves left over from a previous wind) rolling in from seaward, this would be a most delightful anchorage from the viewpoint of shelter; so good, in fact, that the Admiralty (who produced this chart) have actually printed an anchor on the water to recommend it. (This recommendation, in fact, would refer to the bottom being good holding ground for the anchor).

A glance at the soundings, even quite close to the land, shows that we would have plenty of water to anchor a small motor cruiser well tucked in close to the beach at the bottom left. We know it is a beach because it has S printed on it, meaning sand. If you look around the bay you will see other letters printed on the water. They all tell us the nature of the seabed – M in the middle means mud, fS means fine sand, R is rocks, St is stones, and Bo means boulders. Information on all these chart symbols can be found in special booklets obtainable from nautical bookshops or

chandleries and also in the Almanac. This information is essential if you use Admiralty charts as their symbols are rather cryptic. Certain charts published specifically for yachtsmen tend to have the information written out more clearly.

These symbols showing the nature of the bottom are important to us when anchoring, as anchors hold better in certain types of bottom than in others. Generally, sand and thick mud or clay are best as they give a good grip on the anchor. Rocks, weed and soft mud are least reliable as the anchor cannot get a sure grip. Very fine sand can also give a poor grip, but the fine sand here must be all right to merit the anchor sign recommending it as an anchorage. Different types of anchor hold better in different bottoms, as we mentioned in the caption to the photographs.

Finally, we must beware of anchoring where the bottom is foul – ie where old wrecks and rubbish are lying – as the anchor could get jammed and be impossible to raise again. These areas will be clearly marked on the chart as **foul ground** or something similar. Rocky bottoms can also trap anchors, as can mooring chains from nearby buoys, anchor chains from nearby boats, and underwater telephone and electricity cables (which will be clearly marked on the chart). The latter might also land you with a hefty bill if your anchor managed to break them! Give buoys and other anchored boats a wide berth, and if you have doubts about the bottom, use a **buoy rope** on the anchor. This is a light line with a small buoy or fender on the end, attached to the **crown** (bottom end) of the anchor (see figure 44). If the anchor fouls, it can be hauled backwards out of whatever is holding it by pulling on the buoy rope. Make sure the line is long enough to reach easily to the surface at High Water, or the tide rising and lifting on

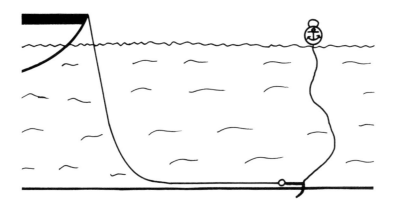

Figure 44

the buoy could loosen the grip of the anchor. Paint an anchor on the buoy so that no one will moor up to it. Yes, it happens!

If we want to anchor close to the beach in Runswick Bay, we must calculate – using tide tables and the twelfths rule – what the actual height of tide will be on arrival. We can then work out how much higher it will rise (to High Water) and how much lower it will fall (to Low Water). The former will enable us to calculate the amount of anchor warp we must put out; the latter

will enable us to calculate how deep the water we anchor in must be so as to ensure that we still float when it falls to Low Water.

If we calculate that, on arrival, the tide will still have 2 metres to fall to Low Water, then we must anchor with at least this depth of water under the **keel** (bottom of the boat). I would suggest a safety margin of 1 metre, so we should look to anchor when the sounder reads 3 metres plus our **draft** (depth of keel below surface) if it reads from the surface. The tide, of course, may be rising when we anchor, but remember that after High Water it will

Figure 45

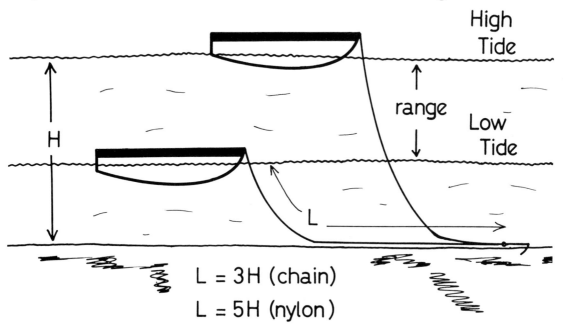

then fall all the way down to Low Water.

If our draft is 1 metre, we will be letting go the anchor in 4 metres of water. However, assuming the tide has, say, 3 metres still to rise to High Water, we know that at High Water we will be anchored in 7 metres of water, and this is the depth for which we must calculate the amount of warp to veer. If we have all chain cable, we must let go at least 21 metres of cable; if we have nylon, this should be increased to a minimum of 35 metres of warp (see figure 45). Remember that at Low Water there will be a lot of warp out, so the anchor must be let go far enough from shore, rocks, other boats and shallow water to allow for swinging round a long way from the anchor.

All these depth calculations will also have to be made if we want to berth alongside a quay in a tidal harbour. Take no notice of the 'local' who tells you there will be plenty of depth at Low Water! Work it out for yourself.

Setting the Anchor

We have stressed the importance of setting the anchor properly in the bottom and laying the warp out neatly for maximum holding efficiency. To actually do this in practice is not difficult, but it does require a little care. Having decided where we want to anchor, we approach the anchor berth slowly, heading into the tidal stream (or wind if there is no stream), and stop the boat in the required place – when the depth is suitable. Then we drop the anchor and go astern slowly, paying out the warp steadily as we go. Bear in mind that the boat will end up some distance from the anchor, depending on how much warp is to be veered. Nylon warp can simply be paid out by hand, but chain needs rather more controlling, unless it is very light. If you have a proper **windlass** with a brake, the brake should be used to ensure that the chain does not run out too quickly, thus running the risk of its piling up on the bottom. If you do not have such a luxury then the chain can be controlled by resting one foot on it, varying the pressure to let it run faster or slower as required. *Never* do this with bare feet or flip-flops.

As the boat gathers way astern, put the gear lever into neutral so that she does not build up too much speed, and continue veering the warp until the required amount is out. Then **snub** the warp by taking a few turns round a cleat or bollard, or braking it hard on the windlass, and let the boat settle. When she has settled, cleat the warp properly, or secure as in figure 46. As the boat goes astern, she will swing out of line due to wind and/or paddlewheel effect, so it will take her a few moments to settle down in line with the warp. When she has settled, go slow astern until the warp lays out ahead of you bar taut, then shift back to neutral. This ensures that the anchor is well dug in, the warp well strung out, and the whole holding the boat securely. Then leave the engine ticking over for a few minutes while you make absolutely certain she is not dragging her anchor along the bottom. Line up part of the boat by eye with a nearby moored boat or some object ashore, directly to one side of your boat, and make sure you are not gradually moving astern in relation to it. Check this from time to time while you are anchored, but make allowance for the natural movement of the boat around her warp. To stop the chain rubbing against the bow as the boat moves around, hang a shaped 'bow fender' around the bow.

Weighing the anchor (hauling it up again) is a simple matter of hauling or winding on the warp until the anchor appears out of the water, then hoisting the anchor inboard over the rail and

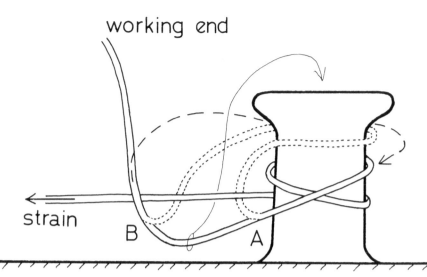

working end

strain

B   A

Figure 46 An extremely useful method for securing to a bollard, particularly when using chain or very thick rope, or when strain remains on a rope after you have taken a quick turn or two to hold the boat. It is often called a 'tugboat hitch' as it is ideal for towing, being very quick, safe and easy to both put on and cast off when a rope is under strain. Take two or three turns round the bollard, as shown, then hold hard at A to keep a firm grip round the bollard if there is strain on the rope. Pull some slack through from the working end with the other hand (keeping the weight at A all the time so the rope does not slip round the bollard), pass a bight under the standing part (the end with the strain on) and loop it over the top of the bollard as shown by the thin arrow. The rope should then lie as shown by the dotted lines. Let go at A and immediately take the weight at B, as the turns tighten round the bollard. Then loop another bight directly over the bollard from the front so that the working end leads as shown by the dashed arrow, and lies across the front of the whole thing as it did originally. The complete process can then be repeated. Casting this off is a simple matter of unwinding the turns, if necessary keeping the strain on all the time.

onto its chocks. A **boat hook** (like a broomstick with a hook on the end) may be found useful for this operation. If everything comes up covered in mud, this should be scrubbed off before the cable goes down into its locker, even if this means piling it temporarily on deck, otherwise it will fester and smell horribly when stowed. If there is any wind or tidal stream, the hauling can be made much easier by going ahead slowly on the engine to take the weight off the warp. Go ahead just enough so that the warp leads vertically down into the water; do not overrun it or you could end up with it round your prop. As chain cable goes down into its locker, try to have someone down below to range it neatly in rows across the chain locker, so that it always lies on top of the chain that is already in. This is known as **flaking the cable down**, and will ensure that the cable does not tangle the next time it is run out. If you are proceeding from an anchorage out to sea, go very slowly so as to give the crew plenty of time to get everything stowed, tidy and lashed down before you meet any waves. A nylon warp should be coiled into a fairly large coil, then the parts lashed together with small line and reef knots. Stow it somewhere secure – lashed to the guardrails perhaps.

Picking Up a Mooring
In most harbours you will find **moorings** – buoys that are permanently anchored to the bottom – and you may

find a vacant one that you can moor up to. This will almost certainly be more secure than putting your own anchor down; you will also swing round it in a much smaller circle than you will with your own anchor. The approach to a mooring should be made just as though you were going to anchor in that spot; although when you go astern to stop, the paddlewheel effect will probably swing your bow over slightly, so aim for the opposite side of the buoy to counteract this.

There are two basic types of mooring. If the buoy is large, with a big metal ring on top, you can tie up to this ring as it is connected directly to the chain which anchors the buoy. If the buoy is small, with no large ring on top, you must pick up the buoy and haul on it until the chain appears, then secure the chain to the boat. This type of mooring buoy is not sufficiently buoyant to hold the chain, so it is connected to it by a length of rope long enough to reach the bottom at High Water.

Clearly, some moorings will be heavy enough to hold your size of boat and some will not. If it is an official visitors' buoy, information on this will be found in the Pilot Book covering that harbour. If not, many buoys have the maximum permissible weight of boat painted on the side. Failing that, lift the buoy and look at the size of chain holding it. If it is smaller than your anchor chain then it is too light for you. Checking the condition of the chain under the buoy is a wise precaution anyway. If the mooring is in poor condition, then almost certainly this will show itself in wear or corrosion of the **shackle** attaching the chain to the buoy. Because of the movement of the buoy there will be more chafe here than on the bottom, and also more corrosion due to it constantly being in and out of the water. Check the parts that rub against each other.

Check as soon as you can, with the harbourmaster or the local yacht club, that the mooring is vacant and that you can stay on it for the period of your visit. Many moorings are privately owned and, although most owners do not mind their moorings being used while they are away, they do like them to be free when they get home! If you are staying overnight, you should set a **riding light** – simply a white light showing all round – to warn others that you are there. Many boats have these installed on the masthead but, if not, you can hang a hurricane lamp (or something similar, that will not blow out in the wind) high up somewhere for'ard. This will also enable you to find your boat when you come back from the pub. In the daytime, a black shape should be hung up for'ard, but a decent-sized round fender will show others that you are anchored.

Ideally, you should secure to the mooring ring with chain, to avoid any risk of chafe. Many people unshackle their anchors, then shackle the anchor chain to the buoy. This is extremely secure, but it does leave the anchor unusable in a hurry should the mooring part company with the bottom. Better to have a separate length of chain the same size for mooring with. After shackling to the buoy, tie the eye of the shackle-pin tightly to the side of the shackle with a piece of wire to prevent it coming undone with moving against the ring (see figure 47). The inboard end can be secured round a hefty cleat, or shackled in a loop round the windlass. If you have to use rope, tie it very tightly onto the ring with a round turn and two half hitches so that it cannot move against the metal and chafe through. Protect it, where it passes through the bow-fitting, with thick canvas or a piece of plastic pipe slit along its length. This should also be done if anchored with nylon warp.

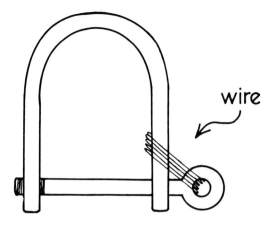

wire

Figure 47 A shackle is a U-shaped piece of metal with a hole in the end of each arm, one of them threaded. It is closed by screwing a pin through the two holes. You will find it in use all over the boat for joining things together – chain to anchors, leadline to lead, moorings to buoys and so on. Whenever it is permanently in position, the pin should always be 'moused' with wire as shown, to prevent any possibility of it unscrewing. Keep the threads of shackles lightly greased to stop them seizing. Use wire of the same, or similar material to the shackle if it is to be underwater, or it may corrode rapidly (see Chapter 13 and figure 75).

Mooring to a large buoy with a ring will be much easier if you secure to it with a **slip-rope** first – you can then shackle the chain on at your leisure. Secure a mooring warp to a cleat for'ard, as shown in figure 33. On arriving at the buoy the loose end can be passed through the ring, returned on board through the same fairlead and made up on the same cleat. When the chain is secure to the buoy, this rope should be slackened off so that the chain holds the boat. It can be left in position and used again when you leave the buoy. Tighten up on it until the chain is slack, then secure it until the chain is removed from the buoy. When you are ready to leave the end can be uncleated and the slip-rope hauled clear of the ring by pulling on the other end.

This slip-rope technique can be used in many mooring situations when a line

has to be cast off from the boat rather than from the shore. Springing out of a berth (Chapter 5) or locking down in a canal (Chapter 8) are two good examples, when all the crew may need to be on board and there may be no one ashore to cast off for you. Try to arrange the warp so that a fairly short length can be cast off and hauled clear; you could get into all sorts of trouble if the boat has to hang around while yards and yards of rope are laboriously dragged through a ring or round a bollard. If a slip-rope has to be passed through a loose mooring ring on the ground, always slip the end that goes down through the top of the ring. If you slip the one underneath, the act of hauling on the top length could jam the bottom one between the ring and the ground. Because of the risk of chafe, a boat should never be moored for any length of time with a slip-rope.

Laying a Mooring

A reduced swinging area can also be achieved by, in effect, laying your own mooring using both your anchors. This is most easily done by dropping one anchor just before reaching your chosen anchoring spot, then motoring slowly on through this spot, paying out the warp until you have veered twice as much as you have calculated that you need for the depth of water. Then drop your other anchor and haul the boat back towards the first anchor, on its warp, paying out as you go the warp on the second anchor. When the two scopes are equal in length, you should be about in the chosen anchorage. Lash the two warps together very firmly *outside* the bow fitting, then veer both warps together until this lashing is well down in the water – below the keel of the boat. The boat will then more or less swing around this lashing, each anchor and warp preventing her from roaming about in either direction. The heavier anchor should always be laid in such a direction as to hold the boat against the strongest wind or tide. In a changing tidal stream the ebb is very often stronger than the flood, particularly in estuaries when it is reinforced by river water flowing seawards. The first part of this technique – letting go the anchor while motoring ahead – can also be done when dropping a single anchor motoring into a flood tide. Then when she swings to lie to the stronger ebb tide, she will lie with the full length of the chain out in a straight line (see page 66).

To lash the two warps together, take a length of small line and tie a bowline in one end. Wrap it round one of the warps, tuck the end through the bowline and haul it tight. Then pass the end round the other warp, up through between the two warps and round the first one. Continue like this for half a dozen turns, each one being a figure of eight that tightly grips the warps together. Haul taut after each turn. Then work back over the lashing with turns right round the outside of both warps, hauling taut after each turn. Finish off with a clove hitch round the warp that is not gripped by the initial bowline.

Getting Ashore

Having got ourselves efficiently anchored or moored up out in the harbour, we are now faced with the problem of how to get ourselves ashore. What we need is a small **dinghy** of some sort that can be carried onboard the motor cruiser or towed behind her. There are various types available, but the basic choice is between a rigid, solid dinghy

Photo 15 A proper inflatable, designed specifically as a cruiser's tender. Notice the built-in rowlocks, and two black fittings on the stern to take an outboard bracket. Between these, on the inside of the boat, is an inflation valve. There should be one for'ard as well, as these boats are generally designed with at least two separate buoyancy chambers so that the boat will remain afloat if one is punctured.

and an inflatable rubber one (see photos 15 and 16). The essential difference between the two is that the inflatable can be deflated, and thus stowed away in a very small space. This tends to make it virtually an automatic choice for a small cruiser, especially as it can also double quite efficiently as a **liferaft** on coastal passages. It does have its limitations, however. It is extremely difficult to row in any but the calmest of conditions, it is very susceptible to being pushed about by wind and waves (can even literally blow away in strong winds if there is little weight in it), and it can be punctured, although modern ones are very tough and reliable on the whole. If you have an inflatable, it is most important that it be a proper 'yacht tender' and not a 'child's toy'. Many of the latter masquerade as the former; they will not, however, be advertised in the yachting magazines or sold by reputable marine chandleries.

Whichever type you have, bear in mind that more yachtsmen are drowned between the pub and the mooring than are ever lost at sea. A dinghy, being small and unstable, can be very dangerous, particularly in the rough waters of an open estuary or large harbour, and even more so at night. Never indulge in horseplay in a dinghy, and never overload it so that it becomes sluggish and bashes into the waves

Photo 16 A rigid fibreglass dinghy, being rowed easily and comfortably by a youngster. Practice makes perfect; get someone experienced to show you the technique first. This young lad should really be wearing a buoyancy aid (see Chapter 7).

instead of riding over them. Even if you have one powered by a small outboard motor, always carry oars or paddles, an anchor and warp, and a baler. At night, carry a torch and shine it about you regularly so that others can see where you are. In an inflatable, carry a pump and emergency repair kit, and be very careful of carrying anything sharp on board. Children should wear buoyancy aids at all times in a dinghy, and adults should not hesitate to wear them (or at least carry them on board) at night or in rough weather (see Chapter 7).

When getting in or out of the dinghy, from or to the boat, always moor the dinghy securely at bow and stern so that it cannot swing about, and step into the middle. Long mooring lines (**painters**) should be permanently attached at bow and stern of the dinghy, and a third, very long one for'ard will be useful for mooring to high harbour walls when the tide is likely to fall a long way. Tidal calculations are just as important when mooring up a dinghy as when mooring or anchoring the boat, and you should always ensure that the

79

Photo 17 A well loaded inflatable dinghy motoring with a small outboard. On a wild and windy night this would be too many people unless the water was very calm and sheltered all the way out to the cruiser.

dinghy painter is secured above the High Water mark so that it does not submerge and pull the dinghy under when the tide rises. Throwing the anchor out a distance over the stern will help to stop the dinghy banging into the wall when moored to one, and will also keep it clear of landing steps that others may want to use. Make sure there is sufficient scope to allow for any rise of tide, and moor the bow painter to one side clear of the steps. Experience will be needed to gauge the right lengths of painter and anchor warp required to keep the dinghy clear of the wall as the tide ranges up and down.

Dinghies can capsize or swamp when unattended or being towed, so anchor warp, baler and rowlocks should be permanently tied to a strong part of the dinghy. Oars and paddles should be lashed down securely when not in use, and an outboard should be permanently attached to a strongpoint with a tough safety line in case the clamps should work loose or you should drop it when fixing or removing. Always secure the line before fitting the outboard. When not in use an outboard's fuel should be shut off, the breather cap closed tightly and the prop tilted clear of the water, partly to protect the prop from weed, ropes or the bottom, and partly to make rowing easier.

When towing a dinghy in confined spaces, keep the painter as short as possible. This will stop the dinghy sheering about, and possibly trying to pass on the other side of a moored boat to the side you are going! At sea, use two painters – one to each quarter of the motor cruiser – to reduce sheering, and fix their lengths so that the dinghy is on top of a wave at the same time as the cruiser. This will reduce considerably the strain on the painters. Having said that, it is always best to carry the dinghy on board at sea, if you can. It is less likely to come to harm there.

7
LIVING ABOARD YOUR BOAT

Two important factors make living aboard different from life ashore, and we must be constantly aware of their significance if our motor cruising is to be both safe and enjoyable. The first is that a boat floats in the water, and for our well-being and comfort we must ensure that she continues to do so. Water belongs outside a boat, and if it gets inside in sufficient quantities the boat will sink. Thus it is most important that we have at least one system for pumping out water. Pumps for this purpose are known as **bilge pumps**, because they pump water out of the **bilge** (the bottom of the boat). Although some types are more reliable than others (being less likely to jam on sucking in foreign objects), all can be improved dramatically by fitting a strainer on the end of the suction pipe that lies in the bilge. This should be easily accessible for cleaning regularly. Try to keep the bilge clear of rubbish anyway; there are very few pumps capable of passing bits of old rag, wood shavings or even water if the **strumbox** (the strainer) is clogged up with them.

All boats should have at least one powerful hand-operated bilge pump – preferably the diaphragm type which is very simple, reliable and repairable – as a standby should the engine or the electrics fail. Usually it is situated in the cockpit, or somewhere where it can be easily operated by the man steering, for everyone else might be furiously baling out with saucepans and buckets in a real emergency. A main bilge pump driven probably by a belt off the engine, or a powerful electric pump, is so useful as to be almost essential. Not only will it shift vast quantities of water compared to the hand pump, but it will do so without occupying the time or energy of a crew member who, if the boat is leaking badly, will be better employed searching for and blocking up the leak! The automatic electric pump, activated by a float switch in the bilge, is particularly useful on a boat that spends long periods of time unattended. It is more than a little embarrassing to be busy for a month or two, then go down to the harbour and find your boat sunk – just for the want of a little pumping. Remember, however, that if the boat leaks a lot, this will soon drain the battery.

The other factor that makes life on a boat so different from life ashore is that if something dreadful happens – like a fire – you cannot simply run out of the front door and down the street screaming for help. So not only must you be far more careful to avoid the risk of fires when out on the water, you must also be equipped and able to tackle them yourself if they do occur. Basic firefighting techniques are discussed in Chapter 12, but here let us consider the equipment we should carry on board, and the precautions we should take to reduce the risk of fire.

There are three main areas of fire risk on board a boat: fuel, especially if you carry petrol on board; gas, if your cooker runs on bottled gas as most do these days; and cooking fires (chip pans and the like). The first two carry the added risk of explosion.

A real danger with both gas and petrol is that, as both are heavier than air, very slight leaks will gradually run down into the bilge to accumulate and mix with the air until an explosive mixture is formed just as in the cylinders of the engine. An horrendous explosion can then be set off by the slightest spark or smallest naked flame. Lighting the cooker or a cigarette, or even dropping a big spanner so that it strikes a slight spark off the engine, will be sufficient. This risk can be reduced virtually to nil by the simple expedient of pumping the bilges regularly (at least daily) until the pump starts sucking air, then continuing to pump for perhaps a dozen strokes. This will pump out any gas or petrol lying about down there.

Other precautions are equally simple. Gas bottles – and you should always have a spare – must never be kept down below, always on deck from where any slight leaks can drain overboard. (After changing them, smear soapy water over the joint. Bubbles will show any leaks.) The same applies to petrol stored in cans. Petrol should only be kept in cans if absolutely necessary – for small outboard motors, for example – and then only in proper, approved petrol cans stored as far from the cockpit (where people might smoke) as possible. Large quantities for a main engine should never be stored like this, only in properly installed and designed tanks. When refuelling, there must be a total ban on all naked lights (cigarettes, cookers, pilot lights etc) however far they may be from the fuelling point; and no machinery of any kind should be running, because of the risk of sparks. This includes fans, electric pumps etc, although spark-free fans designed for

extracting petrol fumes from engine rooms are all right. The nozzle of the delivery pump should always rest against the metal of the filler pipe to prevent the build up of static electricity, which might spark. The filler pipe itself should be earthed to the tank, which in turn should be earthed to the engine, which itself will be earthed to the water. Swill a bucket of water over the deck before opening the filler, so that any fuel spillage will easily wash away.

By adhering to these simple precautions, and always keeping the gas switched off at the bottle when not in use, the risk of fire and explosion will be reduced dramatically. If we then equip the boat properly with firefighting equipment, we will have done all we can to ensure the safety of the boat and her crew from this particular risk.

A number of fire extinguishers should be carried on board, of a type suitable for dealing with fuel fires (the most likely). These will probably be the dry powder, inert gas or foam type, and one should be positioned close to, but outside, the entrance to the engine room; another should be placed similarly in relation to the cooker. These two, together with a fire blanket near the cooker for placing over chip pan fires and the like, should be the absolute minimum. Try to imagine where a fire might start, and place the extinguishers so that you will be able to reach them before the fire does, wherever on the boat you may be at the time. Fire extinguishers should be checked annually by your supplier, as most have only a limited lifespan during which they remain reliable. *Read the operating instructions* on them, *before* you need to use them in earnest – it might be dark, or the fire might burn the instructions!

Accommodation
With those potential horrors under

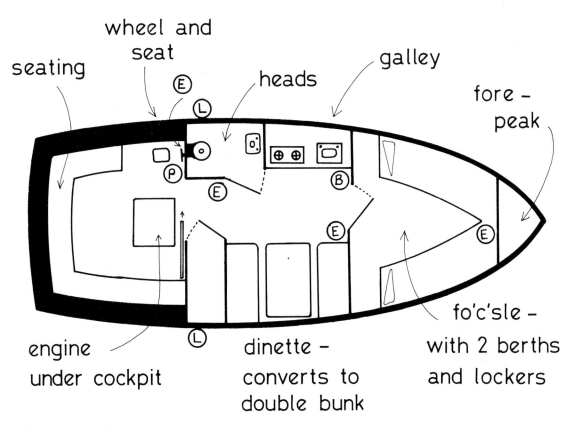

seating

wheel and
seat

heads

galley

fore –
peak

engine
under cockpit

dinette –
converts to
double bunk

fo'c'sle –
with 2 berths
and lockers

Figure 48

Ⓔ suggested sitings for fire extinguishers (*not
too close to possible fires*)

Ⓑ suggested siting for fire blanket (*not too
close to possible galley fire*)

Ⓟ suggested siting for hand bilge pump
(usable either by helmsman, or by another
crew member without getting in helmsman's way)

Ⓛ suggested sitings for lifebelts

control, we can now relax and enjoy the cosy comfort that only a boat can offer. Figure 48 shows the layout of a fairly typical small motor cruiser thirty feet long with comfortable accommodation for four. An inboard diesel engine sits under the cockpit floor out of the way, and there is a small shelter at the for'ard end of the cockpit where the **helmsman** can stand or sit while steering with a wheel. The cockpit has seating around it, under which there are storage lockers. In these are stowed all fenders and warps, leadline, deck scrubbers, fishing lines, buckets and so on, secure against the rolling of the boat yet handy when required. At least one bucket should have a line attached so that it can be lobbed over the side for water to scrub decks, peel potatoes and so on. This needs to be done with some care if the boat is moving, or you could be yanked over the side by the drag of the bucket. Throw it forward so that the bucket lands in the water upside down. As the boat catches up with it, heave it up clear of the water before it drifts astern and begins to drag.

A **boarding ladder** should also be stowed somewhere, and it should be long enough to reach at least a couple of feet beneath the surface when it is hanging over the side. If someone is trying to get on board from the water – a swimmer or a man overboard – this enables him to get his feet securely on the ladder before having to make that strenuous heave to drag the weight of his body clear of the water. Make sure the ladder fits securely over the edge of the deck, and have short lines attached so that it can be firmly lashed in place. Care is needed if you intend swimming from the boat. Never do so when a strong tidal stream is running or you could easily be swept away. If there is any stream or current then keep up-stream of the boat all the time. When children are swimming, have the dinghy in the water and manned by a capable rower, in case they get into difficulties. Young children – or poor swimmers – can have a lot of fun, and gain a lot of confidence in the water, by swimming about in their **buoyancy aids** (see page 86). A good way of testing their efficiency is that over-large or improperly secured buoyancy aids can easily slide over a child's head. Make sure the buoyancy aids are thoroughly dried out afterwards; some types can become waterlogged after long submersion.

Finally, *never* have the engine run-ning when people are in the water close to the boat, even if it is in neutral. Props can turn in neutral if the gearbox 'creeps' and a gear lever can easily be knocked. A turning propeller can make mincemeat of a swimmer, who can easily be drawn into it by the wash. Keep a good eye out for strange swimmers when motoring towards beaches and the like.

Also stowed somewhere in the cockpit should be an emergency tiller, or some device for steering the boat should the main steering gear break down. If it is metal, keep it well away from the steering compass (see Chapter 11). The steering compass, chart table and navi-gation instruments will probably be in the wheelhouse or shelter – convenient to helmsman and lookout, but in the dry.

From the wheelhouse we go through a door into the accommodation, a pro-cess known as **going below**. On the port side, in figure 48, is a small compartment masquerading as a bath-room. There is a toilet (known on a boat as the **heads**, as all you did in the old days was hang over the side at the bow, known then as the head of the ship), and a tiny wash basin; the whole com-partment may even comprise a shower cubicle if you are lucky. A sea-going heads looks, from a distance, much like a small household type. The essential difference is that on completion of the task in hand you do not simply flush it and walk away. Fresh water is in very limited supply on a boat, so water must be pumped in from outside through a seacock. As it is not good policy to have a large hole in the bottom of the boat for the waste to fall through, we also have a second pump to mash it up and push it out through another seacock. The pre-cise details of operation vary between makes of heads – some utilise the same pump for inlet and discharge – so *read* the instructions carefully.

The two seacocks in the bottom of the boat are quite sufficient to sink her in short order if you incorrectly install, operate or maintain the heads. Both should always be kept shut when not in use, so make sure they are easily accessible, or no one will bother. The discharge pipe should go right up to the **deckhead** (ceiling) and bend over before going down to the seacock. This prevents any risk of water siphoning back along it into the boat through the bowl, as water will drain away from the high point and create an airlock. This is not necessary with the inlet pipe, as it is not connected directly with the water in the bowl.

Most rivers and inland waterways these days will not permit sewage to be pumped over the side. In these situ-ations it is necessary to fit a **holding**

tank into which the waste can be pumped and stored. It can then be pumped out later at sea or into special tanks at marinas or boatyards. Or a simple chemical toilet can be used. Whichever you have, a ventilator in the heads is essential.

Fresh water to the basin can either be delivered through a small hand pump situated where the tap normally is, or an electric pump can deliver it through a normal tap. A pressure switch causes the pump to be actuated when the tap is opened, by the release of pressure in the water system. When the tap is closed, the pressure in the water pipe shuts off the pump. If you are very lucky, you may even have hot water, heated by the engine or a gas heater.

Water, in all but the smallest of boats, will be kept in one or more tanks, probably in the bilges or the engine room. A pipe, through which they can be filled, will run from the tanks to the deck, and there will be a breather pipe. Water, I repeat, is precious on a boat. Use no more than you have to.

Opposite the heads in our illustration is a locker in which boots and wet oilskins and so on can be stowed before entering the **saloon** – the name given to the living area in a boat. On the starboard side of the saloon we have a dinette arrangement, a small table surrounded by fixed seating. By lowering the table and putting a shaped cushion on it, we can convert this into a double bunk.

Opposite the dinette we have the **galley**, the nautical name for a kitchen. Perhaps a rather pretentious name too, as it usually consists of little more than a couple of cupboards, a few shelves, a tiny sink and a very small cooker, consisting probably of two burners, a grill and, if you are lucky, a small oven. Water to the sink will be provided in the same way as water to the heads' wash basin, and the drains for both

sink and wash basin will probably go straight out through seacocks. Shut them off when they are not being used. There should be some sort of ventilator in the galley, to remove cooking smells and steam.

You will probably find that all shelves and work surfaces, and the table, have lips to them, an inch or two high. These are to stop things flying about when the boat is rolling or pitching in a seaway. It is most important that all gear is stowed securely against any movement of the boat. Even in harbour, the wash of passing vessels can roll you about. Tidiness is therefore extremely important, and you will probably find small lockers tucked away in every nook and cranny in which to stow your gear. Space, as you can imagine, is very limited on board, and every square inch must be utilised for something. Anything that is susceptible to damp (matches, sugar etc) should be stored in airtight containers. Keep sleeping bags etc in large plastic bags.

For'ard of the saloon is a **bulkhead** (partition wall) with a door leading into the **fo'c'sle** (the small space right for'ard). In the fo'c'sle there are two bunks and some storage lockers. Fo'c'sle, incidentally, is a contraction of forecastle, which was the high bit for'ard in those old galleons. As they were manned by soldiers to do the fighting, they called the fighting positions castles, presumably so that they would feel more at home.

The tiny space right for'ard is generally called the **fore-peak**, and the anchor chain is usually kept here. It can then be known as the **chain locker**. The end of the chain passes up on deck through a hole, and is then shackled to the anchor. The other end of the chain should be fastened to a very strong point inside the chain locker, so that it will not disappear over the side if all the chain is let out. A good policy is to secure the chain to a length of the strongest rope that will pass through the hole to the deck (called a **navel pipe**) and then tie this rope to the strongpoint. Make the rope long enough to reach right up on deck then, should you ever have to move in an emergency when anchored and there is not time to weigh the anchor, you can run all the cable out then cut the rope and go. This is the origin of the expression to '**cut and run**'.

There will probably be an electrical system throughout the boat for lights, pumps, stereos and so on (see Chapter 2). Like water, electricity is precious on

board a boat. If you are not to spend all night in harbour running the engine to charge the batteries, conserve it. Keep everything that is not required switched off at all times.

Boat's Equipment

Besides engines, anchors, warps, heads and so on, there are certain other important items of equipment that should be carried on board. **Buoyancy aids** – buoyant waistcoats that will help to keep a conscious person afloat in the water – should be carried to fit all members of the crew. They should be worn, properly secured, by children at all times, and by adults in circum-

Photo 18 A typical buoyancy aid, with a zip front and extra securing ties. Some types have buoyancy round the back of the neck as well, and those for very young children should have securing ties between the legs to ensure that the jacket cannot slide up over their heads when in the water.

Photo 19 This is a simple and effective life-jacket for use in small boats, that will not restrict the wearer's movements too much. For inflation it is opened out at the front and blown up by mouth. Note the large area of buoyancy behind the neck, to keep an unconscious person's head clear of the water. Some types can be inflated by small built-in gas bottles.

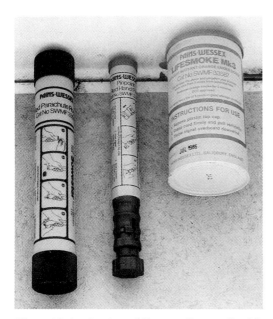

Photo 20 A selection of distress flares, all with detailed instructions printed on the sides – *read them before going to sea.* From left to right we have a parachute rocket, a red hand flare and an orange smoke float (producing dense orange smoke for daytime use). White hand flares will be similar to the red.

stances such as rough weather, night, fog, and by inexperienced non-swimmers. **Life jackets** are rather more complex (and expensive) devices designed to keep an unconscious person afloat with his head clear of the water. They are not essential for the type of cruising that we have in mind. **Harnesses** are very useful for working on deck in rough weather, and for securing children to the boat while they play. Keep safety lines short enough that they cannot reach the edge of the deck.

Flares are rather like large fireworks that can be set off to attract attention when you are in trouble. Three types should be carried on board, in a strong watertight container, and stowed near the wheel for rapid use if needed. **White flares** should be used to attract the attention of a passing vessel for advice or assistance or to warn him of your

presence, while **red flares** should be used only to call for help in a real emergency. There are two types of the latter – **parachute flares** and **hand flares**. The former fires a red flare to a great height and it then drifts slowly down on a parachute. They should be used when no vessel is in sight, as they can be seen at great distances. Hand flares, on the other hand, should be used to show your precise position to nearby vessels. All flares should be fired pointing downwind; this keeps heat and debris from hand-flares out of your face, and enables parachute flares to reach a greater height. Read the instructions carefully (*before* you have to use them – it might be dark then!) and always replace them by the expiry date shown; out of date flares can be dangerous. Old flares should be disposed of carefully. Give them to the police or coastguard – do not put them in the dustbin!

Radar reflectors are curious devices that increase dramatically the size of echo your boat will produce on a ship's **radar** screen (see Appendix 2). Small boats can very easily not show at all on such a screen, so hoisting one of these as high as possible is essential in poor visibility. I would strongly suggest that you have one permanently hoisted when at sea, as even in good weather it can be very difficult to see a small boat from the bridge of a big ship. There are various types available, from the cheap and reasonably effective traditional type to the expensive and very effective modern sort (see photos 21 and 22). For our type of cruising, the traditional type should be perfectly adequate, as long as it hangs in the right attitude. Place the assembled reflector on a table and see how it sits, with an indentation pointing upwards as though to catch rain. That is how it should hang on the boat, so that the radar signals can enter the indentations squarely and be reflected back the way they came.

Photo 21 A traditional-type radar reflector, hung in the correct attitude and permanently fixed to a small mast on top of the wheelhouse. This type can be easily dismantled to lie flat, if you want to stow it away.

Photo 22 The white shape hanging vertically beneath the radar dome is a Firdell reflector – expensive but extremely effective, particularly when the boat is rolling heavily. Note the fog horn at bottom left.

For offshore cruising you should carry a proper **liferaft** in case you should have to abandon ship in foul weather. For our cruising the dinghy should suffice – an inflatable being better for this than a rigid dinghy. When you are at sea, have it stowed or towed so that it can be got into and paddled away from the boat as rapidly as possible. You may have a fire and possible explosion to get clear of. Do not keep an inflatable deflated and stuffed away in a locker! If you do have to abandon ship, take the flares with you, and portable VHF radio if you have one.

Wherever you cruise there is always the risk of someone falling over the side, so two **lifebelts** should be carried in holders, one on either side of the boat close to the helmsman, where he can reach them quickly. If you cruise at night one, at least, should have a light attached to it. Special waterproof flashing lights can be obtained that will switch on automatically when thrown over the side.

A **foghorn** should also be carried. In larger motor cruisers powerful electric ones can be permanently installed, and I strongly recommend these as the small portable ones are not very effective. You must try to imagine the sound travelling to the bridge of a large ship in fog, which is when they are most important. Portable ones can be either aerosol powered or simply blown by mouth.

Photo 23 A well-sited lifebelt, alongside the upper steering position. It can be simply lifted out of its rack and thrown to the person in the water, along with the automatic light that hangs inside it. The traditional circular cork lifebelt is both difficult to get into when in the water and heavy enough to cause considerable distress if it hits someone on the head. This modern horseshoe type is light, soft and easy to get into. There will be an identical one on the other side of the steering position. Both can also be reached easily from the deck. Note the fog horn on the left of the picture.

Personal Equipment

When you are out on the water, remember that you cannot just pop back into the house for anything you have forgotten, so make absolutely certain that you take everything with you that you may need. Check that you have sufficient water, gas and victuals on board, and plenty of warm and water-proof clothing for everyone. It can be surprisingly cold on the water if there is a wind blowing, and working on deck in the rain without proper waterproofs can be most discouraging. Also take towels and complete changes of clothing, just in case anyone does get a ducking. On the other side of the weather coin, the sun on the sea is much stronger than it is on land, due to the extra ultra-violet rays. A cooling breeze can disguise the true burning power of the sun, so take care when sunbathing and use a good suntan barrier cream or lotion. Glare can also be a problem when steering, so sunglasses can be a useful item to carry.

In Appendix 1 you will find a full list of equipment, tools and so on that should be carried on board.

8
CRUISING ON CANALS AND RIVERS

By now you should be familiar with a fairly typical small motor cruiser, and also with the general business of driving one about in open water. Things are rather different in canals and rivers, which tend to be shallow and narrow and winding. Locks and bridges and other boats get in the way and there are certain techniques that we must learn. Let us now look at the particular problems associated with these places.

Rivers

Compared to an estuary a river is generally a rather narrow and winding waterway, often very busy with other boats. Although there will probably be little tidal effect, unless you are low down near the mouth of the river where it flows into an estuary, there will likely be strong currents of river water flowing seawards, and there will certainly be bends, often quite sharp ones surrounded by trees and bushes so that you cannot see boats coming round from the other direction. So things can happen rather quickly on a river, and you need to be alert.

As avoiding action will often have to be taken quickly – on suddenly sighting another boat halfway round a blind bend, for example – it is rarely possible to 'make a bold alteration of course in plenty of time for the other to be quite clear of your intentions'. Recognising this fact (the same applies in busy harbours), the authorities have laid down a series of signals that can be

made on a foghorn to inform nearby boats of any sudden alterations of course you are about to make. These can be extremely useful in busy places and you should know them instinctively. They are as follows:

1 short blast	I am altering course to starboard
2 short blasts	I am altering course to port
3 short blasts	My engines are going astern

Note that three short blasts does not necessarily mean that the boat is going astern. A large or heavy boat may continue moving forward for quite some time, after putting the gear lever into astern, due to its momentum through the water. A very large tanker, for example (not that you are likely to meet one in the upper reaches of a river) may take nearly a mile to actually stop after going full astern on its engine. During the process, paddlewheel effect and wind could combine to swing the vessel all over the place. It is important to bear this in mind at sea, in large harbours and commercial waterways. Clearly a large vessel in such circumstances, due to its restricted manoeuvrability, would have right of way over your small, easily manoeuvred motor cruiser. If you approach too close to him he is most unlikely to go astern to try and avoid you for the simple reason that he would then lose control of his ship and absolute mayhem would ensue! He would probably sound 'at least four short blasts' on his foghorn or siren which, put politely, means 'are you taking sufficient avoiding action?'. Certain authorities may have additional local signals and information on these will be found in Pilot Books (see Chapter 11).

These are the most important signals, but you may well come across overtaking signals, especially in a commercial waterway. A vessel intending to overtake you will sound two long blasts, followed by one short if he wants to pass down your starboard side, or two shorts to pass down your port side. You can acknowledge this by sounding one long, one short, and another long and another short. A short blast lasts about one second and a long one about five seconds. These signals, too, are extremely useful in crowded waters, as is the custom of sounding one very long blast on approaching a blind bend. This will warn vessels coming the other way of your approach, and they should sound a prolonged blast in return to let you know they are coming. By and large, you should keep to the starboard side of narrow channels.

Overtaking other boats can be fraught with dangers in a narrow river, and not only because of the risk of meeting an oncoming vessel before you have got past. If the river is very narrow or very shallow (one and a half times the depth of your boat or less), the increased speed necessary to overtake another boat quickly before the next bend can have alarming and unpredictable effects on your boat's handling.

Two distinct factors can cause boat-handling trouble in these circumstances. The first – encountered in very narrow steep-sided rivers, but mostly in canals – is called **canal effect**. You will rarely experience this in rivers, unless they are extremely narrow, so we will discuss it in the section on canals that

follows. Shallow rivers, however, and even very shallow open water, can give rise to what is known as **shallow water effect**. The lack of depth restricts the flow of water round the propeller, causing eddies and swirls that can make the behaviour of your boat quite unpredictable and uncontrollable. It also causes the stern to drag itself deeper in the water, so running the risk of grounding, or even catching the prop on the bottom. The faster your speed, the worse this effect becomes. It is also at its worst with bulky or flat-bottomed boats as these restrict the flow of water round the propeller even more than will a sleek and narrow yacht, for example. It can be easily recognised as it causes a high, and often breaking, stern wave to form behind the boat.

The other thing that excessive speed does, over a period of time, is erode away the banks of rivers due to the large wash that is created. So keep your speed down. Most rivers have speed limits anyway, and many large harbours also.

You should avoid getting too close to the banks while under way as they will slope and the depth close to the bank will probably be considerably shallower than the depth in the centre of the river. It is quite common, however, to moor against the bank of a river, assuming there is sufficient depth for you to float; this can be checked with a leadline if necessary. There will be little chance of finding handy bollards or mooring posts to tie up to, however, so you should carry a couple of stout metal spikes that can be hammered into the ground for you to tie the boat up to. Head and stern ropes are normally sufficient in a river, although springs might be advisable if there is a lot of passing traffic or if the current is strong, as they will hold you more securely in position. Bear in mind that depths can alter due to flood water, or tide if you are in the lower reaches of a river. Information on all such matters should be obtainable from the local authority for the particular waterway.

If there are tidal streams or strong river currents, care is needed when negotiating such things as bridges and intersections. As mentioned in Chapter 4, streams can be bent, slowed down or accelerated by anything in their way, particularly important on narrow rivers being the fact that a boat is very difficult to control when travelling downstream. Where obstructions such as bridge buttresses restrict the width, the stream accelerates through the gap and accentuates this problem. It is important that you line the boat up carefully and accurately before shooting downstream through a narrow gap. Keep a reserve of power in hand for rapid manoeuvring should you begin swinging sideways onto a buttress, and do not be afraid to give her full throttle if necessary to straighten up and shoot through the centre of the gap. Because of these problems, all craft travelling downstream have right of way over those stemming the tide in such situations. If you are the latter, make certain the way through the gap is clear right through and way beyond before proceeding, as boats travelling downstream may be moving at considerable speed over the ground. Large bridges in busy waterways may even have traffic lights controlling these gaps, although small boats can probably take an inshore passage through to keep clear of the commercial traffic. Look ahead and think ahead all the time.

Canals

All the foregoing will also apply to making a passage through a canal, except that there will be no strong river current, and certainly no tidal effect. Canals are, however, usually extremely narrow (often barely wide enough for two large boats to pass) and generally very shallow. The depth of a canal will vary with the rainfall and precise information should be obtained from the canal authorities before endeavouring to pass through, especially in a hot dry summer. Check also on the maximum permitted dimensions of vessels.

Canals also go up hill and down dale. This poses a problem for the water which, if left to its own devices, would simply run away off the hills and fill up the dales. The authorities get round this problem by building the canal in a series of level steps (see figure 49). To get from one level to the next a boat has

Figure 49

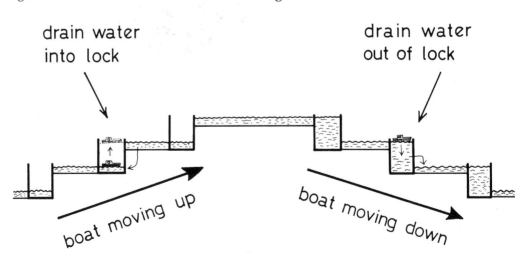

to pass through a **lock**, which is a short section of the canal partitioned off by two sets of gates (see figure 50). If a boat wishes to pass from the lower level to the higher level, the water inside the lock is drained off until it reaches the same level as that outside on the low side. The lower gates are then opened and the boat goes into the lock, where it ties up. The lower gates are then closed and **sluices** (holes in the gate) are opened in the top gates. The water pours from the higher level through these sluices until the level in the lock

is the same as that outside on the higher level. The upper gates are then opened and the boat motors out into the higher level. To go downhill the process is reversed (see figures 49 and 50).

If you consider this process for a minute or two, you will realise that water is constantly being run down from the higher to the lower levels. Only rain keeps the high levels topped up, so that problems are caused in long spells of dry weather. The upper reaches of the canal get very shallow, and you will often find that the number of times the locks can be opened per day will be limited, so as to conserve the water in the higher levels.

Sometimes these lock gates are operated by lock-keepers and some-times we have to work them ourselves. The precise working details vary from canal to canal and full information should be obtained from the canal authorities beforehand. You will find operating the lock gates, if you need to, hard work but fun. To help conserve water, you should always close all sluices and gates after leaving a lock, unless another boat is about to enter.

We will now discuss the seamanship aspects of working through locks, as terrible troubles can be caused if the job is not done properly. The first problem can arise during the approach, before you even get to the lock. If the first gate – upper or lower, depending on whether you are going up or down the levels – is open, you can simply go straight into the lock and tie up alongside the wall, or another boat if the walls are full of boats. Try to pick a boat bigger than yours as you will be hanging onto his shore lines during the locking, as well as bouncing around against him when the water comes swirling in. Locking down is fairly straightforward and little strain on boats and warps, as the water level simply goes down without swirl-ing about. Locking uphill, however, is

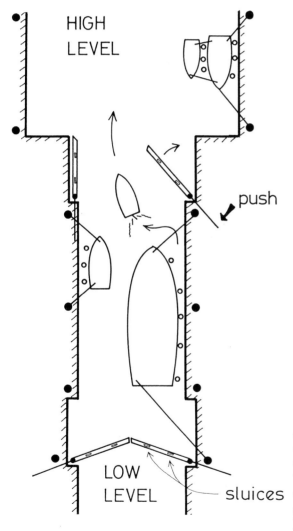

Figure 50

quite different, as the water often comes boiling out of the sluices to swirl and roar about all over the lock. There will then be considerable strain and snatching on warps and boats; so good, strong warps and plenty of big, fat fenders will be required. If you moor up against a boat much smaller than yours, the weight of your boat swinging and bashing against her, even when well fendered, could easily cause damage.

If the first lock gate is closed, however, you may have to wait a while for the lock-keeper to appear, even out the levels and finally open the gate. Usually there is a small jetty just outside the gate and you should moor up here if you can. If this is very crowded with boats, you may have to jill about on the water while you wait, and this can be quite difficult if there is any wind blowing, due to the lack of room for manoeuvring. Do not be tempted to moor against a canal bank as these are usually sloping mounds of rocks and you will almost certainly damage your propeller if you get too close. You must look ahead as soon as the lock comes into sight. If the entrance is closed and crowded with boats, slow right down until you barely have steerage way and creep towards the lock. If you have to stop, do so well before you get entangled with all the other boats. If there is a wind blowing across the canal, keep well over to the weather bank to allow for drifting. If you get blown too close to the leeward bank, there will not be room for you to motor clear without banging your propeller on the rocks. If you have to get someone ashore to open the gates and there is no jetty to moor against, gently push your bow against the bank, keeping the stern well clear, and make the person jump ashore. Make sure he gets the level of water in the lock the same as the level on your side of the gate before attempting to open it! The gates always open towards

the higher level, and remain at an angle to each other when closed (see figure 50). This ensures that the pressure of the higher level holds them closed. It is not possible to open them unless the levels are equal, or virtually so.

Enter the lock slowly and carefully. If you do not stop in time, you will get a hefty bill for any damage to the gates, and any other boats! Get strong head and stern ropes ashore as quickly as possible and secure to both shore and boat. Make sure they are long enough to reach down to the lower level if you are locking downhill! There must be a crew member tending each warp, to haul in the slack as you rise or pay it out as you fall. The latter is particularly important if you are to avoid ripping cleats or bollards out of the boat. Warps must never be tied securely to the boat when she is about to descend a lock, but just turned round a cleat or bollard and the end held in the hand. This will be sufficient to hold the boat steady, and there will be no risk of the warp jamming. The water level can drop very quickly in some locks, so great attention must be paid to this. The warps must be able to run freely round the cleat or bollard, and must be tended constantly.

With all the boats in and safely moored up, the gates can be closed and the water run either in through the top sluices (if you are locking up), or out through the bottom sluices (if you are locking down) until the level is the same as the outside for which you are heading. The other gates can then be opened, the warps cast off from the shore and the boat motored slowly and carefully out of the lock. Do not be in too much of a hurry to get out as the gates are invariably opened just before the levels are quite equal, and there will be a flow of water and some turbulence through the opening gate for a moment

94

Photo 24 A busy lock packed with sailing boats in from the sea. At the top right of the picture can be seen the indentation in the lock wall into which the gate fits when open. You can see the gate itself on the other side of the lock.

or two. Let the water settle down or you could find yourself being carried sideways into the gates or the bank.

After entering a lock, make certain the gates and sluices are closed properly behind you before opening the sluices at the other end, or all the water will pour away! If locking down, it does not matter which sluices are opened first in the lower gate, but if you are locking up you will find it beneficial to open first the sluice closest to the wall against which you are moored. This will set up an initial swirl of water that will tend to run between the boat and the wall

and thus hold the boat away from the wall on her warps rather than bash her against it. Let the water run in gently to begin with; the turbulence will decrease noticeably as the depth increases, and you can then open the sluices more fully. Turbulence can also be experienced if a large vessel motors out of the lock ahead of you. Keep your warps firmly secured until she is well out of the way. Large vessels also often leave their engines running ahead while moored in the lock, and you must watch very carefully for this wash sweeping you sideways if you enter behind one.

If you have to open gates yourself, do not try to push the beam with your arms; you will be there all day! Lean your back against the beam and use the full weight of your body to get it moving. When it is fully open, wedge the locking bar into its socket on the ground to stop the gate closing again by itself. Much time can often be saved when working through a series of locks short-handed, by hauling the boat through on her warps rather than getting back aboard and motoring her out of each one, then mooring up and coming ashore for each set of gates. Watch must be kept, however, for protuberances on the walls against which the boat could catch, and also (when locking down) for the shallow sill extending some feet from the top gates.

Having successfully negotiated the lock you will probably go round the next bend and find a bridge. You should be aware of it, as all locks and bridges will be marked on the chart of the canal that you should be able to obtain from the canal office before entering. If the bridge has to be raised or swung for you to get through, there will probably be a sign before the bend instructing you to WHISTLE, but if not a toot on your horn as you approach will hopefully bring out the bridge-keeper to open the bridge for you. The comments about keeping the boat under control on the approach to a lock apply here also. Approach slowly and keep well back until you see the keeper appear. He will probably wave you on, then open the bridge at the very last moment, just before you crash into it! Do not assume that the bridge will open unless you have seen the keeper wave you on. He may be having a cup of tea, or have stopped for his lunch. It is quite normal for locks and bridges to be inoperative during the lunch break, and the times of this will be given in the booklet or chart for the canal. Keepers also usually observe normal office hours, and it is worth remembering that if you have a **flight of locks** (a number of locks together, one leading directly into the next) to negotiate, the keeper will only let you enter if he is certain he can get you

right through and out of the other end before his knocking-off time. Careful timing can thus make a tremendous difference to your passage time through a canal, particularly as speed limits generally have to be observed.

Finally, let us have a look at canal effect, mentioned briefly on page 91. If you watch a motor cruiser powering along in open water you will see it pushing up a bow wave on either side of the bow – water being displaced by the boat as she pushes through the water. If the same boat travels at speed through a narrow canal there is nowhere for this wave to go. It cannot spread out sideways and gradually die down, there is no room. Thus the wave builds up and is pushed ahead of the boat, kept within the confines of the canal banks. This can be seen quite clearly if the boat is going too fast, as the water level quite some way ahead of her is raised appreciably, while that alongside both sides of the boat is lowered correspondingly. The water is also raised astern of the boat. In extreme cases you can actually see the water being sucked away from the boats' sides.

In theory, so long as you remain at the same speed and exactly in the middle of the canal, this will not affect your handling. In practice, if you veer very slightly towards one bank the pressure of the wave ahead of you will push your bow away from the bank. And this will not be a gentle controlled push, but a sudden and violent shove that will probably crash you into the other bank before you realise it is happening. If you do manage to correct the swing with the rudder, you will certainly over-correct. Within seconds your boat will be veering wildly from bank to bank totally out of control. Your bow will probably crash into both banks, as will your stern, and your propeller will churn into the rocks and there will be nothing you can do about it other than put the gear lever into neutral and pray. If you go hard astern to try and slow down, the paddlewheel effect will almost certainly add its twist to the general mayhem, unless you can use it to oppose the swing. If you are experienced enough to be able to do this, you are very unlikely to have allowed the situation to develop in the first place.

The only real cure for canal effect is to watch the water very carefully all the time, ahead of you and at the sides. If you see the level building up noticeably ahead of the boat, slow down, steadily and gradually, until the water levels even out. At the same time, ease the boat back into the middle of the canal if you are over to one side, as the further from the banks you are, the less will be the effect. Light and unresponsive steering is an early warning of the build up of canal effect. If you feel the steering 'go funny', slow down slowly. Any sudden movement of rudder or throttle may start you swinging. Remember that if the water is very shallow, shallow-water effect may come into play and make everything even worse. It is important to understand these effects, although in practice your boat has to be quite near the maximum dimension for the canal before they become a serious danger.

Canal effect has to be watched carefully when passing another boat coming from the opposite direction. Do not follow your instincts and steer close into the bank to give him room, as you might suddenly sheer away from the bank and into him. Pass as close to the other boat as you can; your respective bow waves will keep you apart.

Finally, never forget the wind. On a long open stretch of canal a side wind could easily blow you down onto the bank before you realise what is happening. Keep slightly to weather of the centre of the canal (not too far or canal effect may grab you if your boat is large for the canal) and be prepared to steer into the wind if you see that you are drifting across. When passing other boats keep to starboard, as mentioned in connection with rivers.

Canal cruising can be great fun, as there are considerably fewer worries and responsibilities for the skipper than there are at sea; but it does require care and knowledge. Without these it can be a nerve-wracking nightmare. There are a great many things that can go wrong for the inexperienced.

9
CRUISING AT SEA

The most striking difference that you are likely to notice when you first go out to sea from inland waterway is the presence of waves. They roll along the sea almost incessantly – sometimes small, sometimes huge – and they will roll your boat about with varying degrees of discomfort, and sometimes danger.

But waves, like people, are complex creations, and it is not always the big one that is the most dangerous. Many factors govern the size, shape and behaviour of a wave and if we are to handle them with confidence and in safety we must understand these factors.

Waves

The first thing to realise is that a wave, unless it is breaking, is not a solid mass of water being blown along the sea by the wind. Waves are caused by energy from the wind and this energy travels through the water much as radio or sound waves travel through the air. The air is not pushed forward but simply displaced up and then down as the wave energy passes. Sea waves are just the same. It could be likened to the passage of a mole under your lawn; he does not (unfortunately, if you are a keen gardener) push the soil along in front of him, but pushes it vertically upwards into mounds as he passes.

Thus waves, by and large (we will come to the exceptions shortly), do not 'bash into you' but simply lift you up and lower you down again as they pass.

And if we lived in a perfect world and your boat was a champagne cork instead of a complex mass of design features, that would be the end of this chapter! However, as Einstein realised, the inherent regularity in our universe is destroyed by the simple fact that everything interacts with, and thus changes, everything else. Waves out at sea are no exception to this.

Let us take as a starting point the ideal wave train (see figure 51) – a regular succession of identical waves caused by a regular, unchanging flow of wind – and see how real life differs from this, and why. Then we will discuss how best a seaman can cope with the realities of waves at sea.

The first thing that upsets our ideal wave form is the fact that the wind is never constant in strength and direction. Every time the wind varies even slightly, it sets off a different wave train – different sized waves moving in a different direction. As you can imagine, this causes all sorts of vagaries on the surface of the sea. When two or more waves meet at the same time in the same place they combine to form one large wave equal to the height of all of them added together. When the crest of one wave meets the trough of another they cancel each other out to leave a patch of completely flat water, or a smaller wave equal to the difference between them. And if you visualise thousands and thousands of different wave trains charging around the ocean doing this all the time, you begin to

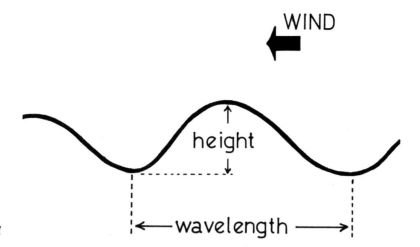

Figure 51

wonder how it is possible for a boat to go to sea at all!

Most of the time, however, these differences are very slight, and we simply find that the sea is not regular and that the wave heights and directions of movement constantly vary a little. Now and again, though, the wave trains combine to form a giant wave perhaps four or more times the average height of the sea. These are the 'freak' waves that one hears about from time to time, but as the quadruple-sized wave occurs something like once in every 300,000 waves most of us sail for a

lifetime without ever seeing one. Bear it in mind, but don't panic.

However, as was said earlier, it is not the size of a wave that makes it dangerous, but its behaviour. In the deep, open sea the biggest of waves ramble along peaceably, minding their own business, and are very rarely a danger to a properly handled seaworthy vessel. It is when a wave encounters an obstruction that it can turn nasty. The basic reason for this is that the energy in a wave reaches deep down into the water a distance approximately equal to the wavelength (see figure 52). If this

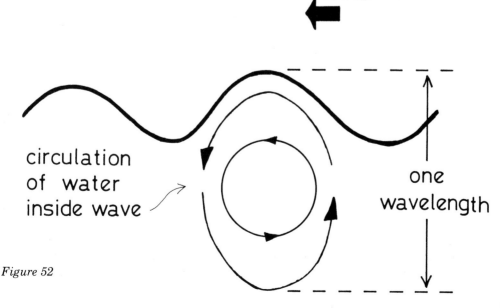

Figure 52

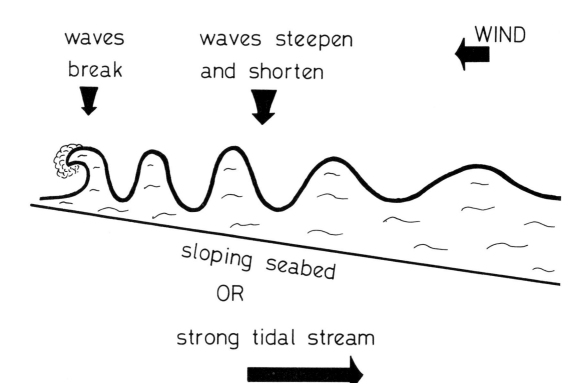

waves
break

waves steepen
and shorten

WIND

sloping seabed
OR

strong tidal stream

Figure 53

lower part of the wave is slowed down by shallow water or a tide or current running against it, the upper part keeps going. At the same time the wave is pushed upwards and grows higher, especially in shallow water. The result is waves that get steadily bigger, steeper and shorter until eventually they fall over themselves and break (see figure 53). We now have, for the first time, an actual body of water moving forward and downward and, as sea water weighs approximately 1 ton per 35 cubic feet (very roughly a dinghy full), it is not hard to see why small vessels can easily founder in breaking seas. This is the reason why the sea gets suddenly rougher when the tide turns and the tidal stream begins to run against the wind – referred to as **wind over tide**.

This basic problem can be further compounded by tidal eddies and uneven

sea bottoms, which can cause waves to steepen or break randomly and in all directions creating a very confused and dangerous sea in certain circumstances. Headlands, fast tides, shallow banks and river **bars** (shallow bank across the entrance) can all cause dangerous and often confused breaking seas in strong **onshore winds** (winds blowing from seaward), and should be avoided in all but reasonable conditions. Charts and Pilot Books will tell you where these dangers exist and they should be heeded carefully (see Chapter 11).

Handling a Motor Cruiser in Waves
Even out at sea, however, there are certain techniques that we should employ for riding waves. Although a cork will simply appear to bob up and down on the passing of a wave, a boat is rather more complex in shape, as well as heavier, and its motion in a seaway will be somewhat less simple. However, for our practical purposes we can avoid

100

hydrodynamic theory and make three basic statements:

1 If heading into waves, a powerboat will pitch up and down as the wave first lifts her bow then drops it and picks up the stern.

2 If heading across the waves, a powerboat will roll from side to side as the wave first picks up one side then drops it to pick up the other.

3 If heading away from waves, a powerboat will tend to 'corkscrew' – rolling and pitching together. The reason for this is that as the wave first picks up the stern it also tends to push it forward due to the forward movement of water at the crest. As the bow is likely to be ahead of the forward-moving water, the boat will tend to gripe – the bow digging in and the stern being swung across and forward. If the waves are not from directly astern this gripping will be accentuated and make it quite difficult to keep the vessel running straight. In extreme cases this **broaching**, as it is called, can swing the boat completely side on to the waves, in which position she can be capsized or swamped by a big following wave beam on, as she will not have sufficient speed to provide stability. This is why turning in a big sea can be dangerous. If you ever have to do this, watch the approaching waves and make the turn so that a calm patch arrives when you get beam on.

All this may sound like gloom and doom, but let us be clear that it takes some skill to handle a powerboat in a big following sea and that it is not a game for those straight out of inland waterways. Having said that, it is a game that can be learnt by practising with small following seas. You soon learn to feel when a wave is about to pick up the stern, and which way it will swing it. The secret then is to put the rudder over just before the boat starts to swing. Once the wave starts to carry the stern, the rudder will become almost useless. A burst of power will often help, so in a big following sea you must never use full power, as a reserve of throttle must be kept for such action. In general you should keep your speed down to well below that of the wave so that it will pass under you quickly. The faster you are going, the longer you will hang about on the front of the wave and the more chance it will have of broaching you. You will soon know if you are going too fast as the steering will go light and you will get the distinct feeling that you are not in control of the boat. You will be right – you're not; slow down.

Motoring beam on to a sea is generally more uncomfortable than dangerous, as considerable stability is imparted by the forward speed of the boat. It is this stability that is lacking when you broach. You will find that the amount you roll will vary with your speed, and a little experimentation will often disclose a speed at which the boat will be surprisingly comfortable in even quite a big sea. Very often an increase of speed, more than a decrease, will improve stability. A slight alteration of course can also have a marked effect.

The real danger when motoring beam on is of developing a **synchronous roll**. This happens when the natural rolling of the boat finds itself in phase with the passing of the waves. Each time a wave arrives it reinforces the roll and the latter will increase dramatically getting heavier and heavier with the arrival of each new wave. Eventually the boat will roll right over if nothing is done to stop the synchrony. Fortunately the onset of this is easy to spot and the remedy simplicity itself. Normally waves will arrive at all sorts of stages of a boat's rolling – some will accentuate the roll imparted by the previous wave and some will stop it or slow it. Thus a boat will roll unevenly, sometimes heavily and sometimes hardly at all. While she does this all is well. The moment you notice that the roll is getting steadily worse with every wave, suspect synchronous rolling and immediately alter course to a different angle with the waves – if beam on – or change speed noticeably. Either course of action will break the synchronisation between rolling and wave arrival and put you to rights again.

Motoring head into the waves is probably the least troublesome way to proceed, although the pounding in a steep sea can be most uncomfortable and a considerable strain on the hull. Once again it will benefit you to experiment to find the most comfortable speed, which will not always be the slowest. If this does not reduce the pounding to an acceptable level, a slight

alteration of course to bring the waves to one side of the bow will greatly improve things. This will have the effect of lengthening the distance between crests and thus the boat will ride more easily. Motoring at dead-slow speed on this course is the recommended way of **heaving to** in a powerboat should the sea get too big and rough for safe or comfortable progress in any direction. It is also the best way to ride the wash of a large ship passing close, which may produce steep and breaking waves.

One problem you may encounter motoring into a head sea is the propeller coming out of the water as the bow dips into the trough. Without the water to turn against the prop will immediately race wildly and this will do no good to engine, gearbox or prop. The last might even fall off. If the prop does race badly, cut the power immediately until you feel it regain the water. Try to adjust course and speed to keep this effect to a minimum.

This problem particularly besets high-speed planing boats in rough seas, as their small and fast-revving propellers are generally very close to the surface (particularly outboards). The constant thumping as a high-speed boat bounces from wave to wave can be very

Photo 25 You can see quite clearly here the steep waves set up by the wake of a large ship. Small boats should endeavour to meet them bows on, as this little yacht has. At sea the wake from a big ship could interact with the waves to cause quite a confused sea, possibly dangerous to a small boat; in such circumstances a large vessel should not be passed too close astern. In a narrow river the wake could build quite alarmingly as it runs into shallow water outside the main channel, causing moored and anchored boats to roll violently.

wearing and uncomfortable, as well as putting great stresses on the hull, and the lack of slow-speed steering control – particularly with the small rudders of a twin-screw inboard boat – can make life very difficult in big following seas. Up to a point the planing boat can outrun the waves, bouncing from crest to crest; but the time comes, as the sea builds up, when she is in danger of bouncing straight into the back of a wave instead of onto the top of it. She could then bury herself and be swallowed up by the one following. She must then adopt conventional tactics, and will have great difficulty in retaining sufficient steerage control at the slow speeds necessary. The skipper may have to tow long warps astern in order to slow her down, their drag enabling him to use sufficient throttle for steering. The largest possible warps should be used, strung in a bight from one quarter and back to the other with a weight in the bight if necessary to keep it all down in the water. The bight should be as far astern as possible, in case it should cause a sea to break.

Finally, rough seas expose the slightest imperfection in a boat and her systems – not to mention the crew! Everything must be securely stowed and lashed down, and in these situations it is absolutely vital that the engine performs without a hiccup. A common problem in rough weather is dirt in the bottom of the fuel tank being stirred up and sucked down the fuel line. Prevention of this, and general engine-room maintenance, are discussed in Chapter 13.

Predicting the Conditions

Clearly, being able to predict wind strength and direction before we go out to sea is of paramount importance, particularly on a coastal passage during which we may be many miles from the nearest shelter. We want to know what the waves will be like, before we go out, for the whole duration of our passage. Strong winds and big, dangerous waves can spring up very quickly, and the sea could easily be too big for us to cope with safely long before we have time to get into a sheltered harbour. Added to which, many harbour entrances are exposed to the sea, and in rough weather can be extremely dangerous to enter with onshore winds. We may well find sea conditions in the shallow water close to shore far more dangerous than those offshore in the deep water where the waves are not breaking. In such a case, it will be much safer for us to remain offshore and heave to in deep water, heading very slowly into the waves at a slight angle to their direction. This is one of the reasons why the maximum load of fuel should always be carried, and why you should find out the most economical revs at which you can motor. With offshore winds, however, sheltered calm water will be found close inshore.

It should not be hard to see that some experience is needed in order to be able to judge these things. Until you have gathered this experience you should only go out in quiet weather. There are all sorts of weather forecasts available to help us decide what sea conditions will be like – on radio, on television and by telephone from Coastguards and Meteorological Offices (see Chapter 10). The weather forecast will also give us details of the other important factor that affects our passages at sea – the visibility. In poor visibility or fog, motoring around at sea can be a very hazardous business, partly because of the difficulty of safe navigation when we cannot see the land, and partly because of the danger of collision with other vessels. In my view, fog is by far the greatest danger to a small boat at sea, and you should never put to sea when there is any risk of it until you are extremely experienced – and even then only if you have the right equipment to cope with it (see Appendix 2).

Fog

If you do get caught out in fog there are certain precautions that you can take to minimise the risks. Navigational risks are dealt with in Chapter 11; the risk of collision can be reduced considerably by taking the following actions:

1 Reduce speed such that you will be able to stop, or at least take sudden avoiding action, should another vessel loom out of the fog. Take a fix if possible, so as to obtain an accurate and up-to-date position (see Chapter 11).

2 Keep a sharp lookout and listen for the sounds of engines or foghorns. A lookout posted right for'ard can best do this as he will be far from the noise of your own engine. He can also sound your own foghorn if it is a portable one, and should do so in answer to any others he hears. The sound signals that different types of vessel make in fog are given in Appendix 4; they should not be confused with the manoeuvring sound signals mentioned in the last chapter, which are purely for use when vessels are in sight of one another. Do not, however, be deluded into thinking that sounding a foghorn and listening for those of other vessels will automatically prevent collision. Sound travels in very strange ways through fog, sometimes going for miles and other times not going any distance at all. You may not hear a foghorn until it is very close, but you will probably hear a big ship's engine, especially if you go below and put your ear against the hull.

3 Keep out of **shipping lanes**. These are clearly marked on charts as being routes followed around the coast by the bulk of large shipping. These vessels usually proceed at full speed in fog, glibly assuming that their **radar** sets will show echoes from all the boats around them. If your boat is small or wooden the chances are that, even with a radar reflector rigged, she may not show up on a radar screen unless the latter is very well adjusted and tuned and is manned by an expert. Neither, regrettably, can be relied upon. The best place for a small boat in fog is, safe navigation permitting, close inshore in shallow water where the big ships cannot go. The risk of collision with other small boats doing the same thing is far less serious than the risk of being run down by a large ship, and if it all gets too much for you, you can simply anchor and wait for the fog to lift. Switch on your echo-sounder for the approach into shallow water, and remember your tidal calculations.

4 If you hear the sound of a very faint engine or foghorn, do not be afraid to stop your engine briefly while you listen more carefully and try to judge the direction of the sound. Do not, however, let your boat slow down too much, or you may find, if something suddenly looms out of the fog, that you have insufficient way on to take rapid avoiding action.

5 In shipping lanes or busy harbour approaches insist that all the crew put on their buoyancy aids. If a collision does occur in fog, there is every chance that you will have no time, or sufficient warning, to get a dinghy or liferaft over the side. The simple precaution of donning buoyancy aids in situations where the risk of collision is high could save your lives. If at all feasible, have all the crew on deck or in the cockpit, where they will stand a much better chance of surviving a collision than they will if down below.

Seasickness

Although not as dangerous as fog, or as nerve-wracking as big waves, this can be a most unpleasant by-product of going to sea. While some people are quite immune to it and others suffer horribly however often they go to sea, the great majority suffer a little to begin with, then gradually get used to it. For this reason I would strongly recommend that you do not take any sort of seasick pills until you have been to sea a few times and found out how the malady affects you. If you take pills right from the start you will never know whether you are prone to seasickness or not!

There are, however, certain simple precautions that you can take that will reduce considerably the likelihood of seasickness striking. The first is to avoid any food or drink that is likely to sit uneasily in the stomach, beginning the day before sailing. Tea is the worst drink, followed by coffee. Cocoa, milk and soup are the best. All fried or greasy foods should be avoided, pork chops being reputedly the worst of all. Almost as bad is an empty stomach, so eat heartily, especially before sailing. Porridge, scrambled egg, soups, stews, dry bread and so on will all go a long way to discouraging the onset of seasickness. Hangovers will not; so stay off the booze the night before sailing.

If you are nervous or anxious, the tightening of the stomach that this brings will encourage seasickness. If you think about seasickness, that will also encourage it, as will staying down below too long. Too long can mean as little as four or five seconds. I have known people on deck in perfect health to be racked by seasickness literally within seconds of going below into the cabin. As you can imagine, the ability to withstand seasickness is absolutely essential in a seagoing cook! It is even more important for an engineer, who has also to do battle with the sick-inducing smells of oil and fuel.

So avoid unsuitable food and drink from the day before sailing. Try to sleep on board the night before going to sea as this, even in a sheltered marina, seems to get the stomach used to being on the boat. Eat well before sailing; when you get to sea, keep eating; keep on deck in the fresh air, and keep busy so that you have no time to think about being seasick. The onset of seasickness will be accompanied by a feeling of lethargy and a disinclination to eat. Both must be fought. Force food into your stomach, even if it is only dry biscuits, and make yourself do something that will keep you moving and your mind occupied – but not down below, and certainly not in the engine room. With these simple precautions, most of us can combat seasickness.

The Sea at Night

This can be very frightening and confusing to a beginner, so avoid it until you have had some experience. When you are confident at handling and navigating your boat, you will find night-time considerably less alarming. In fact, it can be quite a rewarding experience out there – just your little boat and the sea and the stars.

Going to sea at night is not especially difficult, but it does have its problems. The navigational aspects are discussed in Chapter 11, and here we will consider the business of seeing and being seen.

To see well at night you must allow your eyes to adjust to the darkness, after which you will be amazed how well you can see. All lights in the boat must be kept as dim as possible, especially in the wheelhouse. Even a small glowing indicator-light on the engine panel can spoil your night vision if it is bright. If a bright white light is turned on, then off again, it will take

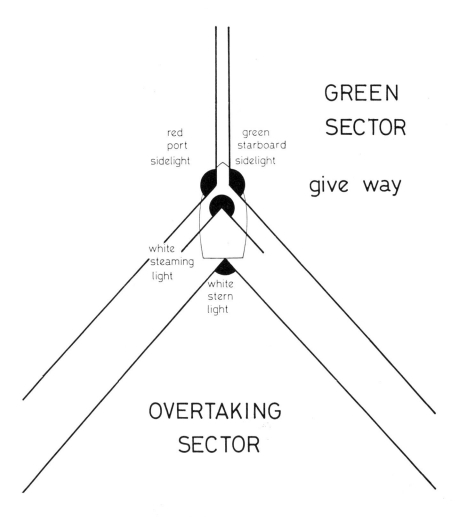

GREEN
SECTOR

give way

red
port
sidelight

green
starboard
sidelight

white
steaming
light

white
stern
light

OVERTAKING
SECTOR

your eyes about twenty minutes to fully readjust to the darkness. The more you can see – waves, coastline, other boats – the happier and safer you will be. Try to steer on a star or shore light rather than slavishly staring at the compass, which you will find extremely tiring after a while.

To be seen you will need a set of **navigation lights** (see figure 54). These are the lights carried by small power craft; other types of boat will show different colours and configurations of lights so that they can be identified at night. Some will show special shapes for identification in the daytime. Full details of these will be found in the almanac.

Figure 54 The lights show only over certain arcs. This is to help other boats judge which part of you they can see, and which way you are heading. The steaming light should be as high and as powerful as possible, as this is the first light others will see. All lights should be properly sited and shielded so that they do not overlap their arcs, and do not reflect into the eyes of the helmsman. Check them well before dark, so that you will have the benefit of good light in which to repair any failures – blown fuses or bulbs, corroded connections and so on. The green sector and overtaking sector are discussed under Rule of the Road (page 107).

Rule of the Road

We talked in the last chapter about avoiding collision with other boats in the restricted waters of rivers and canals. At sea the waters are not restricted, so we do not need the sound signals that we do in rivers etc as we can see another boat coming long before we reach him. Instead, we have an international system of **Rules of the Road** to avoid collision. In detail they are very complex, and full information can be found in the Almanac. The basic rules likely to concern us are as follows:

1 If two powerboats approach head on, both should alter course to starboard to pass clear of each other.
2 If two powerboats approach at an angle and appear to be on course for collision, the one with the other on his starboard side (in his green navigation-light sector) should keep clear – preferably by altering course to starboard to pass under the other's stern, like giving way to a car on a roundabout (see figure 54).
3 If one powerboat is overtaking another, it should keep clear.

This is slightly more complex than it

sounds. An overtaking boat is defined as one approaching in the sector of the stern light (see figure 54). Thus if a boat approaches you on your starboard side close to the junction between stern light and sidelight, it could be debatable whether he is overtaking and thus keeps clear of you, or to starboard and has right of way. If you are in doubt, you must assume that he has right of way, alter hard round to starboard and pass under his stern. Make any alteration to avoid another vessel in plenty of time, and make it bold and pronounced so that he can see immediately and exactly what you are doing.

The overtaking rule applies to any vessel (power, sail or other) approaching in the stern light arc of another. As a powerboat, however, you must keep clear of the following vessels if they approach you in any other arc – sailing boats, fishing boats and any boat restricted in its manoeuvrability by size, draft or the work it is doing such as dredging, cable laying or minesweeping. The latter category is defined precisely in the almanac, but in practice it should be quite obvious when another boat is hampered in its manoeuvrability. If in doubt, keep clear. And do not go closer to another boat than you have to; cable layers and dredgers can

Figure 55

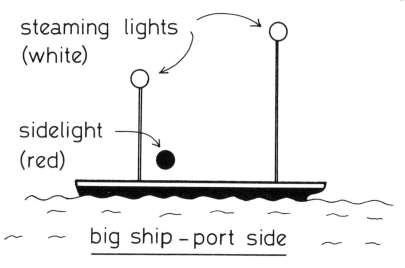

have wires and cables strung out to anchors all over the place, and sailing and fishing boats are very likely to make sudden alterations off course for no apparent reason. Even motor cruisers (your own included) and larger ships can have sudden engine or steering breakdowns. Leave them plenty of room just in case.

To check if you are on collision course with another boat line her up with something on your boat – a guardrail stanchion perhaps – then stand quite still and watch her for a few minutes. If she moves towards your bow from the stanchion, she will pass ahead of you. If she drops back towards your stern from the stanchion, she will pass astern of you. If she remains in line with the stanchion, she will hit you (remember Chapter 4, figure 21). The same test can be made more accurately by taking a bearing of the other boat with a hand-bearing compass as you would if taking a fix (see Chapter 11). Check the

Figure 56 Channel marks are not always the neat cans and cones as shown on the left, and in the photographs. Spar buoys, beacons, home-made buoys (often old beer barrels), and withys (thin sticks jammed in the mud), will often be found marking the sides of channels. Where possible they will be painted the same colours as the proper buoys (although home-made ones can be rusty and quite indistinguishable), and topmarks (cone and can-shaped, and coloured accordingly) may be found on all of them. Withys must be followed with care, as they are often posted alternately on opposite sides of the channel. Beacons are likely to be standing on rocks so give them a wide berth. Check the chart.

bearing every few minutes for a while. If she remains steady on the same bearing, she will hit you (or you her)!

A large ship over about 150 feet will show two steaming lights, the for'ard one lower than the after one (see figure 55). This can be a great help in telling which way she is pointing, and in giving an immediate indication if she alters course. Sidelights often cannot be seen on a big ship until the latter is too close for comfort, so the positions and movement of her steaming lights will enable us to take avoiding action in plenty of time. Experience is needed in order to interpret accurately the movement of steaming lights, but in general we can say that if a vessel is coming towards us and they swing closer together, she is altering course in our direction. If they are in line, she is pointing straight at us, although this does not necessarily mean that she is on a collision course. If they move apart, she is turning away. If the vessel is going away from us, the opposites apply. Think of her two lights as a transit moving through the water (see figures 21 and 22). They should help you to visualise what she is doing.

Finally, in and around harbours, especially ones with commercial shipping, keep to the starboard side of channels. Better, if there is enough water, keep right outside them. The big ships will follow the channels and will not prove a collision hazard.

These deepwater channels will be

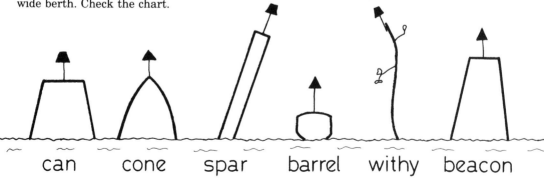

Photo 26 A port-hand buoy. Note the can shape, and the light and radar reflector that many buoys carry. Channel buoys are generally numbered, much like houses in a street, port-hand buoys having even, and starboard-hand buoys odd, numbers.

Photo 27 A starboard-hand buoy. Note the conical shape. The lattice work is to reduce wind resistance, but will appear solid from a distance.

marked by buoys of the type illustrated in figure 56. The port-hand buoys – can-shaped and red – will be on the port side of the channel as you enter the harbour, and the starboard-hand ones – green and conical shaped – will be on the starboard side. Strictly speaking these buoys are arranged according to the flood tide (port-hand buoy to be left to port when travelling in the direction of the flood stream), but in practice this invariably means when entering harbour. Occasionally, however, you may meet these buoys along the coast, so it is as well to remember this.

In the Almanac you will find information on the direction of the flood stream around the coast, and charts will give details of the lights and sound signals shown and sounded by these buoys, for identification at night or in fog. The port and starboard sides of channels may also be shown by beacons (same colour as the buoys) or, in small harbours and creeks, sticks or home-made buoys (which may or may not match the official ones in shape and colour). In some cases they may be shown on the appropriate charts of the area (see Chapter 11).

10
FORECASTING THE WEATHER

There are two main types of weather forecast we can use in order to predict the likely conditions out at sea. There is a specialised Shipping Forecast, specifically tailored for the needs of seamen, and there is the general land forecast, usually more concerned with the likelihood of rain than anything else. The former should be our staple diet, with the latter a useful addition.

The Shipping Forecast

This is broadcast regularly on BBC Radio and details of times, programmes etc are given in Appendix 4. It is always read out in the same format, consisting of:

Gale Warnings: list of areas in which gale-force winds are expected.

General Synopsis: a brief description of the weather chart (such as they show on the television), from which the forecast is calculated. It gives the experienced listener a general picture of the overall weather pattern.

Area Forecasts: these give specific information on wind strength and direction, the general weather and the visibility expected during the next twenty-four hours in the areas of sea marked and named in figure 57. The forecast begins with Viking and works clockwise round to South East Iceland.

Station Reports: these give present weather conditions at a number of observation posts around the coast. The information comprises wind direction and strength, general weather (if relevant), visibility and atmospheric pressure together with whether it is rising, falling or steady. The positions of these coastal stations can be seen in figure 57. Not all these listed stations give reports in every forecast.

There is a considerable amount of information in this forecast, large tracts of which are totally ignored by far too many small-boat sailors. All too often a skipper will check from the map which sea area he is intending to sail in, then listen just to the forecast for that area, ignoring all the rest. And that is why so many of them come unstuck. Let us look in some detail at this Shipping Forecast and see just how much we can learn from it.

There are two most important things you must appreciate first, however. One is that meteorology is not an exact science. A meteorologist would be the first to tell you that he cannot predict precisely what the weather will do next. All he can do is assess, using his training and experience, what he thinks the weather is most likely to do. The two are not the same. The other important point is that by the time the forecast is actually read out over the radio it is already some hours old. If it is broadcast at 1750, it will have been issued by the Meteorogical Office about 1700, and their predictions will have been calculated from a chart drawn from information obtained about lunch-time. The best laid plans of mice and meteorologists can wildly 'gang aft a-gley' in that time.

In principle, the weather is caused by

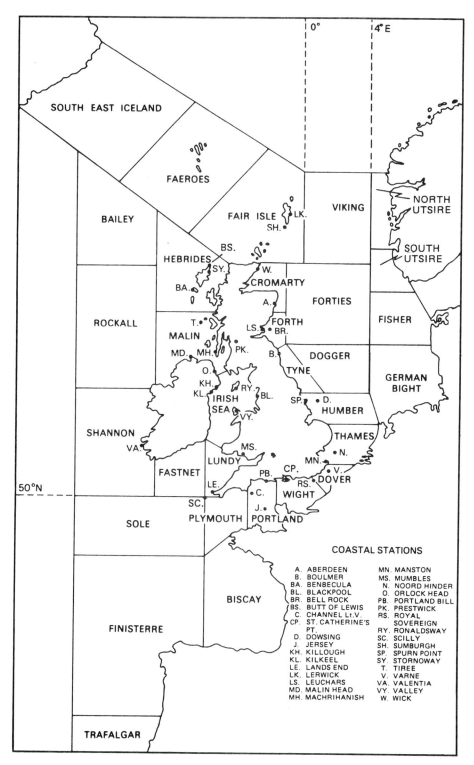

0°   4°E

SOUTH EAST ICELAND

FAEROES

VIKING
NORTH UTSIRE

BAILEY

FAIR ISLE   •LK.
SH.•

SOUTH UTSIRE

HEBRIDES
BS.•
SY.•
•W.
CROMARTY

BA.•

A.•

FORTIES

FISHER

ROCKALL

T.•
MALIN

FORTH
LS.• •BR.

MD.• MH.• •PK.

B.•

DOGGER

KH.•
KL.• IRISH
SEA•

RY.•
•BL.
TYNE

SP.• •D.
HUMBER

O.•

VY.•

GERMAN BIGHT

SHANNON
VA.•

MS.•

THAMES
•N.

FASTNET

LUNDY

MN.•
•V.

PB.• CP.•
LE.•

•C.

RS.• DOVER

WIGHT

SC.•
PLYMOUTH PORTLAND

50°N

SOLE

J.•

COASTAL STATIONS

BISCAY

FINISTERRE

A. ABERDEEN
B. BOULMER
BA. BENBECULA
BL. BLACKPOOL
BR. BELL ROCK
BS. BUTT OF LEWIS
C. CHANNEL Lt.V.
CP. ST. CATHERINE'S
    PT.
D. DOWSING
J. JERSEY
KH. KILLOUGH
KL. KILKEEL
LE. LANDS END
LK. LERWICK
LS. LEUCHARS
MD. MALIN HEAD
MH. MACHRIHANISH

MN. MANSTON
MS. MUMBLES
N. NOORD HINDER
O. ORLOCK HEAD
PB. PORTLAND BILL
PK. PRESTWICK
RS. ROYAL
    SOVEREIGN
RY. RONALDSWAY
SC. SCILLY
SH. SUMBURGH
SP. SPURN POINT
SY. STORNOWAY
T. TIREE
V. VARNE
VA. VALENTIA
VY. VALLEY
W. WICK

TRAFALGAR

Figure 57 (Reproduced from *Weather for Sailing* by Ray Sanderson (Stanford Maritime))

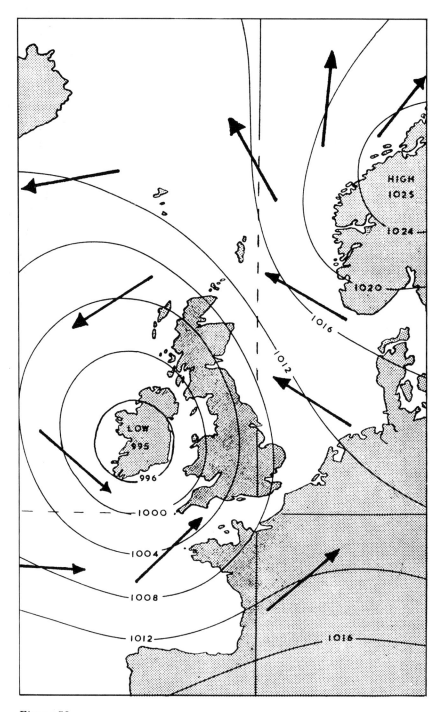

Figure 58

the interaction of regions of different atmospheric pressure. Air, generally, will flow from high pressure regions towards low pressure regions, just as water flows from high places down towards low places. It is, in fact, the mingling of these airstreams, some dry, some hot, some wet, some cold, that causes the weather; and that is as deep as we are going to go into the theories of meteorology.

The General Synopsis tells us about these different pressure regions – where they are, how they are moving, how low or high the pressures are, and how steeply the pressure falls or rises towards their centres. In general, low pressure areas – known as **lows** or **depressions** – bring wind and rain, while high pressure areas – known as **highs** or **anticyclones** – bring light breezes and fine weather. These regions can usually be seen quite clearly on a weather map, surrounded by roughly circular lines (see figure 58). The lines, called **isobars**, are drawn to join places of equal atmospheric pressure, and the actual pressures (in units called **millibars**) are written on the lines which can be seen wandering all over the place on the television weather chart. Although the air flows generally from a high pressure area to a low pressure area, it ends up swirling round the centres of these areas, anti-clockwise round a low and clockwise round a high in the Northern Hemisphere. In the Southern Hemisphere they go the other way round. Thus the wind that we actually experience on the water (which is simply this movement of air) blows more or less along the isobars as you can see from the arrows in figure 58. In practice, the rotation of the earth throws them slightly off course and they end up blowing slightly inwards towards the centre of a low and outwards away from the centre of a high. If you think of water swirling down towards the centre of a plughole, it will help you to remember that the wind blows down towards the centre of a low. It also blows down the low's left-hand side.

The speed of the wind is governed by the steepness of the pressure change. If the isobars are close together, the pressure is falling very steeply towards the centre of a low. The wind will blow very hard down this steep gradient, just as water will flow very hard down a steep hillside. When the isobars are far apart, as they generally are in a high, the wind will blow very slowly across this shallow pressure-gradient. In the area forecasts the speed of the wind (or its strength, as it is more commonly known) is given not in miles per hour, nor knots (see page 43), but in a simple code known as the **Beaufort Scale** (see Appendix 4). This scale also gives descriptions of the likely state of the open sea in such wind strengths. Although Force 8 is given as a gale, it must be borne in mind that Force 6 is a lot of wind for a small boat and is often called a 'yachtsman's gale'. Force 3 or 4 is quite sufficient for your initial forays onto the open sea.

Wind direction is given in terms of north, south, east and west, together with various directions in between. These are shown in figure 59, and a study of this **compass rose**, as it is called, will show the logic of the intermediate directions. North-east is midway between north and east; north-north-east is midway between north and north-east; north by east is just a little to the east of north, and so on. The wind is always described as coming *from* a particular direction: the north wind blows *from* the North Pole, not towards it. That is why it is cold!

Atmospheric pressure is measured on a device known as a **barometer**, and is often referred to as the barometric pressure. There are various types of

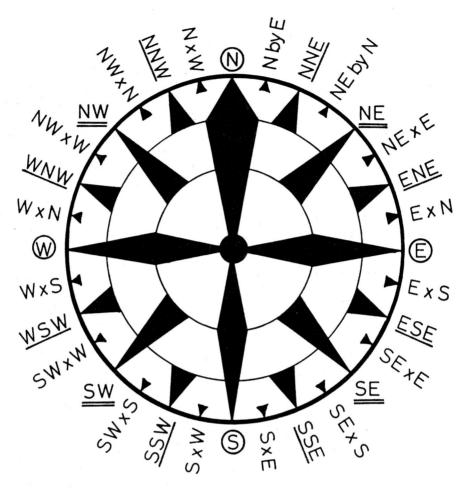

Figure 59

barometer, but the commonest in use on small boats looks somewhat like a small clock. It is absolutely essential that you have one of these on board as it can give you all sorts of information about the impending weather. If, for example, the barometer reading suddenly begins to fall rapidly, you can be certain that this rapid fall in pressure is caused by an approaching deep depression, with its attendant strong winds, perhaps gales, and rain. The barometer will fall until the depression passes, then begin to rise as the latter moves away. This will generally denote a better spell of weather, depending on the situation on the synoptic chart.

Depressions

By and large, depressions approach the British Isles from the west, travelling at speeds of anything up to thirty knots or more. Usually, the deeper the depression, the faster it travels, so the very bad weather tends to pass over quite quickly. As the depression approaches, the barometer falls and the cloud begins to gradually thicken, building up from the west. If the depression is heading to pass north of us (and most of them do go to the north of the British Isles), the wind will **back** (shift anti-clockwise) and begin to freshen up from the south, or even the south-east if the depression is very deep, and gradually **veer** (swing round clockwise) into the south-west, getting stronger all the time. This is the time when the wind is usually strongest, as the depression is nearest to us then (see the wind direction arrows in figure 58). As the depression moves away to the east or north-east so the wind gradually decreases, at the same time veering more into the west or nor'west. The barometer begins to rise as the higher pressure isobars move towards us, and the cloud will move away with the

depression, leaving clear blue skies, dotted perhaps with white fluffy 'cotton wool' clouds.

Often these depressions will contain **fronts** (see figure 60). The fronts mark dividing lines between different types of airstream, and they have the effect of altering the gradual change described above to two distinct changes. Before the warm front the wind will be moderate south or south-east, the cloud will be reasonably high still and just beginning to thicken and there will likely be no rain as yet. As the warm front passes over, you can see from the way the isobars kink that the wind will shift suddenly into the south-west, then the clouds will thicken considerably and it will begin to pour with rain, often reducing visibility quite drastically. At the same time the wind will blow up

Figure 60 The warm front is on the right, marked by half-round blobs. It is so called because it brings warm air behind it – in the triangle between the fronts known as the **warm sector**. The cold front is on the left, marked by points, and so called because it brings cold air behind it. It is the interaction of the warm and cold air masses that causes these fronts. The arrows across the isobars show the wind directions around the low.

much harder and the barometer will slow down its rapid fall. This happens because the isobars in the warm sector are more or less parallel to the track of the depression, so as it passes over the pressure will remain more or less steady. The cloud ceases so abruptly at the cold front that you can very often see a clear line of blue sky approaching from the west as it gets near to you. As it passes over, the wind will immediately fly round into the west or nor'west and the barometer will begin to rise, sometimes quite rapidly. With a strong cold front you often find a sou'west gale followed by a nor'west near gale for some while before it begins to die down. Remember, the steeper the pressure gradient, the stronger the wind; and the steeper the pressure gradient, the more rapidly will the barometer change, be it fall or rise. So watch your barometer at all times, and keep track of how it is moving, either by writing the reading regularly into the logbook (see Chapter 11) or by setting the adjustable mark on the barometer at regular intervals. Appendix 4 gives a rough guide to what the barometer's rate of rise or fall can tell you.

If the depression passes to the south of us we will not have these dramatic frontal changes, and the wind will shift differently. If you look carefully at figure 60, you will see that the wind will start off easterly and will then gradually and steadily back through north-east to about north. The barometer will fall until the wind is about nor'east, then begin to rise. It will rain heavily, continuously and drearily the whole time. Visibility will most probably be poor. If the centre of the depression is forecast to pass over your sea area, you will be given 'cyclonic' winds; which simply means that the wind will veer steadily and rapidly from the southern sector to the northern sector of the depression.

Anticyclones

An anticyclone is quite different from the action-packed depression. Usually much larger, it drifts about rather aimlessly, appearing to form, disintegrate and reform again whenever the mood takes it. With widely spaced isobars it generally produces light winds or calms, and as it does not contain the vigorous, swirling and interacting airstreams that constitute a low, little cloud is formed within it. The summer characteristics of a high are thus light breezes, clear blue skies and sunshine. In short, just what the skipper ordered.

Due to their lack of energy and determination, highs tend to be pushed around and swallowed up by every approaching low of any intensity. Occasionally, however, we find a strong high that stands its ground, forcing all the lows approaching from the west to divert north or south. This is called a **blocking high** and is the cause of the long fine settled periods we sometimes find in summer around the British Isles. In these conditions we often experience what is known as a **sea breeze**, ie wind blowing in from the sea with no regard for the angle of closeness of the isobars, caused by the sun heating up the land and the air close to it. As you will know if you have ever sat with freezing feet next to an open fire, this warm air rises, and it causes air to be drawn in from the sea to replace it. This sea breeze generally begins late in the morning (when the sun has had time to warm things up) and continues until the evening when things begin to cool down and the rising of warm air from the land ceases. During this time it gradually veers, due to the rotation of the earth pushing it off course. On the South Coast it would begin southerly, and gradually veer more into the south-west. If there is an existing wind blowing off the land it will delay, reduce or even cancel the sea breeze, depending on its strength and precise direction.

Of considerable relevance to a motor-cruiser skipper is the fact that, if there is an existing onshore wind, it can be reinforced by the sea breeze to produce quite a strong wind at times. A coastal passage begun on a quiet sunny morning with a light onshore breeze could end with you struggling to round a headland in rough seas (particularly with a strong tidal stream against the wind) and with half a gale blowing you onto a **lee shore** (a shore to leeward of you). The wind strength given in the weather forecast will not take the sea breeze into account, so this is something you have to think out for yourself.

The other danger that can develop in anticyclonic conditions is fog.

The Formation of Fog

On a hot, sunny day the land warms up steadily all day until the sun goes down. If the skies remain clear during the night, this heat is allowed to radiate out into space (clouds act rather like loft insulation, keeping the heat in) and thus the ground, and the air close to it, cools down. The colder the air is, the less water vapour it can hold, so if it cools sufficiently, the water vapour condenses from an invisible vapour into tiny droplets of water, billions and billions and billions of which are what clouds are made of. And fog is cloud at ground level – damp, dismal and extremely difficult to see through.

This **radiation fog**, as it is called, tends to form in patches on low-lying ground and in valleys. When it forms in river valleys it is inclined to roll down into the estuaries and out to sea for perhaps a couple of miles or so (rarely more than five), where it remains until the heat of the next day evaporates it back into the air – generally late in the morning. It can last all day, however, if it is very thick and some cloud forms

during the day to reduce the heat of the sun. Wind will help to dissipate it more quickly.

As with sea breezes, the possibility of radiation fog is often not mentioned on the Shipping Forecast, due to its localised nature, being caused by the land rather than by the meteorological situation on the synoptic chart. Both can often be found predicted in other types of weather forecast, as we shall see later. Both can also be predicted relatively easily and reliably by the man on the spot, ie you, and we will also look later at the forecasting you can do yourself.

Sea fog is quite a different matter, and will be mentioned in the Shipping Forecast. This, as its name implies, is formed at sea by the action of warm, moist air passing over colder water. The cold water cools down the air until the latter can no longer hold its water as vapour which then condenses out as fog. The temperature at which the water vapour begins to condense is known as **dew point**, and it varies with the temperature of the air and the amount of water vapour the air holds. When the temperature of the air is cooled to below its dew point the fog begins to form, just as we saw with the radiation fog. This type of fog is common in the western English Channel in spring when south-westerly winds (warm from the tropics and full of water vapour sucked up during their passage over the ocean) blow in over a sea that is still cold from winter. It is more difficult for a skipper to predict than radiation fog and is far longer lasting as the sun will not burn it up. It will also persist in strong winds (radiation fog will not, as it is low lying and wind will cause it to mix with the warm upper layers of air and so disperse it), and this can allow it to blow into adjacent sea areas where it may not actually be forecast. It can also appear in patches where cold water

117

comes to the surface. The only thing that will remove it is a complete change of meteorological conditions. Thus it is a far greater menace than radiation fog.

Frontal fog is basically sea fog that is formed in the warm air around the warm front in a depression. It will pass with the passing of the warm front, and will probably be mentioned in the Shipping Forecast. **Arctic sea smoke** is a most interesting form of fog that will definitely not be mentioned in the forecast. Neither, however, will it be a danger to you, although you may see it occasionally in the early morning in sheltered spots close to land in shallow estuaries. It is formed when very cold air (after a cold clear night) flows off the land onto the relatively warm water in the shallows. Vapour evaporating from the warm water cannot be held by the cold air so is immediately precipitated out as fog. This fog is then warmed by the water to above its dew point and disperses. It then rises into the colder air and precipitates out again. And so it goes on, the fog appearing to writhe upwards like tendrils of smoke, hence the name. It is extremely unstable and lasts hardly any time at all, but is interesting to look out for when conditions are suitable.

Other Features on the Synoptic Chart

Although the synoptic chart is generally dominated by the existence of highs and the passage of lows, there are other features that you will hear mentioned on the forecasts from time to time. **Troughs of low pressure** and **ridges of high pressure** are simply squashed and elongated versions of lows and highs, and the weather they give is very similar except that ridges can sometimes give cloudy and drizzly weather with poor visibility and often surprisingly strong winds, as the isobars tend to squash up more than in

a high. An **airstream** is formed where a low presses up against a high, the clockwise winds on the edge of the high being reinforced by the anticlockwise winds in a low (see figure 58). This can often give very strong steady winds for days on end, as the low pressing against the high squeezes the isobars closer together. If the high is blocking the progress of the low, they may remain locked in mortal combat until one or the other gives in and moves off elsewhere.

An **occlusion** is a merging of warm front and cold front, found near the centre of a low that is fizzling out – **filling** is the official description (see figure 61). What happens is that the cold front travels faster than the warm front and gradually catches up with it. It does so nearest the centre of the low first, as the two fronts are closest together here, and as the two mingle into an occlusion (or **occluded front**), the energies of both are dissipated and the low begins to fill. Whereupon we all breathe a sigh of relief and look forward to better weather. Or do we?

The wise seaman does not. As the cold front begins to occlude and slow down, its trailing edge sometimes tends to overrun it and form a kink or wave (see left-hand edge of figure 61). This kink in the cold front, if sufficiently accentuated, can rapidly draw a circulation of air around itself and form very quickly into a deep and vicious little low, travelling at great speed in the wake of its dying parent. This **secondary**, or **wave depression**, will often have much stronger winds than the original one, and can form so quickly, and travel so rapidly, that it can be upon you before anyone has had time to see it and forecast it. It is invariably the cause of the 'unexpected gale' that we read about in the papers, wreaking havoc all the way up the English Channel.

You on the spot, however, can forecast it very easily. Be wary of any

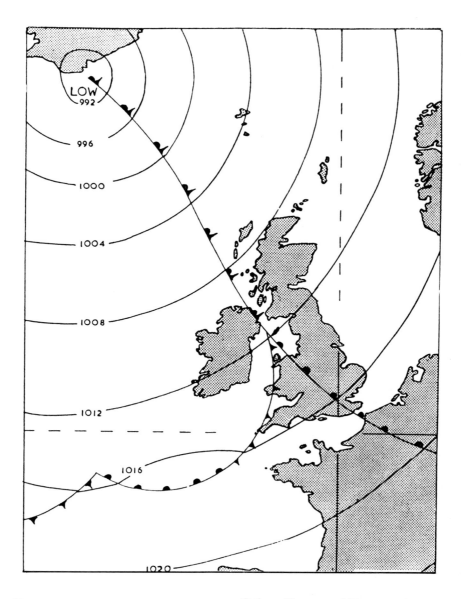

Figure 61

occluding depression. When the cold front goes over, the skies will clear and the barometer begin to rise. Keep a very close eye on the sky to the west and the barometer. If thin high wispy cloud begins to approach, thickening as it comes, and the barometer ceases to rise, then begins to fall, a wave depression is fast approaching, and the best place for you is tucked up in a nice sheltered harbour.

Other Types of Forecast

Although the Shipping Forecast should constitute our main source of weather information, there are various other sources that we can profitably use to supplement it. The synoptic chart shown on certain television weather bulletins is an excellent way of fleshing out the rather meagre details given in the Shipping Forecast's general synopsis. The latter tends only to give the speeds and positions of the major lows and highs, whereas the television chart shows everything – isobars, fronts, occlusions and so on. Regular perusal of this will give you a very good general picture of the weather pattern, which will help considerably in your interpretation of the Shipping Forecast. Bear in mind, however, that it is a very general picture, with the emphasis on weather over the land. Use it in conjunction with the Shipping Forecast, not instead of it. The detailed land forecast at 1755 on Radio Four is also useful for this, information on belts of rain helping you to assess the position and progress of fronts, about which the Shipping Forecast seems curiously reticent.

Forecasts more orientated towards the seaman can be had on local radio stations operating in yachting areas, by phone from certain Meterological Offices and from the Inshore Waters Forecast on Radio Four. Details of all these will be found in the Almanac. If you telephone a Met Office, ask for specific information – speed and direction of wind, probability of fog etc in a particular place at a particular time – rather than simply 'the weather forecast for tomorrow'. If you tell the man where you are going and when, and the particular weather conditions that concern you, you will find him extremely helpful. He will also usually give you a long-range forecast for the next few days or more if you ask. This produces an excellent forecast before sailing, if you can get through on the ever-engaged telephone! The Inshore Waters Forecast is very good for coastal passages. It is similar to the Shipping Forecast, but concentrates on conditions close inshore. It is generally broadcast after the 0033 Shipping Forecast, but is liable to change.

Assessing the Weather Yourself

Wherever you get your forecasts from, never forget the point made at the beginning of this chapter about their fallibility. Having learnt here something of the nature of the weather, you should be able to decide for yourself whether the forecasters are right or not. The main points to watch for are the possibility of a depression speeding up, so bringing the bad weather to you sooner than forecast; deepening (pressure at the centre getting lower), so bringing stronger winds than forecast; or altering course, so bringing to you the bad weather that has been forecast for somewhere else.

You have three basic ways of checking the forecast – your barometer, the nature of the sky and the Station Reports of present weather, given out in the Shipping Forecast. You can also find the present weather by telephoning the local coastguard. The Almanac will give details of phone numbers and whereabouts of coastguards. All these can assist you in gauging the progress of a depression approaching from the west, the usual harbinger of bad weather in British waters. Knowing the speed and direction of movement of a depression (as given in the General Synopsis), it is a simple matter to calculate how soon you can expect the present weather at the Scillies to arrive in, say, the Thames forecast area. Keep a sharp eye on the forecasts in sea areas to the west of yours, for that is the weather that is coming to you when the usual depression is on its way. If the depression speeds up (and your barometer will give warning of this if it begins to fall more rapidly, see Appendix 4), you could all too easily find yourself struggling in a sou'-westerly 6 or 7 that was forecast for areas to the west, instead of the manageable 3 to 4 that was forecast for your area.

The ability to analyse and assess the overall weather situation from all the information available to you – shipping forecasts, television forecasts, land forecasts, telephone forecasts, your own barometer, the amount and type of cloud in the sky, and the existing weather in other places — is a great asset to a motor-cruiser skipper, and it makes him a far more competent seaman than the man who simply listens like a parrot to the forecast for his area. It is an ability that comes with experience, but an experience you can cultivate yourself. Even when you are not going out, listen to the forecasts over a period of days so that you can see how things are changing and developing, watch the sky and your barometer, and assess what you think the weather will do and when. If you get it wrong (which even the forecasts do), try to work out why. You will soon learn.

You will find it a great help to get hold of a pad of **Metmaps** (printed forecast area charts available from chandlers and nautical bookshops) so that you can keep a record of a series of forecasts. You can then look back over them and see how the weather has developed over a period of days. Fill in all the information from the Shipping Forecast, then try to flesh out the synopsis with isobars and fronts to give you a more detailed picture. The barometric readings and wind directions at the coastal stations will help in this, as will the wind directions given in the area forecasts. Check, however, the times at which these items of information are given for, as they vary. You will have to guesstimate a bit to bring them all to the same time. You will also have to learn to write in some rapid form of shorthand due to the speed at which the forecast is usually read out!

There is an official system of shorthand symbols, but it is probably as well to develop your own that you will find easier to remember. Simple abbreviations such as NW (north-west), bec (becoming), v (veering), csr (continuous slight rain) and so on, will be found quite effective. Group areas with the same forecast, eg TDFGB (Tyne, Dogger, Fisher, German Bight) and note Station Reports as Sc-NNE3-6'-1015 ↓ s (Scilly Isles-nor'nor'east Force 3, visibility 6 miles, barometer reading 1015 millibars, falling slowly). You will soon get the hang of it.

11
MAKING A COASTAL PASSAGE

Navigation is the business of finding your way from one place to another on the sea. It can be a complex mixture of art and science, requiring considerable training and experience to carry out competently and reliably. For our purposes, however – a short coastal passage in good weather – the knowledge required is fairly basic and simple. If you wish one day to go beyond this stage, then you must study the subject thoroughly from a specialised navigation manual.

The equipment we require for such a passage is equally basic and simple. There are a great many electronic aids to navigation available these days, and these are discussed briefly in Appendix 2. With the exception of a simple echosounder (not absolutely essential, but extremely useful as we saw in Chapter 6) and a **log** (a device – not necessarily electronic – that measures the distance we travel through the water, and also sometimes our speed), not one of these is even remotely necessary for the sort of passage that we have in mind.

Let us imagine we want to go from Scarborough to Bridlington, two small ports on the north-east coast of England about twenty miles apart. Neither of them is a very suitable place for a beginner to keep a motor cruiser as they both dry out at Low Water and they both open directly onto the exposed waters of the North Sea. However, a passage between the two should teach us just about all we need to know for making a short coastal passage.

Equipment
The first thing we need for this passage is a chart. In fact, we need three – a large-scale one with lots of detail, for getting out of Scarborough and into clear coastal water; a smaller scale one covering the complete passage; and another large-scale one with sufficient detail to enable us to safely approach and enter Bridlington. There are various types of chart we can use, produced by the Admiralty and by some nautical publishers. Figures 62, 63 and 64 show the relevant portions of the Admiralty charts covering these areas. Each chart has a reference number marked on it, the chart of Scarborough Bay in figure 62 being number 1612. Small scale charts (those covering a large area) are often marked with the outlines of more detailed, larger scale charts that cover certain portions of them. The number of the chart is written in the top right-hand corner of the outline, and you can see on the chart in figure 63 the area covered by the larger scale chart of Scarborough Bay (number 1612).

It is important that we use up-to-date charts, or some depths and dangers may have changed, jetties may have been built or knocked down, buoys moved or the characteristics of lights changed. Suppliers keep their charts corrected to date when you buy them, after which you should return them every winter for any necessary further corrections. There will be a small charge for this, but it is very false economy not to have them done. When you are experienced you can obtain the corrections from the suppliers and do them yourself. You can see a note of the latest correction at the bottom of the chart in figure 63. The year in which the correction was made (1983) is followed by the reference number of the correction (2959).

You will also need a Pilot Book covering the area. This is a book with detailed information about harbours and the problems of entering them together, usually, with navigational information on the coastline. It also gives invaluable information on facilities available in harbours, where to anchor or berth, special regulations in force, and so on. It can be obtained from the chart supplier, and should also be corrected annually.

A Nautical Almanac is essential. There are two on the market particularly suitable for our purposes, *Reed's Nautical Almanac* and *MacMillan's Almanac*. They are republished annually and contain a mass of information both essential and useful,

including tide tables and tidal stream atlases for the whole country. They also contain potted information and chartlets of a great many harbours. These are most useful for general planning, but should not be used as a substitute for proper charts and Pilot Books when actually navigating. Fuller details of the vast amount of useful information

Photo 28 A small chart table showing essential equipment. The two sides of the parallel ruler swing apart, always remaining parallel. To transfer a course or bearing across the chart, hold one side firmly on the chart and move the other in the desired direction. Then hold the other and move the first side up to it. Parallel lines can be transferred all over the chart by this means. The dividers are so designed that they can be held and adjusted in one hand. This makes them much quicker and easier to operate than the traditional school type, particularly in bad weather. A small adjustable light hangs over the table, and can be dimmed by means of a variable switch. Some people like red lights at night, while others prefer very dim white ones. Try them both out and see which you prefer. You can make a red bulb by painting an ordinary one with red nail varnish.

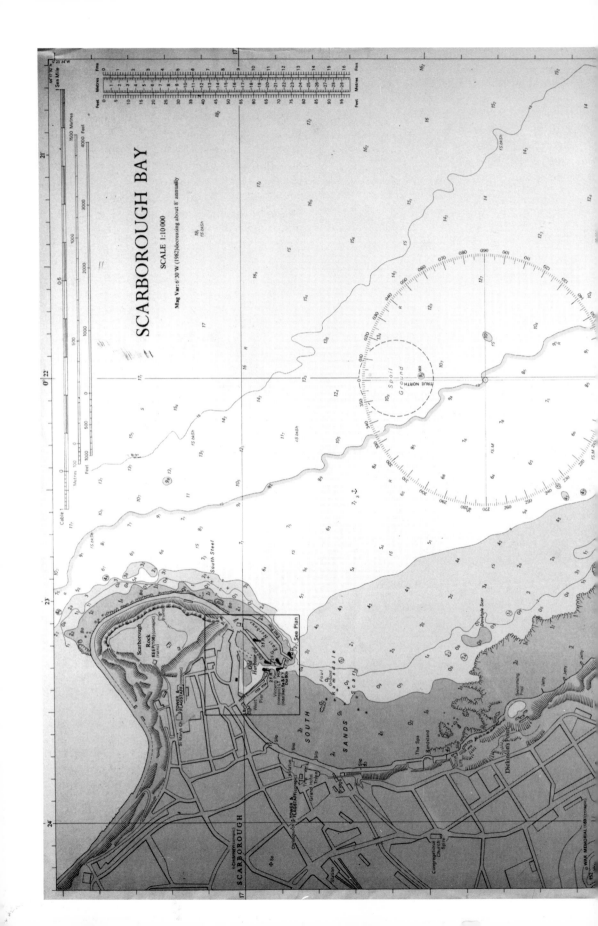

SCARBOROUGH BAY

SCALE 1:10000

Mag Var: 6°30'W (1982)decreasing about 8' annually

SCARBOROUGH HARBOUR

SCALE 1:5000

contained in the Almanac will be found in Appendix 3. Add to this a parallel ruler (for plotting courses on the chart), a pair of dividers (for measuring distances on the chart – the single-handed type as shown is best), a pair of compasses, a couple of soft (2B) pencils, a pencil sharpener and rubber, a small notebook, and a logbook (in which to note down navigational information), and we have all the equipment we need for the chart table.

In the cockpit we want an echo-sounder, a log and a **compass**, together with a pair of binoculars and a hand-bearing compass. There are two basic types of log – the sort that trails over the stern on the end of a long thin rope and the sort that is fitted into the hull. The latter is better on a motor cruiser as it avoids the risk of fouling the propeller with the log line.

A compass is a gadget that shows us the direction of magnetic north. Essentially it consists of a card, usually marked round the outside in degrees from 0 to 360 (although sometimes marked in points as we saw in the last chapter) stuck on top of a magnet balanced on a pivot point. The magnet always swings to point to magnetic north, which is slightly to one side of true (or geographic) north, ie the North Pole. The compass enables us to steer in a particular direction.

The compass can be easily affected by anything metallic, electronic or magnetic, and it is most important that anything of that sort – beer cans, metal-clad batteries, knives, cameras, light meters, radios, electronic navigation devices and so on – are kept at least three feet away from it. Very large lumps of metal such as the engine will affect it at much greater distances, and this must be corrected for by arranging with a **compass adjuster** to 'swing the

Figure 62

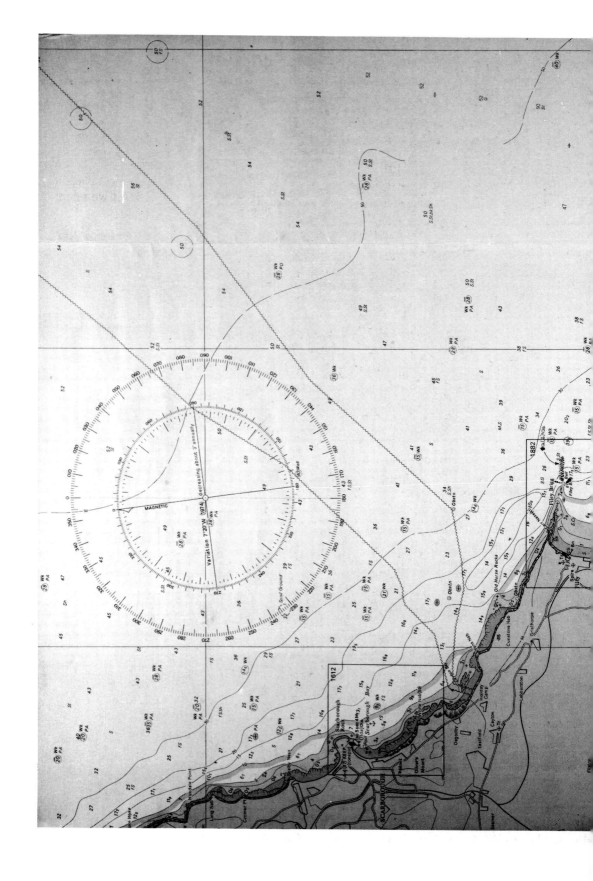

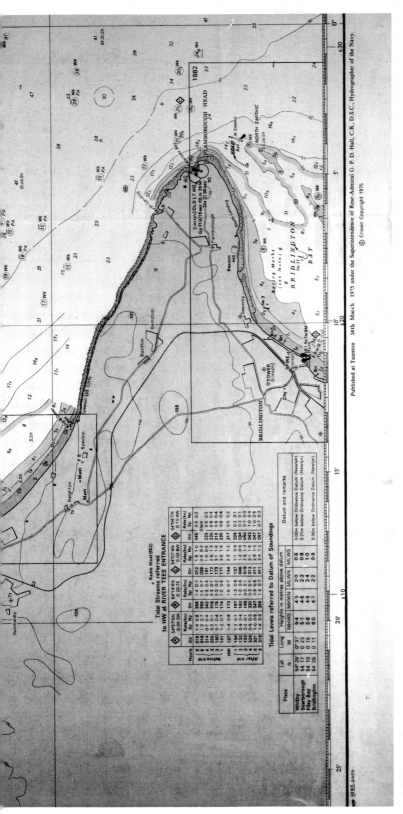

Figure 63

Figure 64a

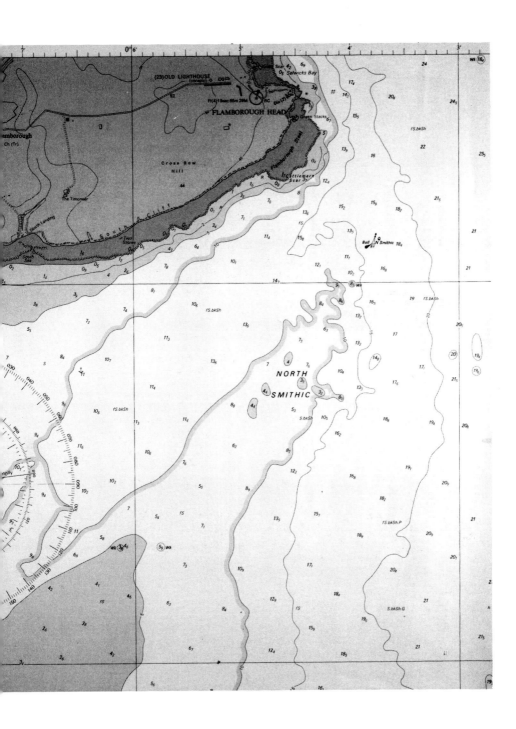

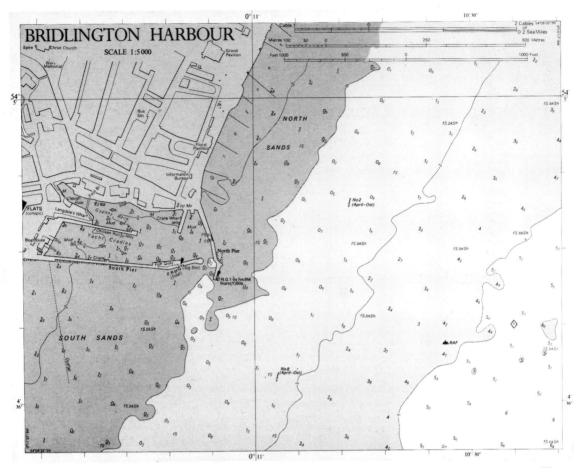

Figure 64b

compass' and check it on all its headings, as the effects will vary with the direction in which the boat is pointing. He then fixes small magnets around the compass to compensate as much as possible for the effects. Any small remaining errors are known as **deviation** and will be tabulated on a card known as a **deviation card** (see figure 65), which should be kept beside the chart table. The errors can then be allowed for when plotting a course by compass. The compass should be swung every other year, or after any major maintenance work that might have moved metal around the boat.

Binoculars are extremely useful for seeing details of things at a distance –

buoys, ships, land and so on. They should not be too powerful or you will find it impossible to keep them steady enough at sea to get a clear image. Seven or eight times magnification is quite sufficient. They should, however, have good 'light-gathering power' so that you can see things at dusk or in the dark. Binoculars classed as 7×50 are the traditional seaman's tool, the 50 basically signifying the size of the lens, and thus the ability to gather light. The 8×30 are commonly used general purpose binoculars, giving slightly greater magnification but less light gathering. If you intend to keep your cruising limited to the extent covered by this book, a pair of these would be perfectly adequate, and would be useful for other pursuits such as racing or birdwatching.

130

A hand-bearing compass is a small compass that can be held in the hand. It has a 'gunsight' at the front and a line marked on the back against which you can read off the bearing of an object aligned with the sight. It is used for fixing the boat's position and for checking whether other vessels are on a collision course (see Chapter 9). You will see how it works when we discuss fixing, later in the chapter. It cannot be

Photo 29 A clear and easily read compass by a well known maker. To read off a course you should stand directly in front of the compass and read off the number in line with the middle white line (known as a **lubber's line**). Because of the distance between the lubber's line and the card, you will get a false reading if you stand to one side. This compass was reading 120 degrees and the photograph was taken from a position to the right of the lubber's line to show the false reading that can be obtained. The card floats about in the compass to allow for the motion of the boat, and the black needle at the bottom will swing against the scale to show how many degrees the boat is rolling from side to side. There will be a light inside the compass to illuminate the card at night. Make sure it is dim. This is only one of many different types and designs of compass, but it shows the principle well.

corrected for deviation, so must always be used in a position well clear of anything that might affect it. Used properly like this, it can be aligned with the centreline of the boat to provide a simple and useful check on the accuracy of the main steering compass.

Planning the Passage

The first thing to do is sit down with the Pilot Book and read thoroughly and carefully all the information and advice it gives about the two harbours and the

DEVIATION CARD Steering compass

Yacht _____

Date _____

Magnetic course	Deviation	Compass course
000	2W	002
015	2W	017
030	3W	033
045	3W	048
060	4W	064
075	3W	078
090	3W	093
105	3W	108
120	2W	122
135	1W	136
150	1W	151
165	1W	166
180	0	180
195	0	195
210	0	210
225	0	225
240	1E	239
255	2E	253
270	2E	268
285	3E	282
300	2E	298
315	1E	314
330	0	330
345	1W	346
360	2W	002

Figure 65

131

coastline between them. Then read it all again. Do not get too bogged down at this stage with the fine details of the passage; concentrate on a general picture of the important facts and main dangers. Then spread out the charts and peruse them carefully, looking for the points mentioned in the Pilot.

The next step is to calculate how to get safely out of Scarborough and into a position in open water from which we can set a course towards Bridlington. This position must be such that we can both confirm accurately that we are in it, and also mark it accurately on the chart. Finding the position of a boat on the water is known as **fixing** her position, and the position then marked on the chart is known as a **fix**. When we fix our position outside a harbour in order to provide ourselves with an accurate departure point, we call it a **departure fix** (see below).

If we now look at the passage chart in figure 63, we will see immediately that it is not possible for us to motor in a straight line directly from Scarborough to Bridlington. We must first pass safely round the outside of Filey Brigg, then down to and around Flamborough Head before we can set a direct course to Bridlington Harbour. The Pilot will tell us all about the dangers off Filey Brigg, and we can also see them on the chart. The ragged-looking line and crosses extending from the point of land and surrounded by a dotted line are dangerous rocks, and we must keep well clear of them. The wavy, watery lines just landward of Filey Brigg buoy (on either side of the 7_4 sounding) denote rough water (known as **overfalls**), almost certainly caused by tidal streams sweeping in from different directions and meeting. If there are strong winds and waves as well, this sort of place can be quite dangerous for small boats, due to the buffeting they get from the steep and irregular waves

that are formed (see Chapter 9).

These overfalls are quite common off all coastal headlands, especially if fast tides sweep by them. The extent, the precise position and even the existence of the overfalls will vary considerably with the rate and direction of the tidal stream, so careful timing of your arrival off a headland can often be crucial to the safe or comfortable rounding of it. Full information must be sought from the Pilot on this matter.

What happens is that the tidal stream tends to sweep directly from one headland to the next, not bothering to follow the curve of the bay between them. A certain amount of the stream does, however, tend to drift into the bay, creating a slight shoreward set which must be guarded against when crossing a bay, particularly in poor visibility when the far headland cannot be seen. This water then piles up at the far end of the bay to be deflected by the headland and pushed out to sea, where it meets the original stream and causes the overfalls. The Pilot tells us that this is exactly what happens off Filey Brigg with a north-west going stream. Clearly the overfalls will be worst at spring tides when the streams are strongest. A similar but less pronounced effect might be experienced with a south-east going stream, due to a back eddy being set up in Filey Bay, running north. You should be able to deduce, however, that an east-going set just south of Filey Brigg will meet the main north-west stream almost head on, whereas it will tend to merge, with little or no disturbance, with a main south-east going stream. Thus ideally (certainly at spring tides or in rough weather), we should time our arrival off Filey Brigg to coincide with a south-east going stream. From the point of view of our passage this is ideal, as it means the stream will be helping us on our way, particularly past the headland where it is likely to be stronger than elsewhere, as headlands also tend to constrict the passage of the water, thus forcing it to run faster.

Filey Brigg buoy is moored clear outside both rocks and overfalls, so we should set our course to pass outside it. It can be identified by its shape (as drawn on the chart), its colour (as indicated beneath the drawing – BYB being black, yellow and black stripes) and the little black shapes stuck on top of it, known as **topmarks**. Note that this buoy is quite different from the channel buoys of Chapter 9, as it does not mark the edge of a channel but the direction of a particular danger. The colours and topmarks on this buoy indicate that it is situated to the east of the danger. Similar buoys with different combinations of colours and topmarks can be placed to the north, south and west of dangers (see figure 66). The shaped blob underneath the buoy shows that it has a light on it, the characteristic of which is written in

brief alongside the buoy. For identification purposes, lights on buoys and lighthouses flash at different rates, in different colours or in different ways; full details can be found in the almanac. This one gives three quick flashes every ten seconds, and it is white, as no specific colour is indicated.

Strictly speaking, buoys should not be relied upon for navigation, especially if they are in exposed positions, due to the possibility of their dragging their moorings and drifting into the wrong position. In this situation, however, we can use the echo-sounder to check that we are in safe water. The line roughly following the coast, just shoreward of the buoy, denotes a charted depth of ten metres. If we calculate the height of the tide and add it to this to get the actual depth of water on that line, we can use the echo-sounder to ensure that we remain in the deeper water to seaward of it, and thus clear of all the dangers.

The rounding of Flamborough Head should be considered in the same way,

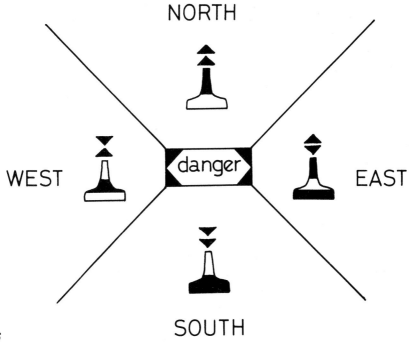

Figure 66

scouring chart and Pilot Book for dangers and for certain ways of identifying that it actually is Flamborough Head when we reach it. The chart would seem to give a clean bill of health as far as dangers go, with no off-lying rocks or shallow water, and no marked overfalls. However, from the way the coast cuts back sharply into Bridlington Bay, it would be wise to assume the possibility of strong tidal streams off the head, and perhaps rough water at certain states of the stream. The Pilot confirms this, with a warning of strong tidal streams, eddies and turbulence close inshore, so a careful study of this information will be needed in order to select the best time for rounding; or to decide how far to stand off in order to avoid them.

The head itself is described in detail in the Pilot to assist in identification (mine even describes the northern side as being the breeding place of numerous seabirds), while the chart gives us the important features. The most noticeable of these are the 'conspicuous' Old Light House and the current operational one (marked by a small star with a light blip, as we saw on Filey Brigg buoy). The notation alongside it tells us that the light shows a group of 4 white flashes every 15 seconds, it is 65 metres above the level of Mean High Water springs (average spring High Water height) and on a clear night is visible 29 miles away. (This is the theoretical maximum; from a small boat you probably would not see it that far away due to the height of your eye above sea level. The higher your eye, the further you can see.) A physical description of the lighthouses will be found in the Pilot.

Just to the south of the head you can see another buoy similar to Filey Brigg buoy, but with different colouring and different topmarks. This marks the north side of the shallow bank known as North Smithic Shoal. The actual depths on this shoal are unlikely to worry us in our small motor cruiser, but they might cause any waves to steepen and break if the wind is blowing from offshore. Keeping to the north of the buoy will enable us to avoid this possibly rough water.

From here it is a simple run across to Bridlington Harbour with no dangers on the chart. The Pilot will tell us the best way to identify and approach Bridlington Harbour, and we must then change to the large-scale charts (see figures 64a and b) for the actual entry. Make sure you identify accurately every feature along the way before assuming that the track is clear of dangers. The Almanac contains details of chart symbols, and the Admiralty issues a special booklet.

Entering and Leaving Harbour

A glance at the large-scale charts of both harbours shows us immediately that virtually all the soundings are underlined, thus denoting that the bottom is *above* Chart Datum, not below it. The actual depth of water at any time will thus be the height of the tide (which is measured above Chart Datum) minus the charted sounding, as discussed in Chapter 6. We can see that Scarborough's East Harbour (which is where we will be, as the Pilot tells us that Old Harbour is strictly reserved for the fishing fleet) dries to quite a height – over 2 metres above Chart Datum – so we must check the height of tide that we will need in order to get out. A glance at the tidal information for Scarborough in the almanac, or on the chart, tells us that Mean Low Water Neaps (average neap Low Water) is 2.3 metres and Mean High Water Neaps is 4.6 metres. Thus the bottom just to seaward of the E in East Pier (dries 2.5m) will be just above the water on an average Low Water Neaps. A rough calculation using the twelfths rule tells us that if we draw 1 metre and are berthed in this position we should be able to get out shortly after half-flood on an average neap tide. [Range = 2.3m. By half tide LW will have risen by half this, ie 1.15m. Height of tide will then be LW (2.3m) + 1.15m = 3.45m. Depth will be 3.45m − 2.5m (drying height) = approximately 1m.]

The drying heights in the outer part of Bridlington Harbour are much less – under 1 metre at the Fish Quay. MLWN at Bridlington is given in the Almanac as 2.2 metres, so we should be able to get into Bridlington just about at Low Water Neaps. We can move further up the harbour if necessary as the tide rises, but the important thing is that we can get in. We do not want to arrive off the harbour and have to hang about waiting for sufficient tide to enter; for this first trip, we want everything as simple and straightforward as possible. Bear in mind, however, that these figures are averages. A neap tide on a particular day will probably be slightly different.

So, if we choose a suitable neap tide for this first coastal passage, we will gain the following benefits:
1 A reasonable spread of time during which we can leave Scarborough.
2 Weak tidal streams during the passage, giving us minimum eddies and turbulence off Flamborough Head and Filey Brigg, a negligible set into Filey Bay, and less likelihood of difficulty manoeuvring in and out of the harbours.
3 Access to Bridlington Harbour at any time.

On this first ever trip to sea, you will have quite enough to occupy your mind without burdening yourself with further, unnecessary, tidal complications. As you gain in experience, so you will be able to cope all the more easily, and these matters will have less

impact on you. The basic principle, however, of carefully analysing all the dangers throughout the passage, and planning your trip to avoid or minimise them (depending on their seriousness), will always remain of paramount importance when coasting in a small boat.

Getting out of Scarborough Harbour and into a suitable position for a departure fix is, as can be seen from both the harbour chart and the approaches chart in figure 62, simply a matter of manoeuvring out through the entrance then turning towards the open sea. We can then take a departure fix and from it plot a course to pass outside Filey Brigg buoy. Figure 67 explains how we take this fix.

We can keep track of our position along the coast by taking a regular series of fixes or we can do it by **dead reckoning (DR)**. This is simply a matter of taking a regular log reading (say every hour) and calculating the distance we have gone from the last position. Mark a line across the course you have steered, plot it on the chart (see below) and note the time. **Estimated position (EP)** is more accurate, being calculated from our course made good (allowing for tidal drift and leeway (see pages 43 and 140) and our speed made good over the ground (see caption 69). It is marked by a dot enclosed by a triangle, with the time. There is little need, as we shall see, for any of these techniques on a simple coastal passage like this in good visibility, when we can always see where we are heading for, and where we are. On longer or more difficult passages they are essential if we are not to become lost.

Not all harbours will be as simple to get out of as Scarborough. Have a look at Eyemouth Harbour in figure 68. Negotiating the harbour itself is simply a question of keeping between the beacons marking the sides of the deep

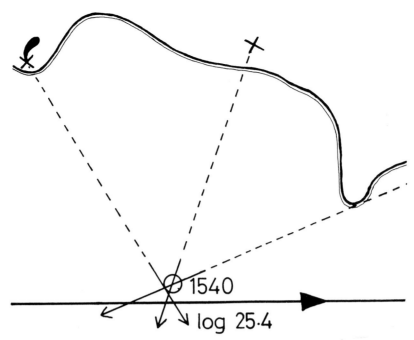

1540

log 25·4

Figure 67 A simple and accurate fix can be obtained by taking with the hand-bearing compass and plotting on the chart, the bearings of a number of fixed objects around us that are marked on the chart. As we must be somewhere along the line of each of these bearings, our position has to be where they cross. If we use three or more bearings, any inaccuracies will show up by their crossing in a small triangle instead of a point. We then assume ourselves to be at the corner of the triangle that is nearest to any danger, so that if we are not exactly there, we are likely to be further from the danger than we think – a simple safety precaution. This example uses a lighthouse, a church and the edge of a headland, all clearly marked on the chart, and far enough apart that the bearings will cut at a good angle. If bearings are too close together, very slight inaccuracies will cause the triangle

(known as a **cocked hat**) to be very long and narrow, thus making the fix almost useless. Fixes can be obtained by crossing all sorts of position lines – depth contours, transits and so on – but they must be all measured as nearly as possible at the same moment if they are to be accurate, otherwise the boat will have moved somewhere else between taking one position line and another. This is a particular problem with high-speed craft, which may have to slow down considerably in order to get an accurate fix. Inaccuracies caused by speed, taking bearings of the wrong objects, identifying objects wrongly on the chart, plotting bearings wrongly on the chart and so on, will all show as very large cocked hats on the fix. You must then recheck everything. Write the time and log reading by the fix, as shown here, then subsequent progress can be checked against it.

channel. Outside the harbour, however, there are a lot of dangerous rocks that we must get clear of before we can take a departure fix and proceed on our way. Pointing roughly north from the harbour entrance is a line on the chart at the end of which is written (Ldg Lts 174°). If you look carefully at the inner end of this line, you will note that it joins up two lights on the western

breakwater. These are known as **leading lights**, and keeping them in line will lead you safely clear of the dangers outside. This, in effect, is a transit, such as we saw in Chapter 4.

A physical description of these leading lights will be found in the Pilot, and this will enable you to line them up in daytime. A suitable departure fix can then be obtained by watching the echo-

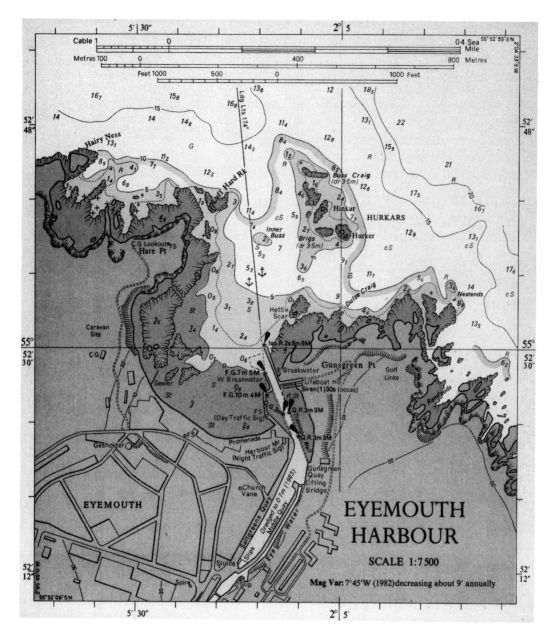

Figure 68

sounder to see when you pass the 15-metre depth contour (making due allowance for tidal height), then taking a bearing with the hand-bearing compass of perhaps the right-hand edge of Hairy Ness shown in the figure. Passing the 15-metre depth contour tells you, as you can see from the chart, that you have gone clear of the rocks on both sides of the leading line and can now safely alter course to the direction in which you want to go. All harbours, of course, will be different, and careful study of the Pilot is essential for safe entry and exit.

Before entering Bridlington Harbour, we must take the same considerations in reverse. We should aim to select a

137

convenient point outside the harbour to which we can motor straight from the previous turning point – Flamborough Head – and from which we can safely approach and enter the harbour. You can see from figure 64 that there is a shallow spit extending southwards from the end of North Pier which could give us problems on a very low tide. To round this and then enter the harbour up the deeper channel could be quite tricky for a beginner, so I would suggest that the way to enter Bridlington would be to arrive when the tide is high enough that you can safely motor straight across this spit. A glance at the depths inside the harbour tells us that if we have sufficient water to cross the spit, we have enough to get alongside a quay in the outer part of the harbour. In strong onshore winds this spit could cause steep and breaking waves.

The initial approach should be to pass far enough south of North Pier that you can see another boat leaving in good enough time to avoid collision. Then round up slowly towards the entrance, keeping a very sharp eye out for any boats leaving, and make the final approach into the entrance only when the piers have opened up so that you can see clearly right the way through the gap. Keep to the starboard side of the entrance channel and proceed slowly into the harbour. In this case the final approach is quite simple, but another harbour (Eyemouth, for example) might require rather more care to avoid obstacles and dangers. Check the chart carefully for these, and read the Pilot. The latter will probably also give you some very useful advice on where to go when you are in. This is often the most difficult problem facing the beginner on entering harbour. If in any doubt, moor up to the nearest boat or empty stretch of jetty, then go ashore and ask the harbourmaster or the yacht club. Do not simply tie up somewhere convenient and wander off to the pub. Some berths will be reserved for fishing boats or coasters, the bottom of a drying berth may be foul or the jetty unsuitable. The positions of harbourmasters and yacht clubs are usually marked on the chart, and information will almost certainly be found in the Pilot or Almanac. Study both well, long before you get anywhere near the harbour, so that you know all the relevant facts on arrival.

Plotting the Passage

Having got out of harbour and into position for a suitable departure fix, we now have to calculate how to steer in the particular direction that we need for the first leg of the passage. If you look at the passage chart in figure 63, you will see at the top of it a pair of circles (one inside the other) surrounded by numbers. These circles are known as **compass roses**, as they show the compass directions on the chart, north being at the top. The outer ring is based on true north (the North Pole) and the inner one on magnetic north (the north shown on your compass). The angular difference between the two is called **variation** and it can be either west of true (as here) or east of true. Variation alters from place to place, and at the same place over a period of time, as you can see from the information at the centre of the rose.

The direction we must steer from just outside Scarborough Harbour to just offshore from Filey Brigg buoy can be found by laying the parallel ruler between these two points, then 'walking' it (keeping the sides parallel) across the chart until it lies against the centre of the compass rose. Where it cuts across the outer ring on the rose we can read off the course we must steer. This, however, will be the true course, and we want the magnetic, as that is what our compass will show. If the date of the variation (shown in the centre of the rose) is sufficiently recent that the change is negligible, we can simply read the magnetic course off the inner circle. If not, we must calculate the up-to-date variation and either add or subtract it from the true to find the magnetic course. There is a simple mnemonic to help us work out whether to add or subtract the variation – CADET. This stands for Compass Add East True, which means that if we are converting a compass course to a true course we must add easterly variation. To go from true to compass we add westerly variation, as we have here. All this applies equally to bearings to be plotted from the hand-bearing compass, as these will be magnetic. The parallel ruler should be placed on the bearing on the compass rose, then stepped across the chart until it touches the object whose bearing was taken.

This, then, gives us the course we must travel along – the **CMG (course made good)**. It can be drawn in pencil on the chart between the relevant points, and the course written beneath the line, followed by CMG. The actual course we steer through the water, however, is likely to be different from this if we have a cross current or tidal stream, or even a strong wind, pushing us off the track. We can calculate the **course to steer (CTS)** as shown in figure 69. Any deviation that the compass shows on this heading must then be applied in order to get the final course that we actually steer on the compass. The variation mnemonic CADET can be

Figure 69 Plot the CMG as shown, from starting point A. Then plot, also from A, the direction and distance that you calculate (or estimate) the tide, current or wind will carry you during, say, one hour (AB). It should be apparent that, in order to make good the CMG, we need to steer a course somewhat down the page in order to allow for the tide pushing us up it – somewhere around the direction of the dotted line. In effect, if the tide sets us up to B during the hour, then during that same hour we have to get from B back to the CMG at the speed we are motoring through the water. If we then set on a pair of compasses the distance we will travel through the water in that hour (our speed), centre the compasses on B and inscribe an arc to cross the CMG, the direction BC will be the course we must steer at that speed in order to be back on the CMG after one hour. If we steer this course from A (roughly along the dotted line) for one hour, at the speed represented by BC, we will crab sideways along the CMG and end up at C. The distance AC will represent **speed made good over the ground (SMG)**. Compare this with doing it by eye in figure 21. Much of the time, in practice, you may be able to do all this by eye, simply by keeping your destination on a steady bearing. If destination remains on a steady bearing, you will collide with it, just as you would a ship (see Chapter 9). DR positions would be marked on the CTS (plotted from A), while EPs would be marked on the CMG, using the SMG along AC rather than the speed through the water (BC).

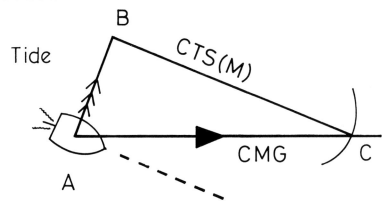

used, although we are actually going from magnetic to compass: we add westerly deviation in order to find the compass course. Whether deviation ought to be added or substracted should be made clear on the Deviation Card (see figure 65). The courses we must steer from Filey Brigg to Flamborough Head and from Flamborough Head to Bridlington are calculated and plotted in the same manner.

Tidal Streams

The best way to find out the rates and directions of tidal streams affecting you during the passage is from the tidal stream atlas for the area, to be found in the Almanac. Tidal Stream Atlases can also be found published separately, but the ones in the Almanac are quite adequate for our purposes. They consist of a number of small chartlets of the area, one for each of the six hours of flood, and six hours of ebb, either side of High Water at some convenient port. For some reason the port of Dover is usually used as a reference for tide times. Each chartlet is covered with arrows and figures giving the direction, and spring and neap rates, of the tidal streams all over the area (see figure 72). If you look up the time of High Water Dover on the day in question (check whether Summer Time has been corrected for), you can then write in pencil beneath each chart the time for which the chart relates.

Some charts give tidal stream information at certain important places. If you look just to the east of Flamborough Head on the passage chart in figure 63, you will see a small diamond shape with the letter C inside it. Another one containing the letter D will be found just off Bridlington. To the left of Bridlington on the chart you will see a table giving the rates and directions of the tidal streams at these places for each of the six hours either side of High

Water at River Tees entrance. Tide tables for River Tees entrance will be found in the Almanac. These 'tidal diamonds' can be quite useful as they give a much more accurate and detailed description of the tidal streams than the Atlas, although they only apply at the position of the diamond.

Much additional information on tidal streams and currents will be found in the Pilot. I cannot stress too strongly the importance of thoroughly reading the Pilot before making any coastal passage, as it gives a great deal of information that will not be found on the chart.

Making a suitable allowance for strong winds blowing you off course is very much a matter of experience. In the quiet conditions that you should be choosing for your first few passages this should not pose any problem. A useful way to check whether you are experiencing any wind drift (**leeway,** as it is called) is to see if the wake is running out directly astern of the boat. If it is running away up to weather of the direction you are pointing, then you are making leeway (see figure 70). The course you are actually making good through the water is indicated roughly by the direction of the wake. This is not in the least affected by the tidal stream, as the boat and the wake are both being moved together over the ground by the same piece of water.

Making the Passage

The foregoing constitutes the basic techniques of planning and preparing a simple coastal passage. Now let us actually make this one, from Scarborough to Bridlington, and see how it all works out in practice. Although your first venture will probably be nothing like this, there will be sufficient information here to enable you to work out your own passage.

The first thing we must do is decide

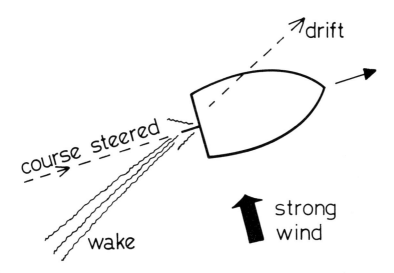

Figure 70

which day to go. We calculated earlier that we would need about 4 metres of tide in order to get out of Scarborough Harbour (2.5m to cover the drying height, 1m for our draft and .5m as a safety allowance). Let us imagine we want to go one weekend in June (1981, as an Almanac for that date happens to be on my desk). If we look up Scarborough in the Almanac we find that the times and heights of the tide are given as differences on those in the main tide table for River Tees entrance. This is quite common for the smaller ports. So we look for a suitable weekend in the tide table for River Tees entrance, and 27-28 June is ideal, the tides being neap and about midday. As the tables are in GMT (Greenwich Mean Time) we add an hour for British Summer Time and find that High Water is at 1212 (4.7m) on the Saturday, with the preceding Low Water being at 0609 (1.7m). Correcting these figures for Scarborough gives us Low Water at 0639 (2.0m) and High Water at 1252 (5.0m) from which, using the twelfths rule, we can calculate that by 1039 we will have 4.25m of tide – comfortably sufficient to get out. See figure 71. It is important to check

```
Scarborough

    LW – 0639    –  2.0m
    HW – 1252    –  5.0m
    ∴ Range      =  3.0m
    1/12 of Range = 0.25m
    2/12 of Range = 0.5m
    3/12 of Range = 0.75m


Thus tidal heights will be:–

    LW – 0639    –  2.0m
    + 1/12 – 0739 –  2.25m
    + 2/12 – 0839 –  2.75m
    + 3/12 – 0939 –  3.50m

    + 3/12 – 1039 –  4.25m

    + 2/12 – 1139 –  4.75m

    + 1/12 – 1239 –  5.0m (HW)
```

Figure 71 Note that the time of High Water (as calculated) is slightly different from the time given in the Tide Table. This is caused by the approximate nature of the Twelfths Rule, and is part of the reason it is so important to allow always a good safety margin in tidal calculations. If you want to calculate the tidal heights during the following six hours, you should start from the tabulated High Water time and height (which can also vary), to avoid accumulating the errors.

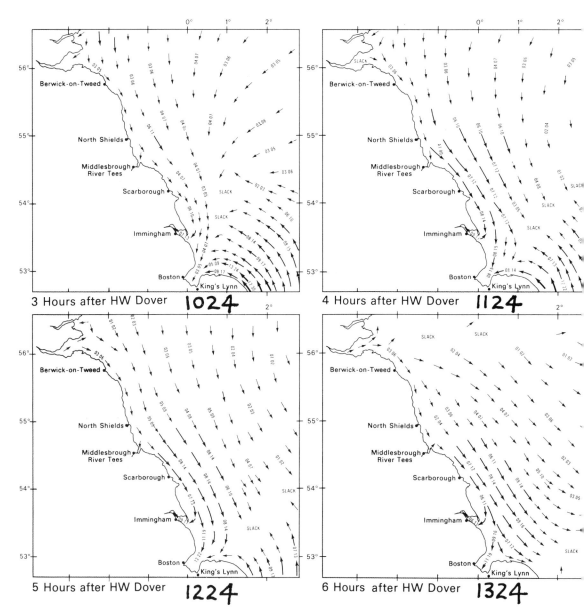

Figure 72

whether tide tables give times in GMT or BST.

We now turn back a few pages to the tidal stream atlas, which we find is based on High Water Dover. We look this up in the Dover tide table, add an hour for BST and find it is at 0724 and then again at 1948. Going back to the atlas we can now fill in the times under each chartlet (see figure 72). A glance at

the four charts shown tells us that we have a fair tide south for the start of our passage, running about half a knot at neaps. If this will take us past the two headlands and into Bridlington Bay, then not only will it speed up our progress, but it will also (as we discussed earlier) eliminate the risk of rough water off the two headlands. Thus we have ideal conditions for our first passage.

So how long will it take us? There are

142

two ways of measuring distances on a chart, and both can be seen on the chart of Scarborough Bay in figure 62. At the top of the chart just above the title you can see a simple distance scale, and these are to be found on most large-scale charts. (A cable is a tenth of a nautical mile, but it is little used by small-boat sailors.) All round the edges of the chart you will see markings and numbers – part of a world-wide grid system covering all nautical charts. The markings running horizontally along top and bottom are called **longitude** and it is measured from 0° at the Greenwich Observatory in London, eastward round the world to 180° East, and westward round to 180° West (these two of course being in the same place). The line running vertically up the chart just to the left of the title is 0° 22′ West of Greenwich (you can see the numbers increase as we go further west). The numbers running vertically up the sides of the chart are called **latitude**, and that begins at the Equator with 0°, running up to 90° North at the North Pole and 90° South at the South Pole. The line running horizontally through Scarborough Harbour is 54° 17′ North. Latitude and longitude are really of academic interest only to us at this stage, except that one minute of latitude is equal to one nautical mile. This, in fact, is the definition of a nautical mile. Thus, distances can always be measured from the latitude scale at the side of the chart.

So, to find the distance between Scarborough and Filey Brigg (our first turning point) we open out the dividers until one point is just outside Scarborough Harbour and the other just by Filey Brigg buoy. We can then place the dividers against the latitude scale and read off the distance – in this case 6.5 nautical miles. On a small-scale chart (covering a large area) it is most important that this measurement be

taken at about the same latitude as the places between which the distance has been measured. The reason for this is that in printing a round globe onto flat pieces of paper distortion occurs, and the length on a chart of a minute of latitude gradually increases towards the Poles. Thus if we put the dividers between Scarborough and Filey Brigg, then measure the distance on the latitude scale up near Iceland, it will indicate considerably less than the 6.5 miles that it is. This is why separate distance scales (as on the Scarborough Bay chart) are only given on large-scale charts (covering a small area) on which the difference in the lengths of minutes of latitude are negligible. It is also why Greenland appears on a chart to be so much bigger than it actually is.

Let us imagine for simplicity that we have a small displacement cruiser capable of 8 knots. With no tidal influence it should take us about three-quarters of an hour to Filey Brigg buoy. The Tidal Stream Atlas gives us a fair tidal stream of about half a knot, but as we will not feel the effect of this until we are well out of Scarborough Bay, the influence it will have on our passage time will be negligible. From there to Flamborough Head we will feel it, as we will be outside any bays. This distance is about 8½ miles so we can say that it will take us an hour, motoring at 8 knots with a ½-knot tide pushing us along. Most coastal passages are conducted, like this one, with the tidal stream either fair or foul, and you will rarely find it necessary to plot vector diagrams for cross tides as shown in figure 69, unless you cross very wide estuaries, or large bays with a strong inward set. The Tidal Stream Atlas, the tidal diamond (D) and the Pilot Book will all tell us that tidal streams at neaps are negligible in Bridlington Bay, so the final leg of 4½ miles from Flamborough Head to Bridlington will be a quite straightforward run of ½ hour or so. Total passage time about 2½ hours, allowing for slowing down on approaching Bridlington. If we leave Scarborough as soon as the tide serves, say 1030, we should be entering Bridlington about 1300. The same tidal calculation as we made for Scarborough tells us that High Water at Bridlington is 1307 (5.1m), so not only will there be negligible tidal stream in the entrance (thus making manoeuvring easier), but a glance at the harbour chart shows that we will have sufficient depth of water to berth more or less anywhere. Bear in mind, however, that actually entering and berthing alongside will probably take half an hour, by which time the tide will be ebbing, so we need to leave a good depth of water under us in the berth in case we are told to move.

So it all looks good. Before we go, however, we must make sure we can get back the next day. Following the same process we find that High Water Scarborough is at 1402 (5.2m) and the next Low Water is 2030 (1.5m). Theoretically we can get back into our berth shortly after 1600 when the tide will have fallen to 4.3m. On an ebb tide, however, this would not give us sufficient safety margin of depth, so we should make it by 1500 at the latest, when we will still have nearly 2½ metres of water over the berth. We will also have the beginnings of the ebb tide to assist us in manoeuvring through the narrow entrance. From the Tidal Stream Atlas we find that the tidal stream will be against us for the return passage, so we allow ourselves an extra half hour and aim to leave Bridlington about 1200. At this time, our calculations tell us, the tide will still be rising in Bridlington Harbour and there will be about 4 metres of it. Thus, if we are to leave at 1200, it is most important that we berth in a place where we will be afloat by then, ie with 4 metres of

tide. If we berth on the Saturday at High Water, there will be 5.1 metres of tide. Thus if we wish to be afloat when there is only 4 metres, we must berth with at least a metre or so of water beneath the keel. I would look for 2 metres to be safe. These 'safety margins' may seem unnecessary if you are mathematically minded, but delays must always be allowed for, especially when entering a harbour on the ebb, and tidal predictions can never be relied on accurately due to unpredictable atmospheric influences, slight variations in charted depths and so on.

So, weather permitting, we will be all ready to sail on the 27th, assuming the boat has been properly prepared, as discussed in other chapters. Information on the availability of fuel and so on at Bridlington will be found in both the Almanac and the Pilot. Also in the Almanac (in the weather section) you will find a list of coastguard stations that you can telephone for a report on local weather and sea conditions. Flamborough Head is one of these, and a call to them before sailing will be both useful and reassuring. They will also make a note of your passage details and keep an eye out for you, if requested, which can be quite comforting should anything go wrong. On top of this the Coastguard Service runs a scheme for recording details of your boat that can be passed to the rescue services should you ever get in trouble or become overdue on a passage. Details of this can be found in the Almanac or obtained from any coastguard station.

The great day dawns. Having carefully followed all the weather forecasts we could over the preceding few days, we are confident that not only will the weather be suitable today, but also tomorrow for the passage home. A phone call to Flamborough Head Coastguard tells us that calm seas, light winds and good visibility prevail down there. So off we go slowly out of Scar-borough Harbour, carefully stowing all warps, fenders and other gear for sea, but leaving the anchor ready for letting go until we clear the entrance. With a careful watch kept for fishing boats belting in and out of the Old Harbour, we proceed out into open water, taking a wide swing round the end of East Pier so that we get good warning of any vessels approaching from the north-east. Then we set course for Filey Brigg buoy.

If we have the type of log that trails over the stern on a line, now is the time to stream it, having got clear of the harbour confines. There is a knack to this. The end that hooks onto the assembly at the stern should be hooked on and the bight of the line streamed over the stern, keeping the impeller at the end on board. When the bight is trailing in the water, the impeller should be thrown clear to one side so that it does not tangle in the bight. It will drag the line out straight, then start rotating. Set the log to read zero on taking the departure fix. If the impeller is thrown over and the line streamed after it, the whole lot will immediately begin to rotate and the mess that will accumulate before the line is all out has to be seen to be believed. Retrieving the line is subject to the same problem, if you simply unhook it from the unit and haul in with the impeller still out there turn-ing. You should feed the disconnected inboard end back into the water as you haul on the line so that the turns can unravel naturally. When you have the impeller in hand, you can then haul the line in without it rotating.

As we will be extremely close to the end of East Pier when we set our course, we can say that our departure fix is 'just off the harbour'. This will be quite accurate enough. With our parallel ruler we draw a line from 'just off East Pier' to 'just outside Filey Brigg buoy', then walk the sides across to the com-pass rose, taking care not to let them slip on the chart or they will no longer be parallel to the course we have drawn. With the rules aligned with the centre of the rose we can read off the CMG at the bottom, where it crosses the true compass rose. The variation is marked for 1974, so by 1981 it will have de-creased by about 20', making it 7° West. If it was any less than this we would ignore it and simply take the course from the magnetic rose. On the true rose we read off the course as 129°. The mnemonic Compass Add East True reminds us that to convert true to compass we add westerly variation. Thus the magnetic course that we must make good is 136°. We write this under the line we have drawn, as CMG 136° (M), the M signifying a magnetic course.

As there is insufficient wind or tidal stream to cause us to drift off this track, this is the course we should actually steer – the CTS, assuming the compass is perfectly accurate. We then check the deviation table (Fig 65) to see if it is, and we find that on this heading (approximately, it is actually tabulated for 135°) the deviation is 1° West. Thus our actual course to steer on the com-pass is 137° (C), the C signifying a compass course.

If we were skippering an aircraft carrier, this is the course we would steer in order to make good 136° (M). In a small boat, however, this kind of precision is not possible. Compasses are generally marked in 5 degree steps, so trying to steer 137° would be both difficult and tiring. The end result would probably be considerable in-accuracy. If we round off the course to the nearest 5 degrees, however, it will not be quite the direction we want to go in, but it will be steered more accur-ately. If necessary, we can alter course somewhere along the line in order to get back towards where we are bound. In this case we would choose to steer 135° (C), partly because it is nearer the course we want, and partly because it takes us slightly further from the dangers of the coastline whereas 140° (C) would take us closer to them. Also, although the tidal stream is almost negligible, what there is of it will tend to push us slightly closer to the coast if anything, so setting our course slightly further away from the coast will counteract this.

From Filey Brigg buoy we set a new course in just the same way to pass safely off Flamborough Head. Rounding a large curving headland like this is best done by simply following it round, using the echo-sounder (on the 15m line) to ensure that we pass well clear of the rocks and shallows at Flamborough Steel. The North Smithic buoy will help us check when we are clear of this and can set a course direct to a point just south of Bridlington Harbour entrance, and we enter the harbour as discussed earlier in the chapter, taking great care to keep a good lookout for fishing boats coming out. If the next place we were heading for were out of sight, we would need to take a fix here to give us an accurate departure point from which to plot a course.

Navigation at Night

The basic techniques of navigation do not alter when it gets dark, but certain things do need to be borne in mind. The main thing is that buoys, lighthouses etc cannot be seen, so we have to identify them by the characteristics of their lights. In some ways this makes matters easier as it is possible to distinguish the characteristic of a light at much greater distance than its physical appearance. On the other hand, relative distances and positions can be very confusing at night. Bright lights can seem much closer than they are, while dim ones seem further away. This is very noticeable on approaching a busy harbour with masses of lights and winking buoys all over the place – not to mention the lights of other boats, houses ashore and so on. It is then most important to study very carefully the characteristics of all the lights in the vicinity so that you can build up a general picture in your mind of what you can see. Equally, it is essential to concentrate on picking out the characteristic of the next buoy from the mass of lights ahead of you. When you do, take a bearing of it with the hand-bearing compass as a guide. As you pass each buoy, you should put a pencil line through it on the chart so as to keep track of your progress. It is very easy to forget which buoy you last passed, even in daylight.

Look out for sectored lights that show only over a certain arc (clearly marked on the chart). These are commonly employed to show the approach to a harbour, a narrow sector of white light usually indicating the safe approach, with coloured sectors either side covering the dangerous water. The bearing along each edge of the safe sector is known as a **clearing bearing**, as keeping to the safe side of the bearing ensures you clear the marked danger. This can also be used with shore objects in the daytime. Plot the bearing of the object from the danger, then steer so that the bearing of the object from the boat keeps you on the safe side of the clearing bearing. Leading lights (as we saw on the Eyemouth Harbour chart) are also often used, and a careful perusal of chart and Pilot Book will uncover all these useful aids to entering harbours at night.

Navigation in Fog

Although there are a number of electronic devices that can assist us considerably in this (see Appendix 2), this is a hazardous business that requires great skill and experience. However well equipped your boat, this must never be regarded as a normal part of seagoing. Fog should be avoided like the plague until you are extremely experienced. Even then, you need a very good reason for motoring about in the stuff.

Having said that, we can all get caught out in it occasionally, so a few guidelines will be helpful. It is most important that your dead-reckoning plot on the chart be kept accurately – a carefully calculated and plotted series of EPs keeping constant note of your position. Bear in mind, however, that this is an *estimated* position. Do not use it to navigate too closely to dangers. Clearly great accuracy in steering and in assessing the effects of tidal streams and leeway is vital.

Even if you have all the electronics, remember that it only takes a fuse to blow and you have lost the lot; so always keep your DR accurate and up to date. If you are not electronically equipped, your echo-sounder or leadline can be of great assistance in determining or checking your position, or at least confirming that you are in safe water. Knowledge of the depth can enable you often to follow depth contours round headlands and into harbours and estuaries where you can always anchor to await the lifting of the fog. Foghorns on lighthouses, particularly at harbour entrances, can be useful; but remember what was said in Chapter 9 about the unreliability of sound propagation in fog.

Use of the Logbook
The Logbook constitutes a record of your passage. What you put in it is a matter for yourself; it should, however, comprise an accurate record of your navigation and the weather. If you buy one, you will find columns ruled for entering such things as course steered, log reading, wind direction and strength, visibility and barometer reading. These should be entered religiously every hour and will assist greatly in your DR (dead-reckoning plot) and your forecasting of the weather. There will also be a column for comments each hour, and in this should go details of all fixes (note log reading at the time), alterations of course (note log reading), buoys, lights, land, harbours sighted and so on (note log reading on passing buoys and beacons etc), together with their times.

Engine-running information can also be entered in the log, but I would suggest that you will find a separate Engine Log more useful. Oil pressure, temperature and RPM readings can be entered regularly, so that any change will be easily noticed. A record can also be kept of all fuel taken aboard, daily fuel- and oil-level readings, amounts of oil put in engine and gearbox and all maintenance done, as well as the time the engine has run for. This will provide an invaluable record of engine performance and hours in use, which will enable you to keep track of engine condition and ensure that essential maintenance jobs are done at the correct intervals.

Navigator's Notebook
This is very useful for all tidal calculations, general passage notes, detailed notes for entering harbours and so on. I would suggest a loose-leaf reporter-type notebook hinged at the top. It can be folded over and laid flat on the chart table while in use, and is considerably more efficient than using odd scraps of paper. When entering harbour it can be left by the side of the wheel for quick reference.

Offshore Passages

After some experience of coastal passages such as the one already described, you may well feel the urge to go farther afield. All the basic navigational knowledge you need for, say, a trip to the Continent, will be found in this book, but certain skills have to be more highly developed. The need for an accurate DR plot becomes vital when you are out of sight of land; the ability to take accurate fixes is most important, a part of which is experience in accurately identifying coastline features from information on the chart. This latter can be quite difficult when very conspicuous objects are not available, as features that look obvious on a horizontal chart are not necessarily so in vertical reality, and vice versa. Much useful information on offshore passages will be found in the almanac, including information on customs in foreign ports and on return home, the flying of courtesy ensigns, as well as a useful glossary in most continental languages.

Other important considerations when making offshore passages include the weather (perhaps the most important of all), and the condition and suitability of the boat and crew. There is far more risk of being caught out in bad weather during a long offshore passage than on a short coastal hop, and boat and crew must be capable of coping in bad weather. On a weekend jaunt across the Channel, you must be able to predict the weather for some days ahead if you are to be sure of getting back on time. The boat must be in top condition, structurally and mechanically, and the crew sufficiently experienced to cope alone a long way from help. Fuel consumption must be carefully calculated and adequate fuel carried. Thought must be given to the question of refuelling at the other end – the availability of the right type of fuel on the day you will be there. Thought must also be given to the provision of proper lifejackets for the crew and a liferaft, which must be professionally and regularly serviced. Thought must also be given to setting up a **watch system**, in which a regular routine of steering, keeping lookout, and having time **off watch**, in which to sleep or rest, is allocated to each crew member. On an overnight passage it is not wise to just muddle along with steering, cooking, keeping lookout and so on. People get very tired at sea, and it is important that they know when they are needed and when not.

Plotting a course to allow for tidal streams is more complicated due to them constantly changing strength and direction during the passage. The effects on steering of both leeway and waves requires some experience to assess, as does **helmsman's error** – the difference between the course ordered and that actually steered by your crew. The debilitating effect of seasickness must not be underestimated, nor the mental paralysis that fear can bring on.

An offshore passage of any length is considerably more than just a long coastal passage out of sight of land, and should not be undertaken lightly, even in the most seaworthy of boats (see Chapter 14). You should read as much as you can from the almanac and relevant books in Appendix 3, then build up your experience gradually. However much you may learn from the written word, life out there is never quite as you envisage, and only experience can convert theoretical understanding into sound practical knowledge.

12
EMERGENCY ROUTINES

However competently you run your boat, there may well come a time when you run into trouble. Some troubles are more serious than others, but virtually all of them, if handled calmly and capably, can be prevented from attaining the status of an emergency. So let us take a look at the likely problems, and consider how best to deal with them.

Grounding

There is little excuse for this as it is so easily prevented. However, it does happen to the best of us occasionally, invariably in our home waters after we have got to know them well! Familiarity has a bad habit of breeding over-confidence and its accompanying carelessness: do try to avoid this.

If you cannot, then at least try to run aground when the tide is flooding. Letting go the anchor (to prevent you from drifting continually into the shallower water as the tide floods in) will keep you calmly in position while you wait for the rising tide to float you. Make sure you let out enough cable to hold you when the tide has risen sufficiently to float you easily.

If you run aground on the ebb, things will be quite different as the tide will be falling all the time. The chances of you getting off before the boat is very firmly stuck are small, but the following actions, if taken quickly enough, may just do the trick if the tide is not falling too rapidly. Clearly you will stand a much better chance of getting off one hour before Low Water Neaps than you

will at half ebb on a big spring tide, when the water level may be falling visibly before your very eyes!

1 Go full astern immediately, at the same time rocking the boat from side to side as vigorously as possible. This latter will impart a twisting action to the keel which will help to free it from the grip of the bottom by digging out a slight channel.

2 If the boat does not begin moving within about five seconds, stop going astern, as the wash from the propeller will tend to build up silt around the keel and hold her more firmly. Try going slow ahead, at the same time winding the wheel back and forth from full lock to port over to full lock starboard and back again. Continue this action for about ten seconds, then go astern and rock her again. This process will tend to swing the keel back and forth and hopefully dig out the silt around it.

3 If this does not get her off, you are probably stuck until the tide rises again. A last resort is to carry away the kedge anchor in the dinghy on a long warp and drop it as far away as possible in deep water. Then try to haul her off by pulling on the warp. If you have an outboard or twin screws, with the exposed and vulnerable propellers that these installations have, this would be your first and only choice of action. Tilt up an outboard before hauling off, in order to avoid the risk of damage.

If you cannot get off, the kedge can be used to haul the boat off when the tide rises again. If you have grounded on a soft or flat bottom then you are unlikely to come to any great harm, so long as there are no waves to pound her up and down. On a rocky bottom, however, there could be a real risk of the hull being holed as it settles onto a rock. Get over the side with a boathook and feel around under the side that is lying down. If you find any fair-sized rocks, try to wedge a mattress or something over the top of the rock as the boat lies down onto it. This could save considerable damage.

Rope Around the Prop

This is a not uncommon problem, sometimes the fault of the skipper and sometimes not. Take great care when handling warps – in anchoring, coming alongside and so on – not to let them drift in the water near the stern. Do not leave ropes lying about on the deck where they could fall or be washed over the side. Careful though you may be, however, there always remains the chance of running over a length of rope that some clown has thrown into the water, or of entangling your propeller in one of the lobster-pot buoy ropes, which infest certain parts of the coastline. The Pilot may give information on their likely whereabouts.

You will almost certainly know if you have. The boat will slow down or stop. The engine will labour and struggle and may even stall (stop altogether). If you suspect fouling a rope you should immediately put the gear lever into neutral and stop the engine. If you are close to any dangers, let go the anchor to stop you drifting, unless a lobster pot already holds you! Then go and have a look over the stern. If you have an outboard, tilt it up. If you are extremely lucky, you may find the end of the rope floating about. If you are even luckier,

you may be able to gently unwind it. Pull on the end of the rope and see if it gives. If it does, then have someone go below to watch which way round the shaft turns as you pull it. They can then physically twist the shaft round as you pull on the rope, and this will help considerably.

The chances of being able to do this, unfortunately, are very small. Usually the rope winds itself into a solid mass round the shaft and prop. If it is synthetic fibre it will probably also melt and fuse into a solid lump. The only answer then is to cut it away, using a hacksaw or rough serrated knife such as a breadknife. An ordinary knife is quite useless. If you have an outboard you can do this by simply leaning over the stern, but have someone hold onto you in case you lose your balance. With an inboard engine you will have to get into the dinghy and lean over the side of that. This can be a precarious operation and must be carried out with some care. If possible have one man standing in the dinghy and holding firmly onto the boat, to stop the dinghy swinging about. Secure it fore and aft with painters as well. Have another man seated securely in the dinghy hanging onto you, and all three wear lifejackets. Then you can lean under the stern of the boat and saw away at the rope, though you may have to lash the knife to a pole or boathook in order to reach it. When you get the rope off, do not disgustedly throw it over your shoulder, or it will float off and do the same to someone else! Finally, *never* work on the propeller without stopping the engine completely. It is not safe to simply leave it ticking over in neutral.

Man Overboard

If you take sensible precautions, such as keeping people in the cockpit in rough weather, or making them wear harnesses, this is unlikely to happen. However, it can, and it does. The action

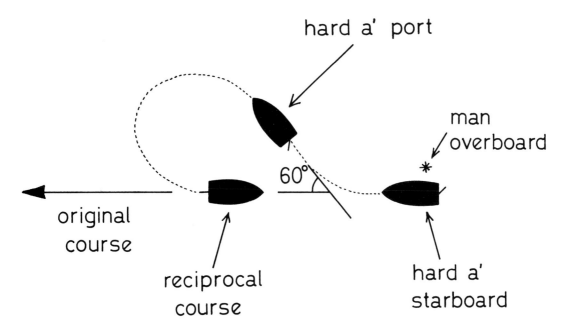

original course

reciprocal course

60°

hard a' port

man overboard

hard a' starboard

Figure 73 With the wheel hard over to swing the stern away from the man in the water, allow the boat to continue swinging until she is heading 60 degrees away from the original course. Then put full opposite wheel on and allow the boat to come right round on full helm until she is on a course directly opposite the original. This should bring you right back to the man. It does *not* absolve you from watching him constantly, but would be a great help if you did lose sight of him. Practise it with a lifebuoy to get a good idea of the time it will take you to return to the man, and the precise angle you should swing from the original course, as this will vary between boats.

that must be taken in order to rescue him is so rapid that it needs to be virtually instinctive. Practice it at every opportunity, using an old life-jacket or something.

Perhaps the most important thing that you must appreciate is the extreme difficulty of finding a man in the water should you lose sight of him, especially if the sea is at all rough. At the cry of 'man overboard' one person should be immediately ordered to watch him – and do nothing else but totally commit themselves to staring at that little head

bobbing in the water, and at the same time hold out an arm pointing in his direction. Stress to your crew when practising, that their eyes should not waver from the man for so much as a split second, or they may never see him again. The importance of this cannot be exaggerated. If you do lose sight of him, call out repeatedly and listen for an answering shout. It should help you locate him.

At the same time the following actions should be taken as rapidly as possible:

1 Put wheel hard over to swing stern and propeller away from the man.
2 Throw him a lifebelt – at night, make sure it has a light attached.

With these actions you have kept the man overboard safe from the prop, kept him afloat and kept him in sight. The immediate urgency is over, and you should now proceed calmly and deliberately to pick him up, without risking anything by rushing. Turn the boat round and head steadily back towards the man, aiming to approach

151

him from leeward so that there is no danger of the wind blowing the boat over the top of him. Figure 73 shows a technique that should return you directly to him. Rig the boarding ladder on your weather side as far for'ard as practicable so that he is kept well clear of the propellers. It must, however, be in a position where the helmsman can see him clearly. Approach slowly and carefully so as to avoid any danger of overshooting and running him down. Have two crew members standing by at the ladder to take an arm each and help him aboard. Unless he is unconscious, or exhausted from being in the water too long, this should be sufficient to get him safely aboard. The moment he is by the ladder, stop the engines completely – do not just put them into neutral – so as to avoid even the slightest risk of his getting near the boat's moving propellers.

If the man is unconscious or exhausted it will be much more difficult getting him aboard. Have one of the crew members (ideally secured to the boat with a line, in case he needs to enter the water) at the ladder in a lifejacket with the end of a line that he can tie round the man (a bowline round his chest under the armpits or tied to his lifejacket) to make sure that he cannot slip away. Bounce him up and down in the water a couple of times to build up momentum before finally heaving him out with a jerk. A fully clothed man in the water without the ability to help himself is a very heavy dead weight. You must think out for yourself how you would cope with this in your own particular circumstances of boat and crew. However, you may be surprised at the monumental feats of strength that a desperate crew member can perform in an emergency like this.

Fire

The business of fighting fires is rather beyond the scope of this book, but there are a few simple guidelines that should stand you in good stead if it ever happens to you:

1 Fuel-fires cannot safely, as a rule, be tackled with water, as the burning fuel simply floats on top of the water. A blast of water is likely to just spread the fire around and make matters worse. It is a good policy to ensure that all the extinguishers on board are suitable for fuel fires; ie foam, dry powder or inert gas.

2 Shut off fuel and gas at tank and bottle as soon as possible in case pipes get ruptured during firefighting. There should be some system for shutting off the fuel from outside the engine room. The same applies to seacocks if connected by plastic piping and you can reach them. Sinking the boat is rather a drastic way of putting out the fire!

3 Do not simply blast off extinguishers in the general direction of the fire. Think of it as a wild animal; attack along its near edge and gradually push it, swinging the jet from side to side, into a corner. Then work inwards, steadily smothering the fire from its edges, making sure that little tongues of it do not escape outwards. Then keep smothering it until you are absolutely certain there is no fire left to spring up again. Dry powder and inert gas do not cool (only smother), so now may be the time to spray the area liberally with water to cool it all down and prevent re-ignition.

4 A galley fire – in a chip pan for example – is best tackled with the fire blanket. Lay it calmly and gently over the top of the pan, making sure it completely seals the edges to stop air getting in. Without air the fire

will go out. Leave the blanket on for half an hour to be absolutely certain not only that the actual flames are out, but also that the fat has cooled down too much to possibly re-ignite. If you do not have a fire blanket (though you should), use a wet tea towel. If it starts to dry out, put another one on top.

Sinking

In detail, this is way beyond the scope of this book, but again there are a few simple tips that could help you save your boat should you ever be seriously holed – through a collision perhaps.

1 Your bilge pumps – however many and however efficient – should be your last line of defence, not, as far too many sailors assume, your first. That should be to find the leak and block it up. If the hole is accessible from the inside of the boat, cover it up. It does not matter how you do it, first stuff a pillow or mattress over the hole and shore up with a table or bits of wood wedged against the deck-head or the opposite side of the boat. In the short term get someone to lean on the mattress, or sit on it, or stick their bottom in the hole! Remember the little boy and the leaking dyke in Holland.

2 If the hole is not accessible from inside try taking a sheet or cockpit cover or something similar, with a rope tied to each corner and drag it underneath the boat until it covers the hole. Lash the ropes to hold it firmly in place, then proceed very slowly.

Engine Failure

If your engine is sound and well maintained (see Chapter 13), the cause will almost certainly be something minor that you can easily fix yourself. Likely causes, and how to cure them, will also

be discussed in that chapter, but it behoves us to realise that even a simple fault may take some time to repair. So check the boat's position before you dive into the engine room. If the water is shallow enough, anchor while you carry out repairs. If it is not, leave someone on watch to keep an eye on your drift, and also to watch for any ships approaching close but clearly not keeping a lookout. Various signals can be made to indicate that you are not under control, but probably the best thing is to fire off a white flare, which will alert the other vessel to the fact that all is not quite well with you. If you have VHF radio you could call him up and tell him to keep clear, using the call, 'Small coaster heading west two miles south of Prawle Point, this is motor yacht . . .'

If you have twin screws, you can continue your passage on one while repairing the other, although you may not always find this quite so easy as it sounds. In certain conditions of wind and sea some twin-screw boats may have great difficulty in maintaining a straight course on one engine. You may have to experiment with different courses and speeds until you find a combination that will enable you to motor in a straight line.

Because of the dangers inherent in an engine breakdown at sea, many single-screw boats have a small spare propulsion unit. This can take the form of what is known as a **wing engine** – a small inboard driving its own propeller on one side of the centreline – or it can simply be an outboard fixed on the transom ready for use if required. Both should be quite independent of the main engine, with their own fuel systems and so on, so that no possible main-engine breakdown could affect them.

If you are unable to effect a repair, and you have only one engine, you may be able to rig some sort of sail from an awning or cockpit cover to get you into a safe haven from where you can go ashore for assistance. Failing that, you will have to call for assistance on the radio or by firing a white flare when another boat approaches. If you want a tow into harbour, agree a fee before you start, in front of witnesses on both boats, or you could end up with an extremely expensive salvage claim against you.

Medical Problems

With the sort of voyaging covered by this book, you are unlikely to be far from shoreside assistance. A well-equipped first-aid kit and a good working knowledge of basic first-aid are all that you should require. A good first-aid book is an essential item to carry on board, and a first-aid section will be found in the almanac, together with a suggested list of contents for the first-aid box. Small ready-made ones that you can buy for home or car are quite useless.

Read the almanac thoroughly before you need to. Better still, attend a first-aid course at your local night school. Countless lives are saved each year by the application of simple first-aid techniques. If something happens that you cannot cope with, white or red flares (depending on the seriousness) or a PAN call on the VHF (see almanac for details) will summon assistance.

Towing

A simple tow in calm water – pulling someone off the mud perhaps – involves little more than attaching a strong rope between strong fittings on the two boats and very gradually taking the weight until the towed boat begins to move. Try not to jerk the rope or you may part it, or pull out of the deck the fitting it is attached to. The towed boat should steer so as to keep the tow rope taut all the time. If there is any wind or tidal stream, you will have to plan your approach very carefully, and get the tow under way as quickly as possible if you are to avoid drifting into trouble. Be extremely careful to keep the tow rope away from propellers; if necessary have someone at the stern holding it in the air until the weight comes on it. If a boat has blown onto the mud, you may find it best to approach bow on and tow her off going astern. That way your propeller will be kept well clear of the bottom, and the tendency for your stern to seek the wind will prevent you being blown sideways onto the same mud. If the boat is drifting in open water, it will generally be found best to approach her bow from leeward.

If you need to tow someone in or out of a tight berth, you will probably find it best to lash him alongside. Secure to him as you would a wall, but keep all warps as tight as possible and position yourself so that your propeller is well aft of his stern, as this will improve your manoeuvrability. When you turn, the drag of the boat alongside will make you turn very tightly towards him and very slowly away from him. You will also take much longer to stop.

Towing at sea, because of the constant yanking that the waves will exert on the tow rope, requires a different technique. Some means of cushioning this jerking must be adopted. There are various ways of doing this, but the simplest is to attach the tow rope to his anchor, then have him veer sufficient anchor cable so that the whole of the tow line hangs quite deeply in the water (see figure 74). Tow at such a speed that it remains in the water and the water will cushion the jerking. You must build up speed extremely slowly or the tow line will spring up out of the water and probably part. Have an axe or very sharp knife handy to cut the tow rope quickly if he suddenly sinks or anything. Guard carefully against chafe where warps pass through fairleads.

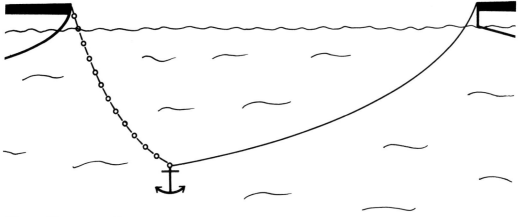

Figure 74

Rescue Procedure

If you should ever get into serious trouble at sea and need rescuing, there are a few things you should remember. Rescue services are there to save life, not property. Lifeboats will generally try to tow your boat in, but you have no right to expect it. On the other hand, they do have the right to claim salvage if they do tow you in – although in practice they rarely do – and that could cost you a large proportion of the value of the boat. If you get towed in by a tug or fishing boat, or any commercial vessel, they will undoubtedly claim salvage. You can reduce the size of the claim by doing as much as possible yourself – supplying the tow rope, directing the operation and so on. However, unless you really know what you are doing, it is probably wisest to leave things to them. If you interfere it could cause such chaos and delay that the resulting salvage claim will probably be bigger rather than smaller.

Helicopter rescues are quite common these days, and the man who comes down the wire will tell you exactly what to do. You can help considerably by lowering any masts or suchlike that could get caught up in the wire. This would cause the pilot to lose control of his machine, to the serious detriment of all concerned. *Never* attach the wire to anything on the boat. Watch out for the very strong down draught from the rotor blades; loose gear will blow away.

Finally, you would be surprised how many rescued people never bother to write a letter of thanks to the local lifeboat secretary or commanding officer of the helicopter's base. A donation to the lifeboat service (RNLI) would not seem to be out of place either, especially if your valuable boat has been rescued.

Distress Signals

There are various ways in which help can be called for if you are in distress. Red flares were mentioned in Chapter 7, and you will find a complete list of distress signals in Appendix 4. Copy out this list and pin it up in the wheelhouse or by the chart table for instant reference should it prove necessary. It is important that you recognise them in case you come across someone else in trouble. If you have a radio-telephone on board (see Appendix 2), you will find the distress procedure to be used given in the almanac and in Appendix 4. Copy this out and pin it by the radio, and make sure everyone on board can work the device in case anything happens to you. You will find more on the subject of distress, urgency and communications generally, in the almanac.

13
MAINTAINING YOUR BOAT

Good, regular maintenance is most important on a motor cruiser, and most things that go wrong do so because of a lack of it. Full information on detailed maintenance and repair is way beyond the scope of this book, and should be studied in the specialist manuals supplied with your equipment – engines, gearboxes, electronics and so on. However, if your equipment (and your boat) is sound to begin with, it can be kept both sound and reliable with a relatively small amount of simple running maintenance that almost anyone can do. Much of it can be delegated to children, and this is an excellent way of teaching them about boats and machinery, as well as inculcating in them the necessary sense of responsibility required by the skipper of a motor cruiser.

The Engine Room

This is the nub of the whole thing – the part of the boat that gets you from where you are to where you are going, and back again. Simple failures in this department cause more trouble to the rescue services than probably anything else. Do not let your engine room trouble them – or you. Before ever you start up the engine, even if only for a day in the harbour, spend ten minutes checking the following:

1 Inspect all water hoses, fuel lines and oil pipes for wear or damage. Check that all hose clips are screwed up tight (they have a ten-dency to loosen up) and that no leaks of water, fuel or oil are apparent. Make sure that no hoses, pipes or lines bear against anything that could chafe and wear them. There is considerable heat, movement and vibration in all parts of the engine room when you are under way, and a reinforced plastic pipe could be cut right through in minutes if it leans against something sharp or hot. All flexible hoses secured with pipe clips should have two clips at each union for added security. Realign or replace any suspect hoses that show wear or signs of cracking with old age. Renew any pipe clips that are rusty or have stripped threads; replace with stainless steel. Do it *now*, not next winter.

2 Check that all electrical wiring is secured clear of chafe points and moving machinery, and that it does not hang near the bilge where it could get wet. Where it runs from a solid part of the boat to the machinery, ensure that it hangs in a loose bight to allow for movement. Check that all terminals and connections are tight and clean. If dirty, dismantle, clean with fine abrasive paper, nail file etc and reassemble tightly. Spray with water-repellent aerosol or smear with vaseline.

3 Check that all drive belts are undamaged and at correct tension (see maker's manual for details). Likely damage will consist of splits

on the inside, across the width of the belt.

4 Check that no loose gear or tools are lying around and that bilge-pump strum boxes are clear of debris.

5 Before opening the cooling-water seacock, remove filter and check that it is clean. Briefly open seacock and check for a healthy blast of water before replacing filter. Close seacock before doing so!

6 Screw down stern-tube greaser one turn (then four-hourly when motoring), then check for leak at stern gland. A very slight leak is normal, but if you have any more than that, consult the boatyard. Screw down grease cups on pumps (including heads), and repeat daily while under way.

7 Check that fresh-water level in header tank (if indirect water cooled) is at correct level. Top up if required. If constant topping up is needed, search for a leak in the system, and fix it.

8 Check oil levels in engine, gearbox and reduction box (with four-stroke engines). Top up as necessary with correct grade of oil (see manuals). If frequent topping up is needed, search for leaks; wipe machinery clean with rags, then inspect carefully all joints while engine is running. If no leak can be found, call in expert advice; it may be an internal problem. Some types of gearbox oil levels need to be checked with the engine running, so read your manuals carefully.

9 Check fuel levels in tanks. You should have at least twice as much fuel as you calculate will be needed for the proposed trip, in case of delays, emergencies etc. If fuel level is consistently lower than expected, check for leaks all the way along the lines. Fuel tanks should be kept as full as possible all the time, in order to reduce the empty space available for condensation. Water in the fuel can be a serious problem. Drain any water and sediment from the sludge trap and check fuel is turned on. Petrol should always be turned off after use, but diesel is better left on to avoid the risk of getting air in the line, which will cause a fuel blockage. This problem does not arise with petrol as it is mixed with air in the carburetter anyway.

10 Check complete exhaust system for soundness and security.

11 With seacock open and fuel switched on, start your engine. Check that cooling water is being ejected and that the correct idling oil pressure is obtained on the gauge within a few seconds. If either is not obtained, stop the engine immediately and investigate the possible cause or very serious damage could result. Check that the ammeter shows the batteries being charged. If all is well, go back into the engine room while the engine is warming up and have a general look round to check for oil, water, fuel or exhaust gas leaks, as well as anything generally untoward. Be very careful to keep yourself and your clothing well clear of the machinery. Test all bilge pumps, including the manual one, and look over the steering gear for serious wear and obvious faults.

12 Check the electrolyte levels in all batteries and top up with distilled water to just above the plates, if they are the lead-acid type. Topping up with water weakens the power of the batteries until the electrolyte has been throughly mixed and charged up, so it should not be done just before starting the engine. The state of charge in the batteries can be tested with a simple little device called a **hydrometer**, which sucks

157

up some electrolyte from each cell in turn and shows the charge of each cell according to how deeply a weighted float sits in it. Ideally, this should be done after shutting off the engine and again before starting it the next time, so that you can check whether the batteries are holding their charge while not being used. They should. If they do not hold the charge, or you have to top up the electrolyte frequently, or any cells show a marked difference in charge to the others, the batteries should be properly tested by an engineer. Losing the charge could be caused by damp or dirty batteries, or suspect wiring, causing the current to leak slowly away to earth, but if you keep the tops of the batteries clean and always isolate them with the main switch when leaving the boat, this should not happen. Ideally, the batteries should be kept in a securely fixed box, fibre glass or lead-lined in case of acid spillage, with a cover to protect the terminals from damp and dirt. Alkaline batteries are very expensive and rather different from the normal lead-acid type, and the makers should be consulted for maintenance. The charge cannot be tested with a hydrometer; it must be done with a **voltmeter**.

13 Have a quick glance at the filter on the engine air intake, to ensure that it is not clogged with dirt, and also make sure there is no hindrance to the passage of air into the engine room. There should be some sort of vent somewhere. Air is most important, not only for feeding the engine, but also for cooling the engine room. Engines like to breathe cool, clean air for maximum efficiency.

14 Return to the wheelhouse and recheck instruments. Check that forward and reverse gears operate, and that the throttle works. Spin the wheel and check that the steering is free but not too sloppy. If it is sloppy, tighten it up – loose steering will cause a lot of wear and strain on the gear.

Written out like this there seems a lot to do. Once you have done it a few times and got used to your installation I doubt if the whole process will take you ten minutes, and it could save you a considerable amount of heartache. Don't skimp, just because it is only a week since you were last out. You will be surprised what can happen in the best of regulated engine rooms between one weekend and the next. And if you find anything wrong, *fix it immediately*, not only because it is a lot easier to do tied up alongside and only a short walk from the chandler or engineer, but also because the trouble could get dramatically worse quite suddenly once you are out at sea. This thorough, routine checking is the sign of a competent and responsible skipper, the one who stands quietly in the background at the bar while others recount their horror stories – because he never has any. You will find excitement comes often enough at sea without your idleness encouraging it.

If you have an outboard engine, much of this detail will be superfluous, but the same principles apply. Check all systems, pipes, connections, wires, levels, etc every time you go out. It is important to realise that a boat operates in an environment far more hostile to machinery than that in which a car operates. You cannot simply drive it around for years on end and put it in for a quick service every other birthday. If you do that, you might not see your next anniversary. On the other hand, if you carry out regularly these very simple checks and the elementary maintenance they sometimes necessitate, and do, or have done by a competent engineer, the detailed maintenance at the required intervals as shown in your manual, both you and your engine room should have long and troublefree lives.

Regular Use

This is the other great secret of trouble-free mechanics and, particularly, electrics and electronics. Without movement and the constant circulation and film of oil, engines will begin to corrode, both outside and inside. Pistons, cylinders, pumps, bearings, all have such tight clearances that the slightest coating of rust or whatever will impede their movement and, ultimately, seize them solid. Damp, particularly salty, air will drift around your electrical terminals and inside your delicate electronic instruments corroding everything in sight, and this corrosion will destroy sensitive electrical connections in places you cannot reach. In no time at all your expensive VHF radio will be useless. The cure for both engines and electronics is to run them regularly. In the first instance this will prevent the delicate moving parts from draining completely of oil; secondly the heat and consequent airflow generated by the bits and pieces inside will keep the damp, salty air away.

If you do not use your boat frequently, make a point of going aboard once a fortnight and running the engine for an hour, and push it in and out of gear a few times. At the same time open all doors, hatches and vents and switch on all electrics and electronics. Let the whole lot run for an hour with plenty of fresh clean air blowing right through the boat. Meanwhile you can go round and check everything else. Pump the bilges, check for leaks at the stern tube, open and close all seacocks throughout the boat (this will help prevent them

from seizing up – a common problem on neglected boats), pump the heads a couple of times, check the mooring warps or the chain if you are on a buoy (make sure shackle is secure and links of chain are not worn where they bear against each other) and so on. You should leave the boat knowing that *everything* has been checked and is working satisfactorily. If you have some spare time before leaving, do a little maintenance. Far better to do things steadily throughout the season than be faced with a long list for the winter. Get the grease gun out and grease the windlass, and anything else with a grease nipple on it. Or pick up a water repellent spray (WD40 or similar) and go round all the electrics in the accommodation. Open up switches, light holders, junction boxes etc, check electrical connections are clean and tight; give a squirt of the magic fluid to keep corrosion at bay. You will soon get into the habit and rhythm of this – you should actually find it rather enjoyable – and the end result will be a reliable and well-cared-for motor cruiser.

The Winter Lay-up

Even if you are one of the hardy souls who 'keep on truckin' right through the winter (and there is much to be said for the odd crisp sunny day at that time of year), don't skip this section as there are some things that even you will have to attend to. Basically there are two ways of approaching the winter. One is to shut up shop completely until the warmth of the spring stirs you from your fireside, in which case the boat will have to be properly and thoroughly 'winterised'. The other is to keep her in commission throughout, even if you do not actually take her away from the berth, in which case, apart from the odd thing we shall mention, all you need do is run things regularly as discussed in the last paragraph.

This regular running of all the equipment should prevent any internal corrosion building up. Condensation in the boat generally can be reduced considerably by ensuring good ventilation throughout the winter. A vent right for'ard and one right aft should produce a continuous flow of fresh air through the whole boat. Let it circulate everywhere by opening all lockers, cupboards, doors etc inside the boat. This will reduce considerably the risk of rotting woodwork and corroding electrics. It will also prevent that damp, musty smell so typical of neglected boats. Cleaning out all lockers (including chain locker) at the beginning of winter will help.

Fresh water can, of course, freeze during winter, and precautions must be taken to prevent this. The fresh-water, closed engine cooling circuit must be treated with anti-freeze (see your manual for quantities etc) just as you would the radiator of your car. Run the engine for a while to thoroughly circulate the anti-freeze, which should also contain a rust inhibitor. It is most important that normal operating temperature is reached, otherwise the thermostat will not open and pass the anti-freeze into the engine. Do not top up batteries unless charging them, or the distilled water will freeze before it has time to mix with the acid. The battery case would be cracked by this.

If your boat lies in sea water it is most unlikely that the raw-water cooling circuit will freeze. If, however, she lies in fresh water, you must disconnect the pipe from the seacock and drain off the water in the system. Also drain the water from the pump, and any pipes and fittings in which it might lie – oil coolers, low bends etc. *Do not forget* to reconnect the pipe and fill the pump with water before starting the engine. If the pump has a neoprene impeller (which most do), it will burn out in

seconds if allowed to run without water.

If you decide not to keep the boat in commission, and lay her up either afloat or ashore, the engine and ancillaries need to be thoroughly and carefully winterised. I suggest that you first have a competent marine engineer thoroughly check the complete installation and test the performance and condition of the engine, giving you a list of all essential work to be done before the next season. While he is there you can have him either winterise the engine for you or tell you how to do it. It is not difficult, but it is most important that it be done correctly and meticulously, and the precise details will vary with engines and installations. You should find information on it in your engine manual and in the specialised books in Appendix 3. If you remain in commission you should also have an engineer test performance and condition of the engine sometime early in the winter, so that you have time to attend to anything necessary before the busy season begins. This will involve expense, but it will ensure that the engine is kept in peak condition, thus saving you worry, trouble, possible serious danger at sea, and probable horrendous expense at some time in the future. If you have to skimp on something, make it the redecoration of the house, *not* the propulsion system of your boat. And remember that the ancillaries – stern gland, fuel system, starter motor, generator and so on – are just as important as the engine itself. Appendix 6 gives a list of work that should be carried out in the winter when you lay up.

Fault Finding
If you look after your engine properly as already described, this section should be redundant. However, detailed fault-finding reference charts are given in Appendix 5, and there are some basic

principles that you will find useful to remember. Chapter 2 described how the various systems in your engine installation work. If something goes wrong, think out carefully which system could be causing the fault. Then go through the system methodically from one end to the other, looking for anything that could be preventing the system from doing what it should do. For example, a petrol engine requires fuel, air and sparks, together with a reasonable cranking speed in order to fire. If it does not fire and cranking speed is reasonable, check fuel, air and electrical systems. Look to see if the air filter is clean. Pull the fuel pipe off the carburettor and see if turning the engine produces a flow of fuel. If it does not, check back through the system for a blockage, inoperative pump, airlock, breather pipe blocked or serious leak – or the fuel shut off or run out! If you have air and fuel, the problem must lie in the ignition electrics. Check first for a spark at the plugs by pulling off any lead and holding it (with heavily insulated pliers) close to the plug terminal. Turn the engine over and a spark should jump the gap. If it does, the plugs must be at fault – probably fouled with oil (two–stroke) or possibly petrol (four-stroke with too much choke). Remove and clean them all with a wire brush, or renew. If there is no spark at the plugs then work back through the system looking for a bad connection, in both HT and LT circuits. Failing this, check points' gap and condition (see manual) and condition of distributor cap – if it is cracked, it will leak the HT away from the plug leads. Turning over the engine in the dark will show a shower of sparks around any crack. It is probably easiest to check the distributor cap condition by simply replacing cap and plug leads with the spare. This is the only way to check the condenser. Having said all

that, the commonest ignition fault is dampness on leads and distributor cap. Dry thoroughly inside and outside of cap, and all along leads, then spray with water-repellent spray.

Check all other faults in the same methodical way. A diesel engine needs a fast cranking speed and spotlessly clean, air-free fuel (read manual for how to bleed air from system). A starting system requires a very high electric current in the starter motor, and the starter cog (known as a **bendix**) to engage with the flywheel. If the starter turns, then jams, free the bendix by turning the end of the starter-motor shaft with a spanner. If battery is charged (test with hydrometer) and all connections (including ignition-switch circuit) are good (a bad connection in the high-powered circuit will feel warm or hot to the touch while the current is flowing), suspect the solenoid and bypass its internal switch by shorting across its connections with a very thick insulated screwdriver or jump leads. A cooling system requires water! Check you have raw water going out over the side. Check you have fresh water in the header tank. Check that the thermostat is opening to allow hot water from the engine into the heat exchanger (put your hand on the pipe from thermostat housing to heat exchanger to see if it is hot). If you have no raw water coming out, stop the engine and check the system methodically for blockages, beginning with the strainer and seacock. Weed sometimes gets past the strainer and blocks the oil cooler next in line. Check for leaking connections or burst hoses. Check whether pumps are working (and clear possible airlocks in them) by opening bleed screws on the top while engine is running; water should come spurting out. If you have an airlock, air will come whistling out first, then water. Extreme shortage of oil in a four-stroke can also cause overheating, as the oil does some of the cooling. If the engine runs too cold, the thermostat is probably stuck open. A thermostat can be tested by heating it in a pan of water to see if it opens; if you have a thermometer, you can even check the precise temperature at which it does. The correct opening temperature will be given in the manual. With extreme loss of fresh water, the temperature gauge may drop below normal after the initial overheat indication, due to there being no water around its sensor.

Rough running of an engine, or sudden stopping, will probably be caused by one of the same faults that prevent it starting. If a petrol engine runs roughly, the chances are that one or more plugs is not firing properly. Sometimes a spark will reach the plug, and even jump the gap when the plug is removed from the engine; but will not jump the gap inside the engine when it is under compression. A faulty plug can be isolated simply by pulling off the plug leads one by one while the engine is running. If you pull the lead off a faulty plug it will not affect the running but, if a plug is working, the engine will run even more roughly. Replace each lead after checking it, if the plug is all right. Use heavily insulated pliers.

Rough running can also be caused by weed or rope around the prop, or by overheating or very low oil pressure – all these problems putting a lot of strain on the engine. Think methodically. If the roughness is regular, it is probably one specific component not working at all – a plug, an injector (test as in manual), or a plug lead. If it is erratic, it will more likely be points, distributor cap, fuel, air, overheating, weed or rope round prop, or very low oil pressure. Anything round the prop is easily checked by putting the gearbox into neutral and trying to turn the propshaft by hand. If you cannot, then something

is jamming it. Sudden loss of oil pressure is likely to be either a serious leak (broken oil pipe somewhere, perhaps leading to the pressure gauge) or a foreign body jamming the oil-pressure relief valve open. This valve opens if the pressure is too great, and diverts the oil straight from the oil pump back into the sump without going round the engine. The manual will show you how to remove and clean the valve. Slight loss of oil pressure may be caused by water or fuel in the oil, thus diluting it. If this is the case, the oil will be white and frothy. Run the engine gently until you get home, then change the oil and filter and find the water or fuel leak – probably the head gasket leaking. It could also be a blocked oil filter; replace and see if it improves. If oil pressure drops seriously, the engine must be stopped immediately to avoid serious damage. Check the points mentioned above.

Finally, if the engine suddenly speeds up and the boat slows down, your prop has probably just dropped off – it can happen! There is not a lot you can do here, unless you have a second engine or an outboard. Outboards have **shear-pins** which transmit the drive to the prop, and these are designed to break if the prop strikes an obstruction. Check and replace the shear-pin. The other possibility is that the gearbox clutch is slipping. If you have the right tools, consulting the manual may enable you to adjust this.

The Hull
Detailed maintenance of a hull is a complex business, and you may well prefer to leave it in the hands of the local boatyard, paying them to inspect and 'do up' the boat each winter. If you want to do it yourself, you must study the specialist books (see Appendix 3). Read also anything on the subject that you can find in your library; much

detailed information is required for good maintenance, and no one book is likely to contain everything that you will need. Whichever course you take, however, you will find that a certain amount of simple preventive running maintenance will pay dividends in terms of stopping corrosion and rot before it can get a grip – maintenance, in fact, as opposed to repair.

Any hull, be it wood, steel or fibre-glass (the three materials you are most likely to encounter), will suffer gradual destruction if water is allowed to penetrate its outer protective coating (paint on wood and steel; **gelcoat** on fibreglass). Wood will rot whether solid timber or plywood; steel will rust just as in your car; and fibreglass can suffer the recently discovered horrors of **osmosis**, in which the underwater part of the hull can break out in a rash of blisters which are horrendously expensive to repair. The foam-sandwich type of construction can, in extreme cases, literally fall to bits if it absorbs sufficient water.

All these troubles can be prevented by maintaining the protective coating, and thus keeping the water out. Any damage to paintwork on steel or wood should be rubbed down with abrasive paper until the area is smooth and even, and all rust has been removed. If any rust remains ingrained in steel, treat with a rust-removing substance. Allow the material to dry thoroughly then give two coats of a suitable priming paint (your chandler or boatyard will advise), followed by one coat of the correct-colour undercoat and one coat of the final finishing paint, which should be of the same type as the paint already on the boat. There are different types of finishing coat, and not all are compatible with one another; once again the local chandler or boatyard should advise. The most urgent and important areas where rot and rust are most likely

to form, are the corners etc where water can lie both on deck and down below – note that rainwater leaks will rot a wooden boat more quickly than sea water. Rot and corrosion will proceed far more rapidly here than on the outside of the hull, except where peeling paint forms a pocket to hold water. Varnished woodwork is treated in the same way, using one coat of varnish thinned with a little white spirit, followed by at least three further coats, rubbing each coat smooth with very fine abrasive paper before applying the next. As with paint, there are different types of varnish and you must use the same sort as is already on the wood.

Damage to a fibreglass gelcoat is treated in much the same way, then repaired with a gelcoat repair kit of the correct colour. Full instructions for its application will be on the packet. Corners and water-traps do not pose the same problems on a fibreglass boat as they do on a wooden or steel one, as the water cannot creep under the gelcoat and lift it off as it can with paint. Any actual damage, however, must be repaired immediately as the water will continue to soak into the fibreglass until it becomes completely saturated. If there is any timber moulded inside the fibreglass – strengthening for engine beds, for example – this will then rot away extremely quickly, leaving you with a very expensive repair job.

Under the waterline your boat will probably be covered with a special thick paint called **anti-fouling**. There are different types of this; but in general it is poisonous to marine growths such as weed, barnacles etc, and is designed to prevent all these things attaching themselves to your boat and growing there. It may not be necessary if your boat is kept in fresh water, but it is essential in sea water or your bottom will very quickly resemble a tropical

163

jungle. This will impair your speed and increase your fuel consumption dramatically. Usually the bottom needs recoating every year, but there is considerable variation in both type and efficacy of anti-fouling paints, and in the fouling you will experience in different places, so local advice should be taken. Clearly the boat will have to be removed from the water in order to do the work, and I would suggest boatyard advice until you have had some experience. Simply putting the boat on a hard and clean beach and letting the tide go down to leave her high and dry will normally give you sufficient time to anti-foul the bottom, as the paint does not have to dry before immersion in water. The boat must be moored or anchored securely fore and aft, and all gear lashed down if she is likely to list a lot. You may have to do one side then

Photo 30 A selection of anodes on a large steel motor cruiser. One protects the rudder, two protect the stern gear, and two more protect a seacock each.

use weights to list her over the other way on the next tide to do the other. Scrub off the weed before it dries or it will stick hard. Scrape off loose anti-fouling, then recoat when the bottom is dry. Drying out on a beach can be tricky, so try to have an experienced local help you the first time.

Osmosis occurs beneath the waterline on some fibreglass boats, due to water leaching through the gelcoat (which is not perfectly waterproof) and reacting with chemicals within the skin. This causes more and more water to be sucked through the gelcoat until sufficient pressure is built up inside to blow the gelcoat out into bubbles. It seems to be caused by poor construction techniques rather than by the material itself, so not all fibreglass boats suffer from it. However, the fact that gelcoat is not absolutely waterproof is clearly an important factor, and the trouble can be prevented by painting the bottom with a special epoxy paint which is considerably more waterproof. The application of this paint, however,

requires a great deal of skill, as well as very precisely controlled temperature and humidity conditions, so it is not recommended to amateurs. It can, thus, be rather expensive and, before considering it, you should take expert advice as the likelihood of osmosis varies considerably with the conditions in which the boat is kept. If, for example, you keep the boat at home and trail her to the water when required, it is highly unlikely that she will be sat in water long enough for the horror to begin. Long periods afloat in fresh water are considered to be the worst conditions, especially if the water is relatively warm.

Steel and wooden hulls can be kept immaculate indefinitely by regular rubbing down and repainting. Fibreglass boats in theory require no attention in this respect. In practice, the accumulation of dirt on the hull causes minute scratches that will absorb dirt to eventually leave the hull looking dull and grubby. The only real solution then is to have it painted with an epoxy paint as mentioned for the bottom. This expensive and evil hour can be put off for a long time by regular washing of the hull in clean fresh water and washing-up liquid. Do not use anything abrasive. When spotlessly clean, the hull can be polished with a good wax polish; this will help to waterproof the gelcoat and also produce a smooth, glossy surface that will both look good and repel dirt. Then simply hose down regularly. Do not use silicone polish as this will be impossible to remove, should you ever want to paint the hull.

Electrolysis

This is a form of electrical corrosion that occurs when two different metals are immersed close together in sea water. The combination of dissimilar metals and an electrolyte (a liquid that conducts electricity) forms, in effect, a battery cell. Electricity flows from one metal to the other through the electrolyte, in the process of which the first metal gradually disintegrates. In bad cases it can even happen on the surface of a single metal, due to tiny cells being formed wherever there is a slight imperfection or impurity. It can be a very serious problem with steel boats for obvious reasons, and also with planked wooden boats because of all the metal fastenings. It can even occur in fibreglass boats on seacocks, propshafts, propellers etc, especially if different metals are used for the various components.

Figure 75 gives a list of metals, and if any two of these are immersed together in sea water, the one nearer the top will corrode. It is clear, there-

```
Electro-chemical Series of Metals

Zinc
Aluminium
Steel
Iron
Stainless Steel (Active type)
Lead
Brass
Copper
Bronze
Stainless Steel (Passive type)
Graphite
Gold
```

Figure 75 A short list of the common metals you are likely to encounter. The further apart in the list two metals in sea water are, the faster will the higher one corrode. If metals have to be mixed underwater, they should be as close as possible in the table. If, for example, a bronze propeller is on a stainless steel shaft (quite common these days), the shaft should be the passive type, not the active. This will reduce considerably the risk of corrosion in the propshaft (which may not be visible). Note the position of graphite, and do not use graphite grease anywhere underwater. Gold is included as it is found in certain radiotelephone earthing plates.

fore, that if zinc is in the water it will corrode in preference to anything else, and this is precisely how the problem is cured in most boats. A lump of zinc, known as a **sacrificial anode**, is fastened to the bottom of the boat close to the metal that is to be protected (generally the stern gear and seacocks), and this gradually erodes while the other metal remains untouched. The zinc needs to be replaced when about two-thirds gone; and it must not be painted, or the erosion will not work. These anodes should also be fitted to the legs of outboards and outdrives, and to steel rudders. (See Photo 30.)

This, in truth, is a considerable simplification of what can be an extremely serious and very complicated problem. I have heard of the propeller falling off a brand new boat within a week of launching, due to corrosion of the shaft! If you experience undue corrosion of stern gear, seacocks or fastenings, you must consult the expert given in Appendix 3 – it is *not* a problem that can be solved by the average local boatyard.

The problem is considerably aggravated by any leakage of electricity from the boat, and you will find that the more electrical equipment you have on board, the more likely you are to experience electrolytic corrosion. The proper earthing of all electrical and electronic equipment is most important – you cannot simply earth things to the engine – and must be carried out by an expert as the precise method will depend on your complete engine and electrical installation. The risks are reduced considerably if you always switch off the battery-isolating switch (which must be double pole) whenever the boat is not being used. This will prevent stray electric currents from leaking out and wandering around the hull. The bonding of all things to be earthed should be done with a single wire that contacts each item in turn, so that the electricity going to earth does not travel through each item on the way. Serious corrosion can be set up in equipment if this happens.

Tools and Spares
It is essential that you carry certain tools and spare parts in case you do have to fix something while you are out (see Appendix 1). Keep tools clean and lightly rubbed with oil or sprayed with WD40, to stop them rusting in the damp environment. Stow them and the spares (clearly labelled and protected) somewhere in the engine room where you can lay your hands on them instantly. Stow all your manuals somewhere clean and accessible, and browse through them regularly so that you become totally familiar with the workings of all your equipment.

14
BUYING A MOTOR CRUISER

This is a very difficult subject, fraught with problems for the beginner due to the vast array of boats available. My initial advice on the matter of buying a boat is, quite simply, don't. Not until you have had at least a little experience on the water, which will help you

Photo 31 A fine sea-going displacement cruiser. Note the solid appearance, the flared bows (to keep spray down and prevent the bow plunging too deeply into waves), the hefty guard-rails and the upper steering position. The windows in the deckhouse are rather large, but they are very strong and well set back from the bow. There will also be a lower steering position for bad weather; note the heavy duty windscreen wipers for clearing spray off the windows. Note the very small, solid windows (**portholes**) in the side. Compare with the smaller sea-going displacement cruiser shown in Photo 1 (page 11).

considerably in judging the type and size of boat that will suit you best.

This chapter describes the various types of boat, their uses and qualities, so that you can form some general idea of the direction in which to look. Then it tells you how to get on the water for a little experience without actually having to buy a boat. Finally, it discusses how to go about actually buying a boat from the huge number, both new and secondhand, that are available. If you proceed towards your dream boat in this patient and orderly manner, you stand a good chance of ending up with what you want at a price you can afford.

Types of Motor Cruiser
By and large, there are two basic types of motor cruiser – displacement boats

Photo 32 A small outboard planing cruiser, suitable for sheltered estuaries and short coastal hops in calm, settled weather. Note the windows close to the water and the lack of deck space and guardrails.

which move through the water like ships, and planing boats which skim over the surface like speedboats. As a general guide we can say that the former are comfortable, seaworthy, economical and slow (perhaps 8 knots), while the latter are uncomfortable, not so seaworthy, expensive to run and fast (perhaps 30 knots). The former type, unless very small, will very likely have an inboard engine due to its economy and reliability, the weight of it being relatively unimportant in a displacement boat. The latter, unless very large, will generally have an outboard engine, or two, due to the very high power output that can be combined with light weight – very important in a boat

that is to rise above the water. Thus if, for example, you want to make fast and frequent daylight passages in good weather, tow water-skiers or simply enjoy the thrill of speed, you would choose a planing boat. On the other hand, if you want to potter about in rivers and canals where speed is limited anyway, are in no particular rush to get anywhere but just enjoy the pleasure of an actual passage, or intend to make longer passages when more experienced, the displacement boat would clearly be more suitable. It is important to realize, however, that a boat specifically designed for use on rivers and canals will not be suitable for the sea, or even an exposed estuary, in anything other than the calmest of conditions.

Types of Hull
The design of a hull for certain conditions, whether it be planing or displacement, is a complex art. The visual

168

differences between a boat suitable for seagoing and one that is not are not easy for a beginner to see, however well he is briefed. Hence the need to garner a little experience and variety of advice before shelling out a lot of money for your own boat. A few guidelines will, however, be found useful.

For sheltered waters, estuary and inland, a displacement boat tends to be little more than a floating box, designed to hold as many bunks, cookers, showers and people as possible. Having no waves or wind to cope with, she can have a fat bow, little draft, lots of superstructure and glass, no flare forward and little power. Planing boats can also have flat bottoms and large open cockpits.

A seagoing boat needs to be fairly deep below the water to give a low centre of gravity for stability in waves. She must be reasonably narrow, with a fairly thin bow, to drive easily through waves, and the bow should be flared to keep down spray, and to prevent it plunging too deep. She needs a fair bit of power to push against waves or strong currents.

No seagoing boat must have too much or too high a superstructure or she might be unstable, and she must have small strong windows well back from the bow, in case solid water comes aboard. She must have reasonable deck space for working anchors etc, strong guardrails, and a small cockpit in case waves come aboard and fill it up. A large cockpit full of water could make her unstable.

Planing boats should have a moderately deep vee-shape to their hulls to avoid slamming into the seas, and to provide stability when they heel over; and a raked bow to ride over waves without plunging deeply. Shallow vee hulls give maximum lift and efficiency in calm waters, while deep vee hulls give less lift but better seakeeping.

Medium vee hulls are a good compromise for most seagoing pleasure craft.

An excellent type of seaboat is that known as **semi-displacement** or **transitional**. A displacement boat that lifts out of the water, she can travel almost as fast as a planing type. She has a fine, flared bow and is fairly flat and wide underwater at the stern so as to rise out of the water at speed. They are often used for pilot boats and suchlike.

Consider all these comments and compare the boats in the photos on pages 9, 11, 27, 34, 52, 164, 167, 168, 170, 172, 176 and 178. You must think carefully about the use you want to make of your boat before choosing a hull type.

Types of Engine
In my view, the standard set-up for a motor cruiser should be a single inboard four-stroke diesel engine – with, if feasible, a small wing or outboard as standby – because of its simplicity, reliability, economy of operation and easy availability of fuel. It is also protected from the elements and easy to get at for maintenance, and the single propeller is tucked up underneath the boat where it is relatively safe from damage by ropes, rocks, lobster pots and grounding.

Twin engines are considerably more expensive and complicated to install, maintain and operate, but do give much greater manoeuvrability. They are useful in relatively large (30 foot up) planing boats which, because of hull shape and small propellers and rudders, can be difficult to manoeuvre at slow speeds. The propellers, stuck out at the sides of the boat, are very vulnerable to damage.

Outboard engines are virtually essential in small planing boats and very small displacement boats; particularly if these are to be trailed behind a car, due to their very small size and

Photo 33 A typical inland waters cruiser. Note the shallow draft, fat bow with no flare, mass of cabin top and glass, lack of guard rails and deck space, etc, etc.

light weight for a given power output (a merit of the two-stroke engine). They also have the advantage of taking up virtually no room inside the boat. They are, however, exposed to the elements with a very vulnerable propeller, and not easy to maintain at sea since they are hung outside the boat although, when lifted, the propeller is accessible. Usually two-stroke petrol, they use oil and expensive fuel, have vulnerable ignition electrics, and tend to foul their plugs with oil. The fuel is not as widely available as diesel, particularly in the average harbour, and the proportion of oil to petrol in the fuel mix for two strokes is very critical, as is the type of oil used.

Petrol inboards, because they are less reliable than diesels due to their complex ignition electrics and have a much more dangerous fuel, are not very common. They are, however, smaller and lighter for a given power and are thus sometimes found in small boats. Petrol/paraffin engines start on petrol then change over to paraffin. They are more economical than petrol engines, but probably even less reliable, having both ignition electrics and fuel that is prone to foul the plugs.

Outdrives combine inboard engines with outboard drives and propellers. As the outdrive unit pokes out of the transom, the engine itself can be installed right aft, thus saving a lot of space in the boat. Although the outdrive unit shares the exposed vulnerability of the outboard, it does manage to combine shelter for the engine with easy access to the propeller, and it is becoming quite popular in smaller boats for these reasons, together with the saving of interior space. As the full weight of the engine is right aft, however, the hull does need to be designed specifically to take this configuration.

Electric drives are becoming popular in river and canal cruisers, and have considerable merits in that they are very light weight, virtually silent in operation, clean and safe (no fuel) and simple to install. They are still rather in their infancy, but as batteries get smaller and more powerful so that longer periods of motoring become possible before recharging, they will very likely become the norm for this type of cruising, where no great power is necessary and charging points easily obtainable. They would not do, at least in the foreseeable future, for estuary or sea cruising.

Water-cooled engines are quieter and less obtrusive than air-cooled ones, which have large, noisy fans and require vast quantities of air. They are best suited to open boats.

Construction

This was discussed in the last chapter, so all I will say here is that so many boats have been built in fibreglass in recent years that circumstances will probably force you into buying a fibreglass boat whether you like it or not. Although it has been proved not to be the magic, maintenance-free material that it was originally touted to be, there is little doubt that a well-built fibreglass motor cruiser in good sound condition has a great deal to recommend it, in terms of cheapness and simplicity of maintenance.

Size

Your bank manager will probably be in a better position to advise you on this than I am! Clearly, the bigger the boat, the more expensive it will be, and the depth of your pocket will probably be the deciding factor. However, the biggest boat you can afford may not necessarily be the most suitable. Not only do larger ones cost more to buy, they cost considerably more to run, not only in terms of fuel and maintenance, but also harbour dues, mooring fees, insurance and so on. They could also be too big for you to safely handle, especially if you are short-handed.

There are three main factors to be considered – the size, strength and capability of the crew; the areas in which you wish to cruise; and whether you wish to keep the boat at home and trail her to the water each time you go out. If the latter, then you are immediately limited to something light, under about 23 feet and almost certainly powered by an outboard. If you are Mum, Dad and the children, then anything over 35 feet will probably be a bit much for you to handle, until you are rather more experienced. If you intend keeping the boat afloat in a marina or on a mooring and want to do the odd sea passage, living on board for perhaps a week in the holidays, then Mum, Dad and the children should be looking for something around 23 to 30 feet. This should give the necessary accommodation, the ability to cope with some waves (assuming suitable design), reasonable economy in purchasing and operating, and not be too large to handle in safety. If you just want to sunbathe, swim and water ski with your girlfriend, then a 15-foot planing boat with an outboard will suit you fine.

Age

To buy new or secondhand? My advice to the beginner is to buy the best secondhand boat of the type he wants that he can afford. Buying old or unusual boats is not a game for the inexperienced, and buying new is horrendously expensive, as well as possibly being a gamble if the design is untried. If you go for a well-known make that has been around for some time, then you can be fairly sure that it has been tried, tested and found good. You can also be fairly sure that it will be readily

Photo 34 A planing cruiser big and seaworthy enough for coastal and offshore passages in moderate weather. Note the large wake pulled up by this type of boat when it is not planing: care needs to be taken in such circumstances if very small boats or dinghies are nearby.

saleable should you want to change after a season's experience.

If you browse through the advertisements for secondhand boats in magazines such as *Motor Cruiser* and *Motorboat and Yachting* you will soon get to know the familiar names of the well-established boats, together with the sort of prices they command. You can learn a great deal from these magazines, not only by reading the articles, some of which at this stage may be rather technical for you, but from the advertisements for new boats. Although I do not recommend that you buy a new boat, they will give you ideas on the general type that you seek, as will the boat tests that the magazines

regularly undertake. If you live in a nautical area, a browse in the windows of chandleries and yacht brokers will also show you a wide variety of craft, usually with photographs and much information on equipment and so on.

The amount of equipment that you will probably get with a good secondhand boat is another reason for buying one. The cost of buying all these, usually essential, items can make a horrifying addition to the quoted price of a new boat.

Getting Afloat
This, suggested earlier, should be done before buying a boat. Even a small amount of experience, and some feel of being out in a motor cruiser or two, will help you immeasurably in choosing the sort of boat you want. There are three basic ways of going about this – joining a boating club near the place you intend to keep your boat; hiring a holiday cruiser; and taking a motor-cruising course at one of the schools advertising

in the yachting magazines.

Joining a club, having members with motor cruisers (it does not have to be a motorboat club, many sailing clubs have members with motor cruisers; approach the secretary and ask), will immediately put you in the company of many enthusiasts who will like nothing better than to tell you all about motor cruising in the area, and their own motor cruiser in particular. If you are lucky, they will take you out for a trip. You will undoubtedly get shown around a variety of boats, and be told the benefits and snags of each. You can learn a great deal like this, so long as you bear in mind that people extol the virtues of their craft and ignore her defects. You will soon learn the defects of one boat from the owner of another! This experience may well be quite sufficient to enable you to settle on a particular type of boat. You may even be offered a suitable one to buy! If you are, be sure to make copious enquiries among the other members as to its condition and suitability; it is certainly not unknown for a rogue to try and unload his heap of junk onto a new member, then skip the fold. So be careful.

If you cannot manage this, narrow your choice down as much as possible, then find a similar boat in the holiday catalogues and hire it for a week. Although you will be limited to sheltered waters, being inexperienced, you should still be able to learn a lot, not only from the boat you are in, but also from the other boats you see and the people you meet.

Taking a course at a motor-cruiser school will be quite pricey, but you will get expert, professional tuition, the experience of a well-found and well-run motor cruiser, and expert advice on your choice of boat from an experienced professional who has no axe to grind in his recommendations. There is much to

be said for this course of action if you do not mind the expense.

Buying the Boat

Having finally decided on the boat you want, it remains only to find a suitable one and buy her. There are many ways of doing this but I would strongly recommend that, as an inexperienced beginner, you buy one through a reputable and well-established yacht broker. You will pay rather more this way, but you are far less likely to be fleeced, as a good broker has his reputation to consider: he is unlikely to sell you a dud. Tell him the sort of boat you want, and ask him to supply you with details of anything that comes up. Like an estate agent, he will probably shower you with dozens of quite unsuitable boats, but somewhere in amongst them is likely to be the one you want. Bear in mind that the asking price for a boat is much like that for a car – far higher than the expected price!

Having found a likely contender, I would suggest, if it is not too far away, that you go and have a quiet look at her on your own first, or if possible, with an experienced friend. You will not, obviously, be able to go aboard and have a good root round, but you will be spared the pressure and patter of a salesman hanging over your shoulder. Take your time with this initial look – unless you are instantly repulsed, in which case you have saved everyone a lot of time and trouble. The more time and trouble you can save the broker in these early stages, the more time and trouble he is likely to give you when you really need it. I believe it is called human nature. You should know from the information whether she is basically what you want. What you need to find out from this initial foray is whether you actually like the look of her, and whether she appears to be well cared for and in decent condition. Does she seem to have the sort of hull you are looking for, the right amount of cockpit and deck space? Does she look well maintained, or run down and tatty? Is the paintwork cracked and peeling, or the gelcoat scratched or damaged? Do you take to her?

If she does not impress you, go home and look for another boat. If she does impress you, go home, ring the broker and tell him you are interested and arrange an appointment to view. Don't tell him you have already seen her. This will give you an advantage on viewing day, as you will be able to concentrate on the details, having already seen and approved her general image.

Your job, as a beginner, is not to survey the boat in detail, but to decide whether she fits the purpose you have in mind, and to gain a general impression of the quality of construction and maintenance. Is the internal joinery and so on sturdy and nicely finished? If it is, the hull probably is too. If the engine room is neat, clean and well kept, the machinery itself probably is also. If you like what you see, you should say thank you very much, then go home and think about it. I would not bother with a trial at this stage. With your lack of experience, ten minutes round the harbour will tell you nothing about anything.

If you are still enthusiastic the next day, you should get hold of a reputable marine surveyor – not one recommended by the broker – and arrange for him to make a 'preliminary inspection' of the boat in your presence. This will be very much cheaper than a full survey, but will be sufficient to show up any obvious problems, and enable you to decide whether it is worth proceeding with further survey expense. Now is the time for a short sea trial if you can arrange it, as ten minutes round the harbour should tell an experienced surveyor a great deal about the boat. If

all is well here, then you must shell out for a full and detailed survey. Although this is expensive, there is a good chance that sufficient minor defects will be found in even a good boat for you to knock the price down by the cost of the survey.

If all is well with the full survey, you can haggle a price with the broker, then tell him to proceed with the sale. He should handle all the paperwork, arrange finance, insurance etc for you. That is what you are paying him for. If there is any detail you are uncertain of, ask him.

A short while later, you should be the penniless but happy and excited owner of a good and suitable first motor cruiser. But where are you going to keep her?

Finding a Berth
This search should really be conducted at the same time as that for the boat, if not before. The type of boat you choose must be suitable for the place where you want, or have, to keep her. In general, there are three alternatives – at home on a trailer, alongside a marina berth, and on a mooring out in the harbour. The former has the great advantage that it costs nothing, but it does entail towing the boat back and forth to the water every time you want to go out, not to mention the business of floating her off the trailer and back on again. It also limits you quite drastically to the size and type of boat you have – little more than 20 feet and lightweight with an outboard engine. If this type of boat suits you, however, there is much to be said for this approach. Not only is it cheap and saves you having to anti-foul the bottom, but it also enables you to take your boat wherever you like, without having the possible problems and limitations of taking her by sea. If you elect to do this, you will find a book in Appendix 3 that

lists all the places in Britain where you can launch her.

In contrast, a marina berth is generally rather expensive, even if you can find one in the marina where you want to sail. But, although some marinas have certain limitations, most sizes of boat can be accommodated and you can simply drive there, park your car in the marina car park and go off. All sorts of facilities are likely to be available – shops, engineers, chandleries, boatyards and clubs. This type of berth is extremely convenient if your time is limited, but do read the small print. You may be obliged to employ marina staff to do your maintenance, you may have to pay the marina commission if you sell the boat, and there may be a myriad of other bureaucratic nonsenses that you are forced to abide by.

A mooring out in a harbour will give you much the same facilities as a marina, but you will have to go out to the boat by dinghy, which can be quite an inconvenience if you have a lot of

Photo 35 Berthing in a marina is crowded but very convenient with all facilities such as water, shore electricity, etc very close to the boats. Barrows are usually available for moving gear, and the long gangway leads directly to a car park, shower and toilet block, chandlery, marina office and so on.

gear to carry. The facilities, although available, will also be rather inconvenient – not just a short walk away up the jetty. The mooring will, however, be a fair bit cheaper than a marina berth with little risk of small-print regulations if, once again, you can find one. Most harbours seem to be very crowded these days if they have any sort of attraction for boatowners.

Which particular harbour or marina you choose will depend on a number of factors – the distance you are prepared to travel; the berthing charges; the sort of facilities you want; the type of cruising that you envisage doing. Do you want to go straight out to sea (as from Scarborough, for instance) or would you

Photo 36 Moorings out in a river are peaceful and reasonably cheap, but may be a long way from landing places and facilities. In certain places they may also be exposed to wind, waves, strong tidal streams or the wash of big ships. Make sure you know who is responsible for the maintenance of the mooring, and that this is done properly.

prefer a large river or sheltered estuary to potter about in? Do you want access to the inland waterways? You will have to think these things through carefully for yourself. *Sells Marine Market*, listed in Appendix 3, contains full information on all the marinas in Britain.

Trailing Your Boat

This can be a frightening experience for the uninitiated, and it behoves you to learn some of the necessary techniques if you propose to do this. The first thing you must understand is that when a boat is seated on a trailer, the weight of it must be taken on the keel, which is the strongest part of the boat. The adjustable supports at the side of the

trailer should be pushed up snugly under the hull, just sufficiently to balance the boat and hold her still, but not so hard that they take any real weight. If they do, they will very likely be pushed right through the hull when you drive over a bump. The weight of the boat should be slightly towards the front of the trailer, such that it takes a little bit of effort to lift the trailer at the ball-hitch. This will ensure that the back wheels of the car stay on the ground! Do not load the boat with so much gear that it becomes too heavy for the strength of the trailer.

The boat must be lashed down extremely securely, not only to stop it falling off the trailer, but also to prevent it from sliding back and forth along it. Run the lashings fore and aft as though you were securing springs to a jetty, and **bowse** them down as tightly as possible with waggoner's hitches (see figure 76). This, incidentally, is a very useful way of lashing dinghies and suchlike on deck, if your

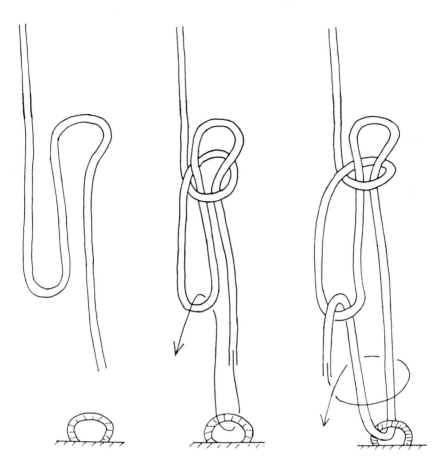

Figure 76 Make a loop in the rope as shown in the left-hand picture, a couple of feet or so above the lashing point. Then make a small eye in the standing part just below the top of the loop, and push the loop through it from the back, exactly as though you were starting a bowline (see figure 30). The standing part must come out from the back of the eye. Pull the eye tight around the loop, then pass the working end through the fastening point and back up through the bottom of the loop, as shown by the thin arrow in the middle picture. Now pull down very hard on the working end to tighten the whole rope (it will slide through the loop as you pull) and secure it round both parts leading to the fastening point with a half hitch or two, as shown by the thin arrow in the right-hand picture.

boat is that big. The lashings must be secured to strongpoints on board (mooring cleats etc), and you should pad the ropes out with something soft like old carpet where they rub against the edge of the deck. If the outboard is on the stern, wrap the propeller securely in some thick material to protect the heads of passing pedestrians from the sharp blades, and hang a strip of brightly coloured cloth from it to make it easily visible. A proper lighting board with back lights, brake lights and indicators, as well as number plate, should be securely fastened to the stern and connected to the car's lighting systems. Gone, I fear, are the days when one could simply chalk the car's number on the stern and drive off!

To launch the boat you must remove all lashings, light board etc and put the

bung in the drainhole, if you have one of these in the stern. Then secure a long painter (bowrope) to the bow and have someone hold onto this while you slowly back the trailer into the water until the boat floats off it. You can then drive the trailer away and pull the boat in by the painter while you get aboard. If the tide is ebbing, do not let her ground or you might not get her off again. To retrieve the boat, back the trailer into the water until it is just deep enough for the boat to float on. Guide the boat onto the trailer until she is in the right position and accurately centred over the keel support; then gradually haul the trailer from the water, all the time manoeuvring the boat to make sure that when she sits down on the trailer she does so in exactly the right place. When she is firmly on the trailer, secure the painter to the front of the trailer and haul her clear of the water and out of the way of anyone else launching or recovering boats. Then you can prepare her for the road at your leisure, without being a nuisance to others. Unless you have special sealed wheel bearings, they should be stripped, cleaned and re-greased after each immersion. Outboards should be flushed right through

Photo 37 Hauling boats out of the water onto a trailer is much easier with a winch, and a trailer that can be angled down towards the water at the back. As the boat is hauled forward its weight causes the trailer to straighten out, and it can be locked in that position with a pin or bolt. Note the spare wheel and the handbrake lever (just behind the man winching).

Photo 38 This is just about the maximum size of motor cruiser that you could conveniently keep at home and tow to the water. She would do well for estuary cruising and short coastal hops in good weather. A fair sized car would be needed to tow her, and some effort would be required to get her in and out of the water. A compromise might be to keep her on the water in the summer, but save on boatyard storage charges by taking her home for the winter.

with fresh water to remove salt. Immerse prop and intake in a bucket of fresh water and run for a few minutes, or fit a hose to the intake (see Photo 42). Wash the boat too.

Manoeuvring the trailer backwards – round corners and through gateways – requires a certain technique. The secret is to forget the car and think only of the trailer and the direction in which you want to swing it (see figure 77). If you want to swing the trailer round in the direction of arrow number one, you need to push the front of it in the direction of arrow number two. Do this by swinging the car as shown by the curved arrow number three. This must not be overdone, however, or you will jack-knife. As the trailer swings towards the desired direction, you must reverse the lock on the car's steering so as to follow the trailer round (see figure 78). The trailer can then be guided by using the car's steering to swing the front of the trailer in the required direction. With a bit of practice you will soon get the hang of it. Keep an eye on where the front of the car is swinging to if space is limited. It is rather like steering the boat on the water; you push the back across in order to align the front with the direction you want to go.

Towing on the road is fairly straightforward, as long as you remember that acceleration and braking will be far less effective with all that weight at the back of you, and that you should make a wide sweep round a corner so that the trailer does not mount the kerb. Remember also that when you try to dodge out of a side turning into busy traffic, the oncoming vehicles will not realise how long you are, as they probably will not be able to see the trailer. Always carry an inflated spare wheel for the trailer. Certain regulations apply to towing trailers on the road, and your local police station should be able to advise you.

179

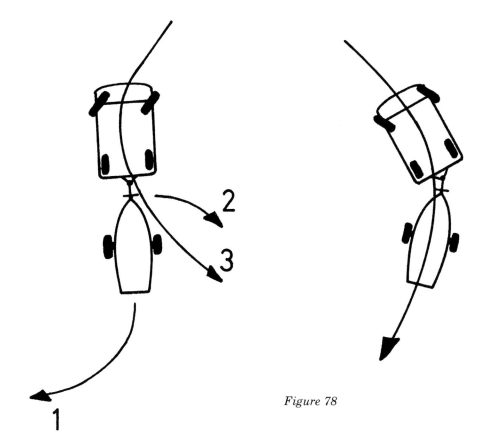

Figure 77

Figure 78

Enjoy Your Boat

I hope you do. There is great pleasure to be had from cruising around in your own motor cruiser, whether you are on river, canal or sea. The better equipped, the better maintained and the better handled your boat is, the greater will be this pleasure. I trust this book will go some way towards helping you achieve the satisfaction of skippering your motor cruiser with confidence and ability.

APPENDICES

APPENDIX 1
EQUIPMENT LISTS

Inland and Sheltered Waters
Main anchor and warp
Mooring warps (4 long ones)
Lifebelts (one with light)
Fire extinguishers
Torches (2 powerful ones)
Boarding ladder
Fenders
Boathook
Bucket on lanyard
Local tide table
Mooring spikes (for rivers, canals)
Warm clothes, and change
Normal domestic items for galley etc
Kedge anchor and warp
Bilge pumps (1 of them manual)
First-aid kit and manual
Fire blanket
Foghorn
Anchor light
Chain (for moorings)
Deck scrubber
Wooden plank (for berthing)
Local chart
Buoyancy aids (and harnesses for small children)
Waterproofs

Coastal and Open Waters
All the above plus the following items:
Navigation lights
Safety harnesses
Dinghy (and liferaft?)
Pair of dinghy rowlocks and spare
Anchor and warp for dinghy
Pair of dinghy oars and spare
Baler for dinghy
Pump and repair kit (inflatable)
Radar reflector
Flares
Steering compass
Log (trailing or built in)
Echo-sounder (if possible)

Nautical almanac
Parallel ruler
Pencils (2B) – ½ doz
Pencil sharpener
Navigator's notebook
Metmaps (or similar)
Barometer
Binoculars (7×50)
Hand-bearing compass
Leadline
Charts of complete area and harbours
Pilot book (of complete area)
Dividers (single-handed type)
Rubber
Compasses
Logbook
Radio (with long wave for forecasts)
Clock or watch
Engine logbook

Spares and Repairs
Batteries (torches etc)
Bulbs (lights and torches)
Diaphragm and valves (bilge pump)
Oil (engine, gearboxes, general)
Distilled water (main batteries)
Fuel and oil filters
Raw-water pump impeller (neoprene)
Injectors and fuel lines (*diesel*)
Shear pins, starter cord (*outboard*)
Vaseline (battery terminals)
Freeing oil
Strong waterproof tape (repair hoses)
Hermetite jointing compound (gaskets)
Hose material
Bulldog grips (joining wires)
Battery jump leads
Fuses (equipment and switchboard)
Foghorn canister (if portable)
Impellers (power bilge pumps)
Grease (stern-tube, general purpose)
Emergency tiller
Drive belts (generator, water pump)

Thermostat
Spark plugs, distributor cap, HT leads, points, condenser (*petrol*)
Waterproof spray
Insulating tape (electrical repairs)
PTFE tape (repair leaking joints)
Stern-gland packing
Hose clips
Emery boards and abrasive paper
Clean rags
Hand cleaner

Tools and Equipment
Spanners to fit all nuts on boat
Water-pump spanner
Small chain wrench (remove filters)
Small crowbar
2lb hammer (mooring spikes)
Hacksaw and spare blades
Vice (that clamps to table)

Sharp knife and marlinspike (KEEP HANDY IN WHEELHOUSE)
Oilstone (sharpening tools)
Hydrometer (check batteries)
Gas-bottle spanner (gas stoves)
Bits of electrical wire
Ball of terylene string
Nuts, bolts, screws etc
Stillson wrench
Mole grips
Pliers (stub and long nosed)
Screwdrivers (selection)
Claw hammer (general use)
Files (selection)
Wire brush
Feeler gauge (check clearances)
Primus prickers (primus stoves)
Sparkplug spanner (petrol engines)
Seizing wire
Odd lengths of rope

APPENDIX 2
ELECTRONIC NAVIGATION AND COMMUNICATION AIDS

Radio-telephone

There are two types that you are likely to come across – VHF and MF. The latter is bulky, very expensive and has a fairly long range. It is not necessary for coastal work. VHF, however, is very compact and cheap, with sufficient range for coastal work, and is a most useful device to have onboard the larger boat. Hand-held portable sets are also obtainable.

Although often touted as a 'safety aid' for making distress calls, VHF has far wider-reaching uses than this. You can call up harbours before arrival to arrange berths and check that entry is clear; radio stations for weather forecasts and 'link calls' into the shore telephone system; coastguards for present weather conditions; ships if you are unsure of their movements; fellow skippers to arrange rendezvous and so on. Full details of facilities, procedures and so on will be found in the almanac, but a few points should be borne in mind. VHF is not a toy to enable bored skippers to chat all day without getting a telephone bill. It is a professional communications system for vessels at sea; it should be used as such, according to the procedures given in the almanac. Licences are required for both set and operator, who must show that he is familiar with these procedures.

Photo 39 A neat VHF radiotelephone situated right by the wheel. Channels are changed with the big knob in the middle, and the number of the selected channel is displayed in the window just above it. The various other controls and facilities will be explained in the manual.

A large number of channels are available, each of which has its own particular use: adhere to these uses, and keep your messages brief; others may be waiting to use the channel. Channel 16 is reserved for distress calls and making initial contact with another station *only*. Do not chat on it – you could cause the death of a fellow seaman. Radio stations, coastguards and ships listen in to this channel all the time, and you should do the same; you might hear a distress call from someone near you. Make sure that at least one other crew member can operate the set, and have the distress procedure written out clearly and posted up beside it. (See Appendix 4.)

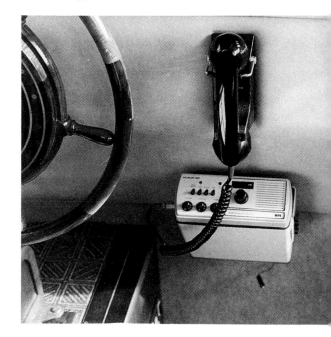

185

Radar

This device can detect solid objects and display them as blobs of light on a screen rather like a small TV set. In capable hands it can be invaluable in the dark and in poor visibility, for both navigation and collision avoidance, but it requires skill and experience to tune and operate the set properly. If you tune a TV channel wrongly, you can end up watching ITV instead of BBC; tuning a radar set wrongly can give you the same level of misinformation.

Radar works by bouncing radio signals off objects and detecting the echoes, which vary in strength considerably, depending on the object they are bouncing off. Strong echoes will come from big steel ships, high cliffs, tall harbour walls etc. Weak or non-existent echoes will come from small boats, wooden boats, fibreglass boats, buoys without radar reflectors, low coastlines and so on. Small objects can be swallowed up in the mass of echoes from rough seas. The picture that is painted on your radar screen is not necessarily the same as your actual surroundings, so care and skill are both required for interpreting the picture properly.

Radio Direction Finding (RDF)

This gadget enables you to take compass bearings of certain radio stations marked on the chart, with which a fix can be constructed as it can with visual compass bearings (see Chapter 11). It is particularly useful in poor visibility, but it has its limitations over and above the basic problems in fixing already discussed. Fuller details of techniques, procedures, limitations, errors and uses will be found in the almanac, along with lists of the special radio stations that can be used. In general, however, RDF bearings are inaccurate and unreliable at long ranges, very short ranges, at night and when they cross land between the station and the boat.

Photo 40 A fairly typical small boat radar mounted at eye level in the wheelhouse. To exclude light and ensure a clear picture, you must press your face against the shaped rubber around the screen. The variety of controls will be explained in the manual.

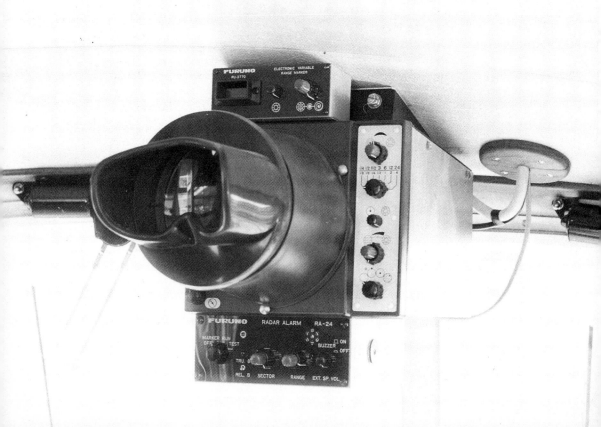

Photo 41 The very small and neat console of the Decca Navigator. Latitude and Longitude are displayed electronically in the windows at the top. This machine can perform a variety of useful tasks besides simply showing your position, and full details will be found in the manual.

They are difficult to take accurately at the best of times, without some experience, and even more so in rough seas or when travelling at speed. Magnetic and electrical influences on the boat can make them go haywire, and a set must be properly installed and calibrated if it is to be any use at all. RDF is, however, much cheaper than the two following devices although far less useful.

Decca Navigator
This is quite a different thing from RDF, being a compact box of tricks that gives, reliably and with extraordinary accuracy, a continuous digital readout of your latitude and longitude. It is, however, rather expensive. The same system in a different form is probably in use on virtually every commercial and fishing vessel operating within the Decca area, which covers most of the coastal waters around Britain and Europe. It works, in simple terms, by measuring differences between special radio waves transmitted from certain stations spaced out around the country.

Satellite Navigator (Satnav)
This, like Decca Navigator, is a small box that gives you a continuous readout of latitude and longitude, this time calculated from the positions of passing navigational satellites. Where Decca, however, produces a virtually continuous series of accurate fixes, Satnav produces a fix each time a satellite passes over (about once an hour), then continuously updates this by DR (course and speed have to be fed into it) until the next pass. Course and speed also have to be fed into it for each fix (as it requires a rough DR position from which to work) and must be maintained

during the time it takes the box to calculate the fix. Thus it is more complex to operate than Decca, less accurate, and far less versatile for coastal work. It can, however, be used worldwide, which Decca as yet cannot, due to its limited coverage. For cruising around Britain and Europe, Decca would be far superior, at roughly the same price, although a new satellite system being developed, that will produce more frequent fixes, could be a serious contender when it becomes available.

Autopilot

This, although not strictly in the same category as the preceding equipment, is included because it is electronic and a great asset on long passages. Quite simply, it will steer the boat on a particular compass course for as long as it is supplied with electricity. It will not get tired, seasick or fed up. It will not eat or drink anything, it will not argue with you and it will not get drunk every time you call into harbour. On the other hand, neither will it keep a lookout or alter course to avoid anything in the water. Thus it is vitally important that you keep a good lookout while on autopilot, something that big ships seem all too often not to do. Although rather superfluous on short coastal passages, you will find it a great boon on a longer journey, as steering gets very tedious after a while.

You will find more detailed information on all these devices in the almanac, and also in the electrical and radar books in Appendix 3. If you buy a boat with such equipment fitted, write to the manufacturers for operating manuals if they are not on board. It is most important that you know how to use them properly. Bear in mind the comments made in Chapter 13 about the influence of electrical equipment on electrolytic corrosion. This type of equipment must be properly installed and earthed in order to reduce these effects. They may also suffer electrical interference from the engine or ancillaries. The suppression of this interference should be dealt with by an engineer.

APPENDIX 3
SOURCES OF INFORMATION

Main Reference Books

Makers' manuals for all equipment on board

Nautical Almanac (*Reeds* or *MacMillans*), which contains details of:

Collision regulations
Fog signals
Communication methods (radio, morse code, flag signals, light signals etc)
Weather forecasting
Light characteristics
Coastguard stations
Distress signals
Tide tables
Harbour information
First-aid
Lights and shapes
Manoeuvring signals
Basic chart symbols
Electronic navigation aids
Rescue organisations
Basic coastal navigation
Tidal stream atlases
Pilot books and chart lists
Glossary of nautical terms
and much, much else of use and interest.

Engineering

Goring, Loris. *The Care and Repair of Marine Petrol Engines* (Adlard Coles, 1981)

Thompson, Chris. *The Care and Repair of Small Marine Diesels* (Adlard Coles, 1982)

Warren, Nigel. *The Outboard Motor Handbook* (Stanford Maritime, 1977)

——. *Marine Conversions* (converting vehicle engines) (Adlard Coles, 1982)

Watney, John. *Boat Electrics* (David & Charles, 1984)

Wilkes, Kenneth. *Radio and Radar in Sail and Power Boats* (Nautical, 1980)

Maintenance

Blandford, Percy. *The Care and Repair Below Decks* (Adlard Coles, 1980)

Verney, Michael. *The Care and Repair of Hulls* (Adlard Coles, 1979)

Navigation

Tetley, R. M. *Small Cruiser Navigation* (David & Charles, 1984)

Wilkes, Kenneth. *Practical Yacht Navigator* (Nautical, 1986)

Weather

Sanderson, Ray. *Weather for Sailing* (Stanford Maritime, 1986)

Watts, Alan. *Instant Weather Forecasting* (Adlard Coles, 1968)

Medical

Counter, Dr Richard. *The Yachtsman's Doctor* (Nautical, 1986)

Ropework

Jarman, Colin & Beavis, Bill. *Modern Rope Seamanship* (Adlard Coles, 1976)

MacLean, William. *Modern Marlinspike Seamanship* (David & Charles, 1982)

Motor Cruisers

Sells Marine Market (Sells Publications, 1984)

Warren, Nigel. *Small Motor Cruisers* (Adlard Coles, 1975)

Equipment Suppliers

Sells Marine Market (Sells Publications, 1984)

Makers' manuals (for spares etc)

Marinas

Sells Marine Market (Sells Publications, 1984)

Launching Sites
Goatcher, Diana. *Where to Launch Your Boat* (Barnacle Marine, 1986)

Electrolytic Corrosion
M. G. Duff & Partners, Chichester Yacht Basin, Birdham, West Sussex.
A good surveyor with specialised knowledge of your type of boat.

Magazines
Motor Cruiser
Motorboat and Yachting
Practical Boat Owner

APPENDIX 4
USEFUL DATA

Communications
Morse Code and Phonetic Alphabet

A — ALPHA   . —
B — BRAVO   — ...
C — CHARLIE   — . — .
D — DELTA   — ..
E — ECHO   .
F — FOXTROT   .. — .
G — GOLF   — — .
H — HOTEL   ....
I — INDIA   ..
J — JULIET   . — — —
K — KILO   — . —
L — LIMA   . — ..
M — MIKE   — —
N — NOVEMBER   — .
O — OSCAR   — — —
P — PAPA   . — — .
Q — QUEBEC   — — . —
R — ROMEO   . — .
S — SIERRA   ...
T — TANGO   —
U — UNIFORM   .. —
V — VICTOR   ... —
W — WHISKY   . — —
X — X-RAY   — .. —
Y — YANKEE   — . — —
Z — ZULU   — — ..

When using VHF radio, these words should be used to spell out call signs and difficult or foreign words.

For further information on Morse Code, see the almanac.

International Code – Single Meanings

  A — I have a diver down – keep clear
  B — I am taking in, discharging, carrying dangerous cargo
  C — Yes, affirmative
*D — Keep clear of me, I am manoeuvring with difficulty
*E — I am altering course to starboard

F — I am disabled – communicate with me
G — I require a pilot
(by fishing boats at sea) – I am hauling nets
*H — I have a pilot on board
*I — I am altering course to port
  J — I am on fire with dangerous cargo – keep clear
K — I wish to communicate with you
L — You should stop your vessel instantly
M — My vessel is stopped and making no way
N — No, negative
O — Man overboard
P — (in harbour) – vessel is about to sail (at sea) – my nets are fast on an obstructon
Q — My vessel is healthy and I require free pratique
R — (no meaning except by sound in fog – see *Fog Signals*)
*S — My engines are going astern
*T — Keep clear, I am engaged in pair trawling
U — You are standing into danger
V — I require assistance
W— I require medical assistance
X — Stop what you are doing and watch for my signals
Y — I am dragging my anchor
Z — I require a tug
(by fishing vessels) – I am shooting nets

All these signals can be made by any means but normally code flags are used by day and morse lamp by night. The ones marked * should not be made as sound signals except in fog or when manoeuvring at close quarters, when they have special meanings. See *Fog Signals* and *Manoeuvring Signals*.

These single letter meanings are urgent and important signals and should be known by all seamen.

Coloured illustrations of the code flags will be found in almanacs, and can be obtained from chandlers on waterproof cards.

R/T Distress Procedure
Set transmitter and receiver to international distress frequency (MF – 2182 kHz: VHF – Channel 16) Then transmit distress call:
'MAYDAY MAYDAY MAYDAY this is (Boat's name three times)'
Send all that three times, then:
'MAYDAY this is (boat's name)' – followed by:
1 position of boat
2 nature of emergency and assistance required
3 any other information that may be of help
then listen. If no reply, repeat the whole message until someone replies with:
your boat's name three times
'this is'
name of station answering call.

For trouble other than grave emergencies, the same procedure can be used by substituting one of the following words for MAYDAY.
PAN—very urgent message concerning safety of ship or crew (this is the one for urgent medical advice)
SAYCURITAY—important messages concerning navigation or weather (report floating wreckage etc)

Best chance of being heard during silence periods – three minutes after every hour and half hour.
Give position as bearing and distance from well known landmark, headland, lightship etc if possible; as lat and long are prone to error.

Keep set tuned to distress frequency when not in use.
Have cards placed by set with procedure and phonetic alphabet for instant reference.

For details of all radio-telephone procedures such as link calls into the shore telephone system, intership calls, berthing information and so on, together with list of all stations, frequencies, etc, see the almanac.

Important Signals
Distress Signals
  1 Gun or explosive signal fired about once a minute
  2 Continuous sound of foghorn
  3 Red flares – rocket, parachute or hand
  4 Orange smoke signal (usually from hand flares)
  5 Flames on the vessel (rag on boathook soaked in paraffin)
  6 SOS sent in morse by any means (light, sound, radio)
  7 The word MAYDAY on a radio-telephone (see *R/T Distress Procedure*)
  8 International code flags – N above C
  9 A square flag and a round shape hoisted together
10 Slow, repeated raising and lowering of arms outstretched
11 Built-in alarm signals from radio transmitters
12 Signals from emergency radio transmitters
13 Ensign hoisted upside down
14 Ensign made fast high in the rigging
15 Article of clothing attached to oar, blowing horizontally

Use the most obvious ones (top of the list) if you possibly can. The last three are final measures if nothing else is available.

Use them only in a situation of grave danger. For urgent advice (medical etc) use the call signals following if at all possible (ships in sight, for instance).
If ashore and you see a distress signal, dial 999 and ask for Coastguard.

Danger Signals
The following signals (usually made by lighthouse, lightships, coastguards etc) mean 'You are standing into danger'.
Code flag U
Code flags N above F
U in morse by light or sound

They may also fire a gun, white flare, rocket sound signal showing white stars or explosive sound signal repeated.
Light vessels may fly code flags P over S, to mean 'Do not come any closer'

Call Signals
K (code flag or morse by light) – I wish to communicate with you
L (code flag or morse by light or sound) – You should stop your vessel instantly
The latter is most likely to be made by a lightship or house, the sound signal being used in fog, light at night, and flag by day.

Fog Signals
Power vessel under way – 1 long blast every 2 minutes
Power vessel stopped – 2 long blasts every 2 minutes
Vessels sailing, towing, fishing, not under command, or otherwise restricted in manoeuvrability – 1 long and 2 short blasts every 2 minutes (Morse for D)
Vessel towed (if manned) – 1 long and 3 shorts every 2 minutes (straight after tug's signal) (Morse code-B)
Vessel at anchor – 5 seconds ringing of bell per minute: if over 100 metres this is rung for'ard and followed by 5 seconds on a gong aft. Can also sound 1 short, 1 long and 1 short to warn approaching vessels. (Morse code-R)
Vessel aground – same as at anchor but with 3 distinct strokes on the bell before and after the ringing.
Pilot vessels – besides suitable signal as above, may sound 4 short blasts (Morse code-H)

Manoeuvring Signals (vessels in sight of one another)
1 short blast – I am altering course to starboard: .
2 short blasts– I am altering course to port: ..
3 short blasts– My engines are going astern: ...

Note the Morse code E, I and S. These signals may be supplemented by the same morse letters by light. Three short blasts does NOT necessarily mean the vessel is actually moving astern as yet.

Vessels intending to overtake sound:
___ . to pass to starbord
___ .. to pass to port

Vessel agreeing to be overtaken sounds:
—.—.

Vessel unsure of other's intentions sounds: at least 5 short and rapid blasts:
.....

Vessel approaching blind bend sounds: 1 very long blast _____

Short Blast is of one second's duration
Long Blast is of about five second's duration

Rule of the Road
Power vessels meeting:
— head on: both alter course to starboard
— otherwise: keep clear of vessels on starboard side
— overtaking: keep clear

Power vessels keep clear of:
— sailing vessels
— fishing vessels
— vessels not under command
— large vessels in restricted spaces

Any overtaking vessel keeps clear of all types

Tidal Information
Twelfths Rule
Tide rises or falls:
　　1 twelfth of range in first hour
　　2 twelfths of range in second hour
　　3 twelfths of range in third hour
　　3 twelfths of range in fourth hour
　　2 twelfths of range in fifth hour
　　1 twelfth of range in last hour
Range of tide is difference between High and Low Water heights
Soundings on chart are measured below Chart Datum
Tidal Heights are measured above Chart Datum
Soundings when underlined are above Chart Datum (in feet or tenths of metres) and known as *drying heights*
Heights of lighthouses etc are measured

above Mean High Water Springs

Spring Tides give big High Water, small Low Water and fast streams

Neap Tides give small High Water, big Low Water, and weak streams

Tides are roughly 50 minutes later each day

Minimum Scopes
chain—3 times greatest depth
nylon—5 times greatest depth

Size of Anchors
bower—bit bigger than length of boat
kedge—bit smaller than length of boat (in feet and pounds)

Size of Chain
up to 25 feet— 5/16 inch
25–35 feet – 3/8 inch
35–45 feet – 7/16 inch

Weather Information

Gale Warnings

Imminent –
   within 6 hours of time warning is issued by Met Office

Soon –
   6 to 12 hours from issue of warning

Later –
   more than 12 hours from issue of warning.

   (Note that warning will have been issued some while before the time of broadcast. Gale warnings are broadcast on Radio 4 at the first change in the programme and after next news bulletin. They are also broadcast by coast radio stations on VHF and MF.)

Weather Forecast Times on Radio 4 (1500m/200khz on Long Wave)

Shipping Forecast
   0555, 1355, 1750, 0033 (clock time)

Inshore Forecast
   end of day's broadcasting

Land Forecast
   1255, 1755

Details of forecasts from local radio stations, coast radio stations, Met Offices etc, will be found in the Almanac.

Visibility – Sea Areas

Good –
   over 5 nautical miles

Moderate –
   2 to 5 miles

Poor –
   ½ to 2 miles

Fog –
   less than ½ a mile

Barometer Changes

Rise/fall over 8mb in 3 hours –
   almost certain gale

Rise/fall over 5mb in 3 hours –
   almost certain force 6

(These are very rough guides only. If you are motoring fast towards the depression, the rate of change on your barometer will be greater than the true rate; vice versa if you are motoring away.)

Speed of Pressure Systems in Shipping Forecasts

Slowly –
   less than 15 knots

Steadily –
   15 to 25 knots

Rather quickly –
   25 to 35 knots

Rapidly –
   35 to 45 knots

Very rapidly –
   over 45 knots

The Beaufort Scale

Force	Approximate Wind Speed (knots)	At Sea	Ashore
0	0	*Calm* No ripples on surface. Any swell is not caused by wind	*Light* Smoke rises vertically
1	2	*Light Air* Patches of ripples on surface	*Light* Smoke drifts. Stirring of flags
2	5	*Light Breeze* Surface covered by ripples and waves up to 12 inches	*Light* Wind can be felt on face, rustles leaves and moves flags
3	5–10	*Gentle Breeze* Small waves, 2-3 feet high, and occasional white horses	*Gentle* Continuous movement of leaves, twigs and flags
4	10–15	*Moderate Breeze* Waves increase to 4-5 feet and white horses are common	*Moderate* Dust and paper blown about. Smaller branches swayed
5	15–20	*Fresh Breeze* Crested waves of 6-8 feet. Spray blown from crests	*Fresh* Small trees sway about. Waves formed on inland waters with crests
6	20–25	*Strong Breeze* Waves of 8-12 feet with spray streaks and crests foaming	*Strong* Large branches swayed. Humming in telephone wires
7	30–35	*Moderate Gale* White foaming crests to waves of 12-16 feet, broken away in gusts	*Strong* Large trees swayed. Difficulty in walking against wind
8	35–40	*Fresh Gale* Sea rough and disturbed. Waves 20-25 feet, with 'boiling' patches	*Gale* Branches snapped off, small trees blow down. Extreme difficulty in walking against wind
9	40–45	*Strong Gale* Sea covered in white foam, waves 25-30 feet. Visibility reduced by spray	*Gale* Chimneys and slates blown down
10	50–55	*Storm* 30-40 feet waves. Visibility badly affected	*Whole Gale* Large trees uprooted. Buildings damaged or blown down
11	60–65	*Storm* Air full of spray. Large vessels may be damaged by waves of 45 feet	*Storm* Major structural damage
12	65+	*Hurricane* Waves over 45 feet will damage large ships and may cause small craft to founder	*Hurricane* Extreme damage

APPENDIX 5
ENGINE FAULT FINDING

A Starter will not turn, or turns very slowly
1 Starter battery isolating switch turned off
2 Bad connection between starter motor and battery
3 Battery discharged or with internal fault
4 Bad connection in ignition-switch circuit to solenoid
5 Bad connection inside solenoid
6 Bad connection inside starter motor (probably sticking brushes)
7 Starter motor bendix jammed in flywheel

B Starter turns over, but engine does not fire
1 No fuel delivery
2 No air
Diesel
3 Insufficient cranking speed (see Section A)
4 Insufficient or faulty starting aid when engine cold
5 Air in fuel line
Petrol
6 Insufficient choke on cold engine
7 Excessive choke on hot engine
8 Damp ignition electrics (HT)
9 Bad connection in ignition circuit (HT or LT)
10 Faulty or fouled sparkplugs
11 Pitted or incorrectly set points
12 Faulty condenser
13 Cracked distributor cap/HT lead insulation

C Engine runs roughly, labours or stops
1 Erratic air supply
2 Erratic fuel supply (dirt in fuel or air in diesel)

3 Erratic ignition
  faulty injector (*diesel*)
  see Section B: 8–13 (*petrol*)
4 Engine working too hard
  weed or rope round propeller
  engine overheated (see Section D)
  no oil in engine or gearbox

D Engine overheats
1 Blockage in raw-water circuit
2 Serious leak in either water circuit
3 Thermostat failing to open
4 Faulty raw- or fresh-water pump
  airlock in pump
  broken pump impeller
  slack drive belt/broken shaft
5 Blocked fan filter or air inlet (*air cooled*)
6 Engine working too hard (see Section C: 4)
7 Lack of cooling air in engine room

E Oil pressure drops
1 Serious oil leak
2 Clogged oil filter
3 Dirt jamming oil-pressure relief valve open
4 Water or fuel in the oil

F Generator does not charge
1 Loose drive belt
2 Bad connection in generator circuit
3 Internal fault in battery (engineer to test)
4 Battery-isolating switch off
5 Ignition switch off (*diesel*)
6 Fault in generator (probably sticking brushes; see manual)
7 Fault in regulator (can also cause over-charging; engineer to test)

G Engine will not drive boat
1 Broken shear-pin (*outboard*)

2 Propeller fallen off or seriously damaged (*inboard*)
3 Gearbox clutch slipping
4 Boat is aground!

H Smoke from exhaust
Black
  Faulty injector (excessive fuel) (*diesel*)
  Overloaded engine (*diesel*)
  Over-choked engine (*petrol*)
  Too rich fuel/air mixture (excessive fuel) (*petrol*)
White
  Faulty injector (insufficient fuel) (*diesel*)
  Poor compression (fuel not igniting) (*diesel*)
  Weak fuel/air mixture (insufficient fuel) (*petrol*)
Blue
  Normal colour due to burning oil (*two-stroke*)
  Internal wear (oil burning in cylinders) (*four-stroke*)
Pale Blue
  Normal colour of exhaust (*diesel*)

I Noise from engine
Loud screeching front of engine
  Slipping drive belt (loose or greasy)
  Worn water pump bearings
Regular tapping at top of engine
  Valve clearances too great

Light tinkling inside engine
  Broke piston ring (compression low in that cylinder)
Dry rattle at high revs
  Worn big end bearings (with low oil pressure)
Light rattle front of engine
  Loose, worn timing chain
Heavy rumbling, vibration
  Worn crankshaft, main bearings
Unusual noises around engine
  Loose fittings vibrating
Whining from gearbox
  Worn gears or no oil
Rumble, vibration at stern
  Propshaft misaligned
  Prop damaged
  Propshaft bearings, flexible coupling worn

J Engine performs badly
Fails to reach maximum rpm
  Prop too coarse a pitch
Fails to drive boat at expected speed (or max revs too high)
  Prop too fine a pitch
Lacks power
  Low compression (internal wear – see manual; blown head gasket)
  Generally out of tune

READ YOUR MANUAL
THINK LOGICALLY
See Chapter 2 and page 160

APPENDIX 6
WINTER WORK LIST

Engine: clean and winterise if laying up (see manual); engineer to test condition

Cooling system: clean sludge out of pipes, fittings and thermostat

Lubricating system: change oil in engine and gearboxes while hot; renew filters

Fuel system: drain and clean tank (close cock to keep *diesel* in pipes); clean or renew filters; clean carburetter float chamber; blow through carburetter jets; send injectors for service

Electrical system: take battery, starter and generator ashore if laying up; keep battery charged; have battery heavy discharge tested; check brushes and commutator in starter and generator; remove batteries from torches etc; move electronic equipment to warm dry place ashore

Ignition system: renew sparkplugs, points (inc magneto) and condenser

Control system: inspect, refurbish and grease steering gear; oil or grease all cables and linkages to throttle etc

Drive system: check plummer block, propshaft flange and stern gland (re-pack gland if it has been leaking); check security and condition of propeller (file smooth any small nicks; send away for repair of any major damage); spray prop with lacquer

Water system: drain and clean tank; sterilise tank; leave tank and piping empty if freezing expected

Heads: drain and clean; repack pump glands if leaking; leave bowl and pipes empty if freezing expected

Seacocks: strip, clean and lightly grease; bed in with grinding paste if they have been leaking; leave closed

Outboard: flush with fresh water

Pumps: strip and check impellers (cooling water and bilge); renew gaskets; strip and check diaphragm and valves (hand bilge pump)

Anodes: check, and renew if two-thirds gone

Windlass: clean and lubricate, then cover up from weather

Cockpit: cover with tarpaulin to protect from weather

Liferaft: send away for servicing every two years; keep ashore at other times

Fire extinguishers: have serviced every two years; keep aboard between times

Compass: have professionally swung and adjusted every two years (or after any major work on boat); keep ashore if possible, away from magnets, metal, radios etc

Dinghy: wash with fresh water, repair, paint. Keep ashore upside down and firmly supported; dry, then deflate inflatable – send away for all but very small repairs

Hull of boat: wash with fresh water; repair and protect as required

Bilges: clean with Bilgex (or similar); leave open to ventilate

Lockers: clean out and leave open to ventilate (including chain locker)

Chain: spread out on quay and inspect; paint new markings

Ropes: wash with fresh water, dry, inspect for chafe, hang in ventilated space

Fastenings: check security of all deck fittings and rudder hangings

Buoyancy aids: remove ashore, inspect and store in dry place (life jackets too)

Bedding, food etc: remove and store in dry place ashore

Trailer: wash with fresh water, repair and paint; regrease wheel hubs.

Charts: correct up to date

GLOSSARY

Abaft behind

Abeam directly out to the side of the boat

A-bracket fitting to support the prop-shaft

A'cockbill anchor just clear of the water

Adrift loose; late; broken off

Aft at the back of the boat

Ahead forward; in front of the boat

Amidships in, or in line with the middle of the boat

Arm the lead smear tallow or grease in the bottom of a lead in order to collect sample of bottom

Astern backwards; reverse; behind the boat

Athwartships across the boat

Avast stop (hauling etc)

Awash level with the water

Aweigh anchor is aweigh when just off the bottom

Back the wind is said to back when it shifts anticlockwise – ie from north to west

Ballast weight put low in a boat to create stability

Bar shallow bank across entrance to harbour, estuary

Batten down secure hatches etc for sea

Beam width of boat at widest part

Bear off push off from jetty etc

Belay secure a rope; cancel an order (belay that!)

Below down inside the cabin

Beneaped aground when tide falling from springs to neaps, unlikely to float again for two weeks

Bight a loop or the middle part of a rope

Bilge the inside of a boat at the very bottom

Binnacle stand on which a compass is mounted

Bitter end very end of a rope or cable

Boathook pole with a hook on the end

Bollard large post for mooring boats to

Bow front end of the boat

Bower anchor main anchor (the heaviest)

Bowse down to tighten a rope or lashing

Breastrope short mooring line straight across to shore

Bring up come to anchor

Broach swing broadside to waves

Bulkhead internal partition in boat

Bulwarks solid rail around the deck

Buoy floating sea mark, anchored as guide to navigation

Buoyancy aid foam-filled waistcoat that helps you float

Cable 200 yards; chain connected to anchor

Carry away to be broken

Carry way to move through the water

Cast off let go of a line or mooring

Catenary curve of anchor cable between boat and sea bed

Cavitation loss of drive due to air sucked around prop

Chine angle between side and bottom of planing boat

C.I.E. Compression ignition engine (diesel)

CG 66 coastguard form for giving details of your boat

Cleat T-shaped fitting for securing ropes to

Clutter echoes on radar screen from waves, rain etc

Coaming raised surround to cockpit etc

Cockpit well at the stern for the crew to sit in

Courtesy ensign small ensign of foreign country being visited, flown from starboard yardarm

Covering board wide deck plank next to gunwhale on wooden boat

Crown of anchor bottom end

Crutch U-shaped fitting to hold oars when rowing

Deck the flat surface on top of a boat

Deckhead underneath the deck (inside the cabin)

Deep vee deep, narrow V-shaped hull

Dinghy small open boat, often used as tender

Displacement weight of a boat

Dividers instrument for measuring distances on a chart

Dowse put out – a light or fire

Draft depth of a boat below the waterline

Ebb tide tide flowing out of harbour and falling in height

End-for-end reeve a rope in opposite direction to spread chafe

Equinoctial gales reputedly occur at the equinoxes

Equinoctial tides very big spring tides that occur at the equinoxes

Fairlead smooth fitting to lead ropes from boat to shore

Fair tide tidal stream that is running with you

Fairway a clear, navigable channel

Fall loose end of rope leading from tackle

Fathom six feet; little used now charts are metric

Fender soft plastic sausage to cushion boat against wall

Fetch distance over water in which waves can build up

Fiddle rail round cooker, table etc, to stop things falling off as boat rolls

Fill a depression fills when it loses energy and fades

Fixed navigation light characteristic – constant light

Flake to coil a rope in long, loose figures of eight

Flashing navigation light characteristic showing shorter periods of light than darkness

Flukes the points of an anchor that dig in the bottom

Flood tide tide flowing into harbour and rising in height

Fo'c'sle compartment right for'ard in a boat

For'ard slang for forward; towards the bow

Forefoot curve of stem below water

Foul anchor anchor tangled up

Foul ground rough seabed unsuitable for anchoring

Foul tide a tidal stream that is running against you

Freeboard height of deck above waterline

Galley kitchen on a boat

Gimbals pivoting supports enabling compass, cooker etc to remain upright as boat heels or rolls

Ground tackle generic term for anchors and anchoring gear

Guardrail wire fence around the side of a boat

Gunwhale top edge of boat's side (pronounced gunnel)

Half ebb halfway from high to low water, as tide ebbs

Half flood halfway from low to high water, as tide floods

Half tide halfway between high and low water

Hard chine planing type hull with sharp bend at chines

Head rope mooring line from bow to jetty

Heads boat's WC

Heaving line light line with heavy knob knot on end, for throwing long distances

Helm tiller or wheel; steering position

Helmsman person steering a boat

High Water when the tide is at its highest

Holding ground type and suitability of bottom for anchoring

Hook slang term for anchor

I.C.E. internal combustion engine (petrol, diesel etc)

Inboard towards middle of boat; engine inside boat

Isobar line on weather chart joining points of equal pressure

Isophase navigation light characteristic with equal periods of light and darkness

Jury makeshift (jury rig, rudder etc)

Keel the backbone of a boat at the bottom

King spoke spoke of steering wheel that is upright when rudder is amidships

Knot speed of one nautical mile per hour

Lee shore shore facing towards the wind

Lee side side of boat facing away from wind

Leeward away from the wind

Leeway sideways drift of boat, caused by wind

Lie a-hull shut off engine and drift with wind and sea

Lifejacket a more complex version of a buoyancy aid that will keep an unconscious person afloat

Liferaft special rubber dinghy for abandoning ship

Lighthouse tall building with guiding light on top

Log device to measure distance run through water

Logbook for keeping detailed records of a passage

Loom reflection from cloud of light below horizon

Low Water time when the tide is at its lowest

Lubber's line fixed line on compass representing boat's heading

Make fast secure a rope to cleat etc

Make water to leak

Marlinspike tapered length of steel for undoing shackles etc

Millibar unit of measurement for air pressures

Mooring buoy secured to the seabed for tying up to

Mouse to secure the pin to a shackle with wire

Nautical mile about 2000 yards; equal to one minute of latitude

Occulting navigation light characteristic with longer periods of light than darkness

Offing area of sea away from the shore

Outboard outside the boat; engine fixed outside of stern

Overfalls steep breaking waves caused by irregular currents meeting or flowing over a rough bottom

Painter mooring line permanently attached to bow of dinghy

Parallel ruler a special ruler that can step across a chart to draw parallel lines when plotting courses

Pooped when a boat is overtaken by a large wave that breaks over her stern

Port left hand side of a boat looking forward

Pulpit strong guardrail round bow

Pushpit strong guardrail round stern

Q flag yellow flag flown when customs clearance required

Quarter the after corner of a boat

Race rough water caused by fast currents, usually swirling round a headland

Reeve to pass a rope through a block

Riding light another term for anchor light

Ringbolt bolt with large ring attached for mooring to

Riser cable from seabed mooring to buoy on surface

Round bilge hull that curves gently from gunwhale down to keel

Rowlock U-shaped gap in gunwhale to take oar

Rubbing strake half round timber or moulding to protect gunwhale

Rudder flat plate swivelling at stern for steering

Samson post heavy post on foredeck for mooring or anchoring

Scantlings dimensions of boat's construction members

Scope the amount of anchor warp out

Scuppers large drain holes in bulwarks

Sea legs you have your sea legs when used to motion of boat

Sea returns radar echoes from waves

Seizing secure lashing to hold two ropes together

Set direction in which current is running

Shackle U-shaped metal fitting closed by threaded pin, used for joining chain etc

Shank long arm of an anchor

Sheer vertical curve of a boat's deck line from bow to stern; to swing away from your anchor

Ship water when waves come aboard

Shoal water shallow water

Slack water period at high and low water when there is no tidal stream running

Snub take a turn with cable or warp to stop it running

Sound to take a sounding (measure depth of water)

Spring mooring warp preventing boat moving fore and aft

Stanchion post supporting guardrail

Standing part end of a rope that is fixed to something

Starboard right hand side of boat looking forward

Steerage way sufficient speed for rudder to steer boat

Stem the very front edge of the bow

Stern the back of a boat

Stern rope mooring line holding the stern of a boat to quay

Stock cross piece on anchor to make it fall the right way up

Surge ease warp gradually round cleat when under strain

Swell long smooth waves left behind when wind dies

Tackle rope rove through blocks to increase hauling power

Take a turn turn just enough rope round cleat or bollard to hold boat temporarily

Tender dinghy for getting ashore from boat

Thwart athwartship seat in small boat

Tiller long stick used to turn the rudder when steering

Topsides sides of boat above water

Transducer underwater sensor that collects information and passes it to instrument on board (eg echo-sounder)

Transom a flat vertical stern

Trick period of time spent at the helm

Trim fore and aft attitude of boat in water

Turn up secure a rope round a cleat

Under way when a boat is not attached to the land

Up and down when anchor cable is vertical

Veer to let out cable or warp; the wind veers clockwise

Victuals foodstuffs (pronounced vittals)

Wake trail of disturbances left in water as boat motors

Warp general term for a rope used for mooring or anchoring; to move a boat using warps

Wash waves emanating sideways from the wake

Watch spell of duty for crew (on watch and off watch)

Wear a boat flies a flag, but wears an ensign

Weatherbreeder short fine spell of weather between depressions

Weather shore sheltered from the wind

Weather side side of a boat facing the wind

White horses waves breaking with white foam

Windage area of boat above water that the wind can blow against

Windrode lying to the wind when at anchor

Windward towards the wind

Working end free end of rope, used to tie knots in

Yaw to swing from side to side of course being steered

INDEX

(Page numbers in italics refer to illustrations or captions)

THE ILLUSTRATED DICTIONARY OF NAUTICAL TERMS
Graham Blackburn

Blackburn's new book is a useful and illustrated reference to nautical terms with more than 2500 alphabetical entries, often cross-referenced. Illustrated in Blackburn's inimitable style, this dictionary includes names, terms, parts, and expressions of and relating to the sea and the vessels that sail it.

Also included are the parts and equipment of water-borne craft, old and new, places aboard ship, the names and terms relating to the various states and conditions of the sea, orders, directives, and manœuvres involved in sailing all kinds of boats, the ranks and functions of the people who sail them, the lore, phenomena, and even the slang used in marine life, as well as the places any vessel is likely to find herself.

From *Able Seaman* to *Z. Twist*, and with 615 beautiful line drawings, here is a comprehensive and practical source book of nautical subjects for all lovers of ships and boats, and of the sea.

'. . . recommended to those who need a quick and accurate reference work and it also corrects a few hoary misconceptions.' – *Lloyds List*

'. . . as a foundation for research into marine history this dictionary is a must.' – *Motor Boat and Yachting*

'All the words checked have their national meaning listed. Many line drawings accompany the concise text.' – *Yachting & Boating*

ASTRO-NAVIGATION BY CALCULATOR
Henry Levison

This book shows you in clear and concise terms how the traditional methods of obtaining an astro-navigational fix can be superseded by using a scientific pocket calculator and a new book of calculator tables. Fixing your position can now be achieved more easily, more rapidly and more accurately than ever before. In addition, all this can be done without drawing a line on a chart at all.

No previous knowledge of the subject is necessary, as the opening chapters explain the principles of astro-navigation and the equipment required. Readers already familiar with traditional methods are invited to compare them with this new and alternative approach to astro-navigation.

Subsequent chapters deal with more detailed problems like the geographical position and the running fix, and each contains step-by-step worked examples and also includes a practice exercise. Detailed answers are provided for every exercise and as these can also be completed by traditional methods as well as by calculator, they provide for a practical comparison between the old and the new.

EXERCISES IN PILOTAGE
A Basic Introduction with Tests and Answers
John Anderson

Practice is the answer to sound navigation. This superb practical handbook is designed to teach you how to cope with every eventuality in all possible weather conditions and tides.

John Anderson has taught navigation for over twenty years and shows that it is really a matter of following the correct principles and techniques. He presents a systematic sequence of step-by-step exercises that provides you with all the knowledge and experience you will need. Follow the exercises and learn to navigate any small vessel offshore with safety and confidence.

Clearly illustrated at every stage, *Exercises in Pilotage* gives you everything you need to know about the Rules of the Road, buoys, lights, visual and sound signals, tides, depths, using your compass, distress signals, navigation at night, radar, using navigational equipment, and basic boat handling.

Fun to use and easy to follow: the perfect introduction to reliable navigation.

SHIPSHAPE
Ferenc Maté

Shipshape is the complete step-by-step guide to sailboat maintenance. In its forty-six clearly written and concise chapters, this book tells you all you need to know to keep your boat — fibreglass or wood — in pristine and safe condition, and to maintain its value even after considerable use.

Written with the benefit of a lifetime's experience in boatbuilding and sailing, Ferenc Maté has drawn on the knowledge of experts from boatyards to paint companies, sailmakers, engine repairmen and manufacturers, to make this the most complete book on the subject.

From the moment of launching to weekly, monthly and even yearly projects, *Shipshape* tells you in straight, simple steps how to keep your boat in the best possible condition. Just as importantly, it also tells you how to enjoy doing so.

"A first class contemporary manual" – *Sail*